Eastern Idaho
SWEET SPOTS

Third edition

Hiking, biking, skiing & climbing

Skiers enjoy the deep snows of Alaska Basin in South Teton Canyon.

Eastern Idaho
SWEET SPOTS

Third edition

Hiking, biking, skiing & climbing

Jerry Painter & Matt TeNgaio

TRAIL GUIDE BOOKS

Published by
Trail Guide Books
P.O. Box 148
Weiser, Idaho 83672
and 1439 Riviera Drive
Idaho Falls, Idaho 83404

Manufactured in the United States

Maps and topos by Jerry Painter and Matt TeNgaio
Cover and book design by Jerry Painter and Matt TeNgaio
All photographs by the authors, unless otherwise noted
Cover photograph: East side of Leatherman Peak from the Pahsimeroi Valley. Photo by Scott Stevens

ISBN 978-0-9911561-1-5

A word about safety

It is important to take the proper precautions in all outdoor activities. It is impossible to alert you to every hazard or anticipate all the limitations of every reader or group in a guidebook. Because of this, the descriptions of trails, routes and natural features in this book do not necessarily mean that a particular place or trip or climb will be safe for your group.

It also helps to remember that to fully enjoy many of the trails described in this book a certain level of physical conditioning is required – especially trails, rides or climbs rated as strenuous.

When you follow any of the trips or climbs described in this book, you assume responsibility for the safety of yourself or your party. Under all conditions, excursions require that you pay the proper attention to driving conditions, traffic, roads, trails, weather, terrain, the capabilities of your group members and other factors.

It is also important to remember that the lands described in this book are subject to development and ownership changes. Access and other conditions may have changed since this book was published that may make it unwise to use the exact routes described. Always check for current conditions ahead of time, respect posted private property signs, and avoid confrontations with property owners or managers. We have provided information sources in this book. You are also welcome to contact the authors directly. Staying informed on current conditions and using common sense are the best ways to enjoy fun and safe outings.

Another warning: Climbing involves an element of risk, as do all outdoor activities discussed in this book. Climbing (and other outdoor activities) can be deadly. Learn how to climb from competent instructors and always use safe climbing habits and equipment. People have been seriously hurt and killed in climbing areas described in this book. Remember that problems usually arise from poor judgment, poor communication, improper equipment and bad belaying practices. Be safe.

Acknowledgements

A lot of people helped make this information possible. We would like to thank the many people who went on hiking, skiing, biking and climbing trips with us. We would like to thank our wives, Julie and Brittany for putting up with our obsessions of being outdoors and for often tagging along. A thanks goes out to Dean Lords, Greg Collins, Marc Hanselman, Mike Engle and Bruce Black for information on the local climbing crags. Thanks to the Forest Service and Bureau of Land Management for information and advice. Thanks to all those who got in front of our cameras to provide us with useful photos. If there are any goof ups, blame us and tell us about them. We'll try to get them fixed in the next go around.

Waterfall Canyon above the Upper Palisades Lake.

CONTENTS

Skiing trails

Climbing areas

8

Introduction

It's a common question, "Where's a good place to ...?" Fill in the blank with hike, bike, ski, snowshoe, rock climb, peak bag, etc. Fortunately for those who live in eastern Idaho, there are lots of good answers to that question. Within a few hours of town, you can be in world-class backcountry. This is country that people come from across the continent to vacation in. It's cool living so close.

This book focuses on the outdoor activities and tells you where the sweet spots are. It is not comprehensive. Generally speaking, it fills in some of the gaps that exist in the book "Trails of Eastern Idaho" by Margaret Fuller and Jerry Painter. Think of it as a companion to "Trails of Eastern Idaho." Because that book is confined to Idaho, many great trails and areas are left out that are just across the border in Wyoming.

However, in this third edition of Sweet Spots, several new climbing areas and high quality mountain bike trails have been added to the bounty of trails and crags already documented in previous editions.

We hope that when you buy your mountain bike, a pair of climbing shoes or cross-country skis that you'll also pick up a copy of this book. You may as well know where all the best places are to play with your new toys. This book is the most up-to-date and accurate guide to rock climbing areas from Pocatello to Driggs to Howe. It includes some of the best mountain bike rides in the area. You'll find a full winter's worth of ski trails to explore. If it's hiking you crave, we'll turn you on to trails you'll remember for the rest of your life. One helpful hint: While our maps are useful and often all you'll need, we encourage you to take along a set of Forest Service and/or BLM maps for greater detail of the areas you'll be in. At the very least, they can be helpful driving to the right starting point.

These are some of the sweetest spots for recreating in eastern Idaho and, in some cases, the western states.

Sam Painter photo
Jerry Painter takes in the view along Death Canyon Shelf in the Tetons.

A dayhiker sits above School Room Glacier at Hurricane Pass in the Tetons.

HIKING

A word about hiking trails: You might wonder why we only have a few hiking trails in this book out of the more than 100 trails found in the area. This book is not meant to be comprehensive in its coverage of hiking trails, but rather a companion to the more comprehensive guidebook "Trails of Eastern Idaho" by Margaret Fuller and Jerry Painter. This book fills in the gaps and covers most of the western slope of the Teton Range -- out of the scope of the other guidebook.

HIDDEN LAKE LOOP

GETTING THERE: From Rexburg, Idaho, drive north on Highway 20 about 5 miles and turn east on Highway 33. Drive east on Highway 33 for about 16 miles and turn north on Highway 32. If you come to the town of Tetonia, you've gone too far. Follow this highway to mile marker 11 and turn north (right) on 4700 E. Go one mile and turn east (right) on 700 N. (also called Coyote Meadows Road). There should be a sign for Coyote Meadows. Follow this road for about three miles where it enters the national forest and becomes FR 265. Folow this road until it ends at the Coyote Meadows trailhead.
DISTANCE: 4.5 miles to Hidden Lake; 6.5 miles to Conant Basin; about 18 miles for the loop around to North Bitch Creek and back to Coyote Meadows.
DIFFICULTY: Moderate to Hidden Lake and Conant Basin; a bit harder around to North Bitch Creek.
WHEN TO GO: All summer and early fall. This area is used by hunters in late fall. Access roads can be poor to impassable after heavy rains or snows.

The trail up to Hidden Lake from Coyote Meadows gains only about 900 feet in 4.5 miles. That makes it a perfect beginner backpacker trail, day hike or for getting your horse into shape.
Whenever the trail does climb, the route uses well-made switchbacks and gradual slopes. If you're in shape, you can pretty much go on cruise control most of the way up.
The trail climbs through a mix of forest, mostly lodgepole pine with some fir and aspen mixed in. The first mile follows Coyote Creek then heads up a ridge across the wilderness boundary. There are a few intermittent streams along the way, but many of them dry up later in the year.
Hidden Lake is just a few acres large. It's completely surrounded by timber. In years past there have been some nice-sized trout of the 1 to 2 pound variety in the lake. Remember that you'll need a Wyoming fishing license to legally fish. Hidden Lake is under special camping restrictions — no camping with stock animals or stock grazing.
About one-fourth mile past the lake, the trail comes to Crystal Spring. There is a nice campsite here with a bear proof food box. The large spring provides good water for nearby campers. There are no restrictions in this area.
Most of the trail is inside the Jedediah Smith Wilderness Area. Bikes and motorized vehicles are prohibited inside the wilderness.
The trail continues on to Conant Basin to the northwest. From here the trail forks; one trail goes east over Jackass Pass into Teton National Park and the southern route heads south and loops back to the Coyote Meadows Trailhead.
Jackass Pass is reputed to be the same route taken by John Colter — one of the first white men to enter Jackson Hole — as he headed south in the early 1800s.
Keep in mind if you are camping, that this area is only 10 miles from the Yellowstone National Park border and considered grizzly bear country. Many of the campsites in this area have bear proof boxes or bear poles for hanging your gear. If you camp where there are no boxes or poles already set up, then you should hang your foodstuffs in a bag from a tree limb at least 10 feet off the ground, eat away from your sleeping area and never take food into your

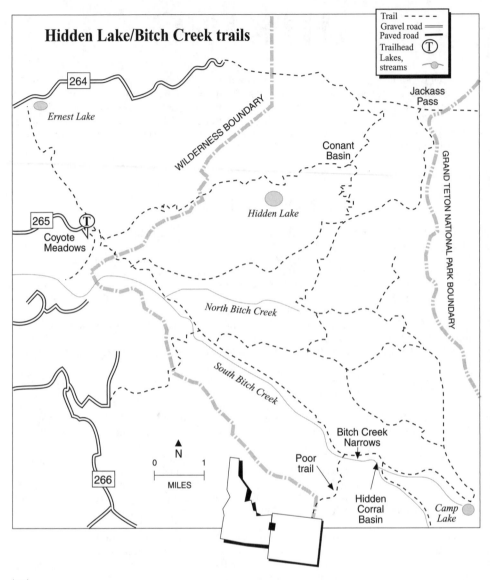

Hidden Lake/Bitch Creek trails

Trail -----
Gravel road ====
Paved road ▬▬
Trailhead Ⓣ
Lakes, streams

264

Ernest Lake

WILDERNESS BOUNDARY

Jackass Pass

Conant Basin

265

Ⓣ

Coyote Meadows

Hidden Lake

GRAND TETON NATIONAL PARK BOUNDARY

North Bitch Creek

South Bitch Creek

Bitch Creek Narrows

Poor trail

0   N   1

MILES

266

Hidden Corral Basin

Camp Lake

tent.

Dayhikers or horseback riders will rarely see any bears. They usually see or hear you first.

HIDDEN CORRAL BASIN / SOUTH BITCH CREEK

GETTING THERE: From Rexburg, Idaho, drive north on Highway 20 about 5 miles and turn east on Highway 33. Drive east on Highway 33 for about 16 miles and turn north on Highway 32. If you come to the town of Tetonia, you've gone too far. Follow this highway to mile marker 11 and turn north (right) on 4700 E. Go one mile and turn east (right) on 700 N. (also called Coyote Meadows Road). There should be a sign for Coyote Meadows. Follow this road for about three miles where it enters the national forest and becomes FR 265. Follow this road until it ends at the Coyote Meadows trailhead.

DISTANCE: It's about 7.25 miles to the Bitch Creek Narrows and another mile beyond to

Hidden Corral Basin. It's close to 2 miles from Hidden Corral Basin to Camp Lake.

DIFFICULTY: Moderate – mostly because of distance – up to the narrows and the basin; beyond the basin the trail climbs steeply up to Camp Lake, less steeper up to the creek's headwaters.

WHEN TO GO: June to October for hiking and horseback riding; skiers would need a ride in from snowmobilers to access the trails in winter. Roads can be poor after a heavy rain or snow. This area is used heavily by hunters in the fall.

One of the most beautiful spots in the Tetons is a gorgeous basin about 8 miles up the South Bitch Creek canyon.

Hidden Corral Basin is so named because it was used by horse thieves around the turn of the century to hide their stolen stock. About 7 miles up from Coyote Meadows, the canyon narrows abruptly. With a few poles stretched across the narrows, livestock were kept safely for weeks in a natural corral until buyers could be found.

Nowadays the canyon and basin are perfect getaways for backpackers and horseback riders looking for some solitude. All but the first mile of the trail is inside the Jedediah Smith Wilderness Area. Bikes and motorized vehicles are prohibited inside the wilderness.

The narrows section forces the creek through several stretches of beautiful cascades and drops. It is especially pretty during high water runoff years in the Tetons.

There are some nice campsites in the basin; a bear proof box is also available.

The hike up from Coyote Meadows requires a stream crossing and has a few ups and downs in the beginning, but for the most part is fairly level, easy trekking. Except for the distances, it's not too tough.

Beyond Hidden Corral Basin, the trail forks. The trail heading south follows the creek and eventually connects into South Badger Creek. The fork heading east climbs up to Camp Lake, then turns north to connect into a series of ridgeline trails. The area around Camp Lake is restricted camping – no livestock grazing allowed. The headwaters of South Bitch Creek is also a restricted camping zone.

GREEN LAKES

GETTING THERE: Drive 5.5 miles north of Driggs, Idaho on Highway 33. When the highway makes a 90-degree turn west, continue going straight. Take the next road right (east) — there are signs to North and South Leigh Creek trails. The road soon becomes gravel. Drive 2.5 miles and turn left (north) at the sign for North Leigh Creek. Drive about 5 miles to the end of the road and a parking area at the trailhead.

DISTANCE: 12.5 miles round-trip to the first lake. Add another 2 miles if you go farther up the canyon to other lakes.

DIFFICULTY: Strenuous. Gains about 2,000 feet in the first 4 miles.

SEASON: July to October. Snow can linger into midsummer on the ridge next to Green Mountain.

This is beautiful wilderness hiking in the upper west side of the Teton range. The trail seems to have it all. The Green Lakes hike is a good all-day hike or overnight backpacking trip.

The trail crosses a footbridge over Tin Cup Creek and almost immediately enters the Jedediah Smith Wilderness Area. The trail quickly begins its uphill climb to the Green Mountain Ridge. Most of the trail is well made. The grades are not too steep, and switchbacks help manage the climb up the side of the mountain.

For the first mile the trail takes you through thick lodgepole and fir forest. There are also some huckleberries to watch for in late summer.

As the trail climbs higher, it takes you through some patches of aspens. Soon the trail begins some wide switchbacks through open treeless areas. The wildflowers here are superb, especially in mid- to late-July.

After about four miles of steady climbing and switchbacking, the trail reaches a ridge and levels off for about .25-miles. This is as high as you'll get on the way to the lakes. Snow often lingers on this ridge until midsummer.

Dayhiking to the first Green Lake in the Tetons.

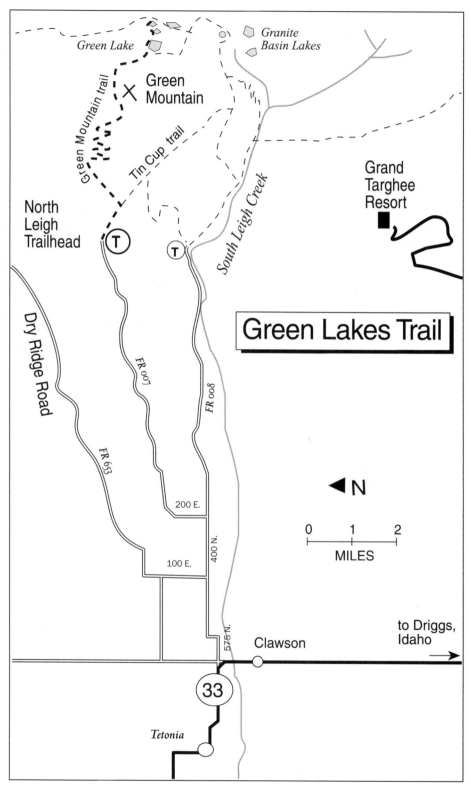

Green Lake

Granite
Basin Lakes

Green Mountain trail

Green
Mountain

Tin Cup trail

Grand
Targhee
Resort

North
Leigh
Trailhead

T

T

South Leigh Creek

Green Lakes Trail

Dry Ridge Road

FR 007

FR 008

FR 653

200 E.

400 N.

100 E.

N

0   1   2
MILES

575 N.

Clawson

to Driggs,
Idaho

33

Tetonia

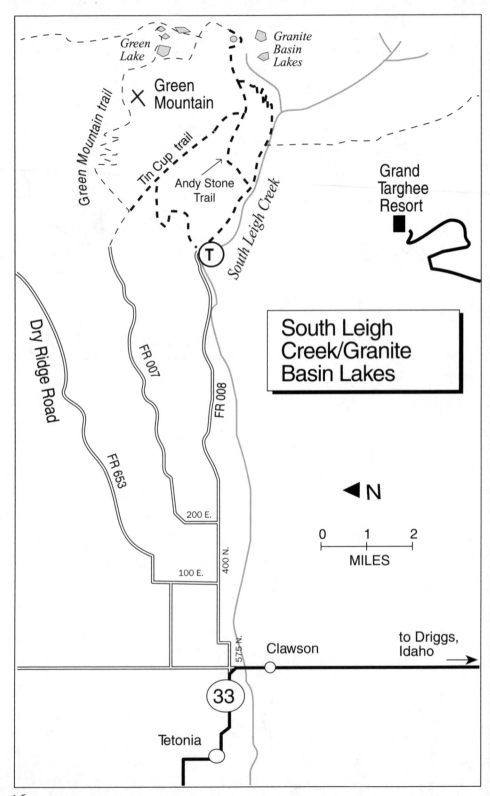

Green Lake

Granite Basin Lakes

Green Mountain trail

Green Mountain

Tin Cup trail

Andy Stone Trail

South Leigh Creek

Grand Targhee Resort

South Leigh Creek/Granite Basin Lakes

Dry Ridge Road

FR 007

FR 008

FR 653

200 E.

400 N.

100 E.

575 N.

◀ N

0   1   2
MILES

to Driggs, Idaho →

Clawson

33

Tetonia

16

One of the pretty alpine lakes in Granite Basin on the west side of the Tetons.

The trail drops down the northeast side of the ridge in a series of switchbacks that go on for about .5 miles. Within another half-mile you arrive at the first Green Lake.

Look for trout and osprey in and above the lake. There is a good campsite on the northeast side of the lake.

There are three more lakes above the first. All three are within about 1.5 miles from the first. These other lakes are about half the size of the first lake.

The return trip is fairly easy once you get past the steep switchbacks on the northeast side of the ridge.

SOUTH LEIGH CREEK/GRANITE BASIN LAKES

GETTING THERE: From Driggs, Idaho, drive 5.5 miles north on Highway 33. As the highway takes a 90-degree turn to the left (west), turn off the highway, continuing north. Turn right (east) at the next road. There should be signs for North and South Leigh trails. The road soon becomes gravel. Continue on this road for 7 miles to the trailhead.

DISTANCE: 1.4 miles to the Andy Stone Trail junction; 2.7 miles to the next trail junction; 4 miles to the switchbacks; and 7.7 miles to Granite Basin.

HOW STRENUOUS: Mostly easy for the first 4 miles from the trailhead to the switchbacks. Strenuous up the switchbacks to Granite Basin (about 2,500 feet gain from the creek bottom to Granite Basin in 3 miles).

SEASON: June to October if you only want to hike the creek bottom; late June or early July to October for Granite Basin.

SPECIAL CONSIDERATIONS: Watch out for stinging nettle along the creek. Snow lingers in Granite Basin until after July 4 most years.

This is a trail with a split personality. The first four miles that parallel South Leigh Creek are gentle and easy walking. But if you are interested in taking off out of the canyon, get ready to huff and puff. These trails climb nearly to the top of the range.

This canyon has more streams than are shown on the map. The trail crosses three good-

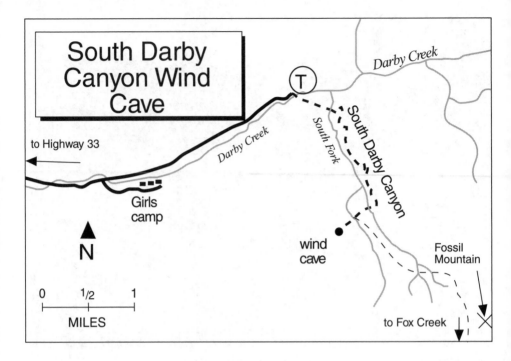

sized streams the first 1.3 miles before you reach the Andy Stone Trail Junction. Most of these streams flow through midsummer, but by late August, some are only muddy spots. Because this is a wet area, be prepared to battle mosquitoes and biting flies.

The canyon is heavily forested with fir and spruce. The trail passes through occasional meadows that are a mass of wild flowers in mid summer.

The trail only draws near the main creek a few times. If you wish to wade or fish the stream, there are a couple of nice places about three miles down the trail and near the junction with the trail to Teton Creek. At this junction there is a large stock/foot bridge over the creek.

If you wish to spend the night, there is a large campsite at the bottom of the switchbacks. There also are some other nice spots at the meadows before the footbridge.

At the top of the canyon await beautiful alpine basin lakes and views to rival any in the Tetons. On the hike up you will see the Grand Teton towering over the ridge. These lakes once boasted trout, but now appear to be empty. The three largest lakes are from three to five acres in size. Beautiful snowmelt creeks cascade down the surrounding cliffs to fill the lakes each spring.

There are two routes to see the Granite Basin Lakes. Both are strenuous and it depends on how you like your poison: all at once or spread out. The Andy Stone Trail climbs right up the side of the canyon with only a few level stretches to let you catch your breath. The other route, a switchback trail at the end of the canyon, seems to take forever to get you to the top. But the switchbacks are well engineered so as not to bite off huge elevation gains at each turn.

SOUTH DARBY CANYON / WIND CAVE

GETTING THERE: From Victor, Idaho, drive 5.5 miles north on Highway 33. Turn right (east) onto a paved road. Look for signs at the beginning of the road for Darby Girls Camp. After a mile the road becomes gravel. After another half mile the road forks. Go right and follow this road about 6 miles to its end, where you may park.

DISTANCE: 3.4 miles to Wind Cave.

HOW STRENUOUS: Gains 1,800 feet, moderately strenuous, but a well-made trail.

WHEN TO GO: Mid-June to October for hiking.

SPECIAL CONSIDERATIONS: Bring headlamp or flashlights for cave.

18

This is a fun trail with a super destination. The wind cave at the end of the trail adds an extra bit of fascination to a hike with nice waterfalls and scenery.

This trail is often called the "Monument Hike" by locals because of a cement and rock monument placed in the upper basin, near the wind cave. The monument is in remembrance of five people who died here after being struck by lightning during a thunderstorm. The group consisted of hikers from the nearby summer girls camp.

The trail starts off with a footbridge across Darby Creek, then begins to climb away from the creek. After about a half of a mile, the trail enters the Jedediah Smith Wilderness and crosses the South Fork of Darby Creek.

After crossing the creek, the trail climbs sharply up the canyon. Most of the tough part of the trail comes in the next 1.5 miles. The last mile climbs at a less-drastic incline.

An interesting phenomenon is that the creek disappears underground for a short way about a mile up the canyon. Late in the season, the creek is often dry until you reach the cave where a small stream flows from the cave's mouth.

The trail continues to climb with a few switchbacks until it is near the canyon rim and into some less-forested terrain. Along this point watch the opposite rim for waterfalls. Late in the season, these can be somewhat diminished or nonexistent.

Hiking down from a visit to the South Darby Canyon wind cave.

As the trail approaches the upper basin, it enters a thickly forested area and turns west. Before entering the trees you should be able to see the wind cave along the western wall of the canyon.

Below the cave are some campsites for backpackers.

The trail forks just before you arrive at the monument. The fork heading up the basin along the creek is not shown on some maps. This unmaintained use trail goes up to the base of Fossil Mountain and drops into Fox Creek Canyon.

From the monument, it's a steep hike up switchbacks to the mouth of the wind cave. During wet, cooler years, snow often lingers around the cave into midsummer. Make sure you bring along flashlights or headlamps to safely enjoy the interior of the cave. On hot days the gusts of wind coming from the cave feel like a giant air conditioner. The cave is really a natural tunnel with wind pouring through from inlets farther up the canyon. The cave goes deep into the mountain and comes out at about the same level along the ridge about .75 miles up the canyon. Between the entrance and exit are some 40-foot drops and climbs that require ropes and caving skills to negotiate.

ALASKA BASIN

GETTING THERE: From Victor, Idaho, drive 8 miles north on Highway 33 to Driggs. Turn right (east) at the main intersection, and follow the signs to Grand Targhee Ski Resort. Drive 6 miles and turn right onto a paved road with a sign for Teton Campground. After a few hundred feet the road turns to dirt. Drive 5 miles to the trailhead/parking lot for South Teton Creek Trail.

DISTANCE: 8 miles one way to the basin lakes; another 2.5 miles up to the top of Hur-

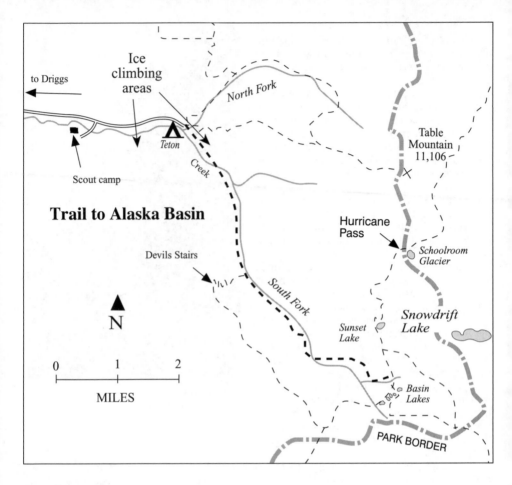

Ice climbing areas

to Driggs

North Fork

Teton

Creek

Table Mountain 11,106

Scout camp

Trail to Alaska Basin

Hurricane Pass

Devils Stairs

Schoolroom Glacier

▲ N

South Fork

Snowdrift Lake

Sunset Lake

0   1   2

MILES

Basin Lakes

PARK BORDER

ricane Pass.

DIFFICULTY: Moderately strenuous for the last 3 miles with an elevation gain of 2,400 feet to the basin lakes.

WHEN TO GO: Late June to October. The trail is usually snow covered through May.

SPECIAL CONSIDERATIONS: If you're backpacking, bring a pack stove. Campfires are not allowed in the basin lakes area.

This is one of the most heavily used trails on the west side of the Tetons, next to the Table (Rock) Mountain trail. What makes the trail so popular is its magical beauty from the lower parts of the canyon all the way to the captivating basin lakes.

Because of its popularity, it is well-maintained and has foot bridges over the major stream crossings.

From the trailhead, the path immediately enters the Jedediah Smith Wilderness. The most striking features in the first few miles are the wonderful wildflowers and the lively creek, that has some stretches where it cascades and drops.

At about 3.5 miles, the trail forks. The trail to the right heads up Devils Stairs. This strenuous trail (not recommended for horses) switchbacks up to a large hanging shelf on the canyon's southwest side. It offers nice views of the canyon below and the surrounding peaks.

The main South Fork trail continues up the canyon alongside the creek through heavily forested terrain.

At about mile 7, you'll pass through some campsite areas. These larger campsites are popular with horsepackers, who are not allowed to camp in the fragile basin lakes area.

At about 7.5 miles, the trail switchbacks over a ridge and into Alaska Basin. Historians believe this beautiful rocky basin was named by settlers who returned from the Alaskan gold rush.

Alpine setting of Alaska Basin is dominated by Buck Mountain to the east.

Look for the bold marmots that inhabit the basin. Remember to hang your food away from marmots and other camp robbers, such as bears.

From Alaska Basin, there are routes in several directions in the range. To get to Hurricane Pass, follow the well-marked trails north to Sunset Lake and the pass. A strenuous .6 mile trail takes you to this beautiful alpine lake with limited campsites. From the lake it's another two miles to the top of Hurricane Pass. The pass offers one of the more memorable sights of the Grand Teton, Middle Teton, South Teton and Schoolroom Glacier.

FOX CREEK

GETTING THERE: Three miles north of Victor, turn east on the Fox Creek Road. Drive 4 miles to the end of the road and park.

The Fox Creek Trail starts out near a rock quarry that is on private property. Some of the first section follows the entrance road into the quarry. Signs lead hikers and horseback riders off the road and onto the south side of the creek to a rocky foot path. There is one sign near the beginning of the trail that says "Fox Creek Pass 10." Don't believe it. At best, the pass is less than eight miles up.

The first five miles up the canyon are mostly easy-going and gentle in elevation gain. The trail travels through lush forest. There are several stream crossings; most are easy to negotiate in late summer and fall. Earlier in the year, hikers will probably want to bring along sandals to slip into for the stream crossings.

After about five miles the trail begins to get more serious in elevation gain. From the trailhead to Fox Creek Pass — about 8 miles — the trail gains a moderate 3,000 feet. At mile five, look for pretty Fox Creek Falls streaming over a rock cliff. These falls are marked on the Jedediah Smith and Winegar Hole Wilderness Map available at the Forest Service office. The falls will be below the trail on the right side.

Above the falls, the trail continues to climb. On your left (north) side of the canyon, Fossil Mountain comes into view. Fossil Mountain is 10,950 feet. As you get closer to the base of the peak, you will notice a prominent notch on the west side between the peak and the canyon rim. This "pass" has a rough trail that leads to the top of South Darby Canyon.

The upper two miles of Fox Creek Canyon offer a few nice campsites.

21

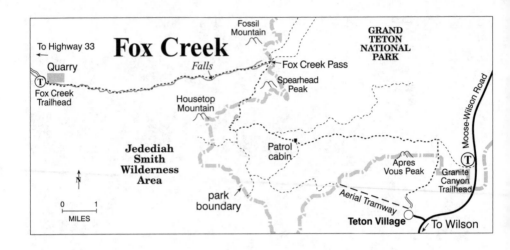

Just before Fox Creek Pass is a junction with the Teton Crest Trail. Here is where the views become wonderful. To the northeast are the Teton's tallest peaks, including the Grand Teton. To the south is Housetop Mountain and Spearhead Peak.

At this junction you have options of heading south to Marion Lake and the top of Granite Canyon about 1.8 miles away or east down Death Canyon or north along the Death Canyon Shelf toward Alaska Basin.

GAME CREEK

GETTING THERE: Finding the Game Creek trailhead can be a bit tricky. About five miles southeast of Victor on state Highway 33, turn east at the sign that says Moose Creek and take an immediate left. After a few hundred feet, the road passes the Moose Creek Road with a large sign pointing to the trailhead. Continue north about one mile and look for a cluster of houses. Turn right (east) on a road between the homes (find the one that doesn't end up being a driveway). Take this road to the end. Near the end of the road, keep left at the intersection and park in an open area just below an irrigation headgate on the creek.

The trail starts on the north side of the creek. You can walk across the bridge at the headgate. On the other side is a sign indicating that the Grand Teton National Park boundary is 6.9 miles up the trail.

The trail up Game Creek is easy going, except for the stream crossings. A couple of the stream crossings have nice fat logs to skip across on, but higher up the trail, you may be forced to take off our boots and wade across. Consider taking a lightweight pair of sandals for these wet crossings. If you go earlier in the summer when the water is higher and swifter, walking sticks are recommended.

The creek begins to do a disappearing act around the 5.5 mile area. The creek goes underground for 100 yards or so, then re-emerges above ground.

Around the 6-mile mark, the trail occasionally does a disappearing act. In places where the trail passes through meadows, grass sometimes fills in the path. If you lose the trail, don't worry too much. If you walk parallel to the creek (on the south side), the trail eventually reappears.

At the top of the canyon, the trail has generous switchbacks to help you climb up to the crest of the Tetons. The route tops out at 10,200 feet. On the ridge you are presented with some nice views of the southern end of the range.

MOOSE CREEK

GETTING THERE: From Victor, Idaho, drive 3 miles southeast on Highway 33 and turn

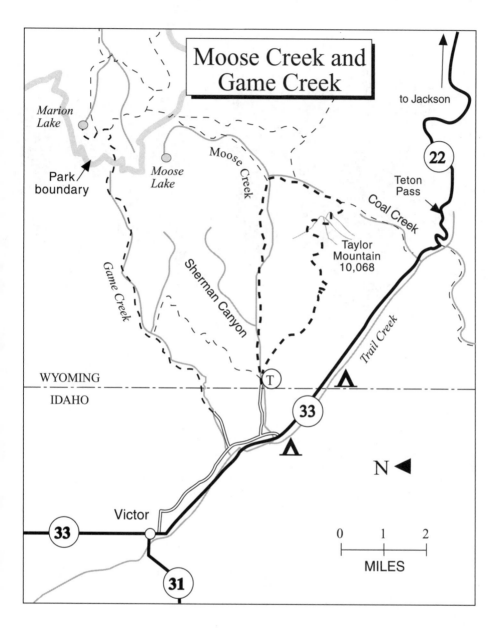

Moose Creek and Game Creek

left on the Moose Creek Road; drive .3 miles and turn right (east) and drive to the end of the road and park.

DISTANCE: 4.4 miles up to Moose Meadows; 5.8 miles to the falls; 8 miles to Moose Lake.

HOW STRENUOUS: Mostly easy, gains 800 feet to meadows.

SEASON: Late May to October.

SPECIAL CONSIDERATIONS: The water is clear and shallow making it easy to spook the trout.

The Moose Creek Trail offers a fun hike up a classic mountain canyon featuring a good-sized trout stream, beaver ponds, a large meadow, waterfall and small lake.

This trail takes you into the Jedediah Smith Wilderness Area. The trail starts out tough for

Dayhikers soak up the views at the top of Game Creek canyon.

the first 1/8 of a mile until it climbs up to an old dirt road along the south side of the creek. From here the next mile or so is fairly easy hiking. The road eventually narrows down to a trail. The canyon is thickly forested with Douglas fir, spruce and lodgepole pine. Willow brush clogs the creek bottoms.

The trail crosses the creek on a nice footbridge at the second mile. If at first you don't spot the bridge, keep looking. The horseback riders usually walk through the water. After the bridge, the trail climbs sharply for a quarter of a mile. At the three-mile mark is a small meadow fed by a spring and backed up by some busy beavers.

At 4.4 miles up the canyon, the trail comes to Moose Meadows. This huge meadow is several acres wide. The area is laced with beaver channels and slack water.

There are a few campsites at the meadows.

Past the meadows the trail begins a steady uphill. Just past the meadows, the trail crosses the creek. There is no bridge here, so plan on getting wet feet.

Another 1.4 miles up the trail is a nice waterfall. When the trail takes you through a rocky section, watch the creek canyon from the trail for a narrow gap that the water falls through.

Grand Teton National Park is about 1.7 miles from the falls. The trail forks about .5-miles before the park boundary. The trail following the creek hooks west and leads up to beautiful Moose Lake. If you wish to camp at the lake, bring a pack stove. No fires are allowed around the lake.

INDIAN CREEK

GETTING THERE: Drive 19 miles southeast of Swan Valley on Highway 26 and turn left (east) into the middle of a wide canyon with a sign marked "Indian Creek." Follow the good gravel road for about 2 miles and turn right at the fork to go to the South Fork trailhead or left at the fork to go to the North Fork trailhead. There are some nice car camping sites along this road. This road can be slippery and mucky after a heavy rain. Two miles from the fork, you come to a trailhead parking area, kiosk, pit toilet and area for off-loading horses.

DISTANCE: About 8 miles from the South Fork trailhead to above the lake basin area. About 6.5 miles from the North Fork trailhead to the top of the canyon.

DIFFICULTY: Easy for the first 2 miles; strenuous in the upper canyon.

Moose Creek falls.

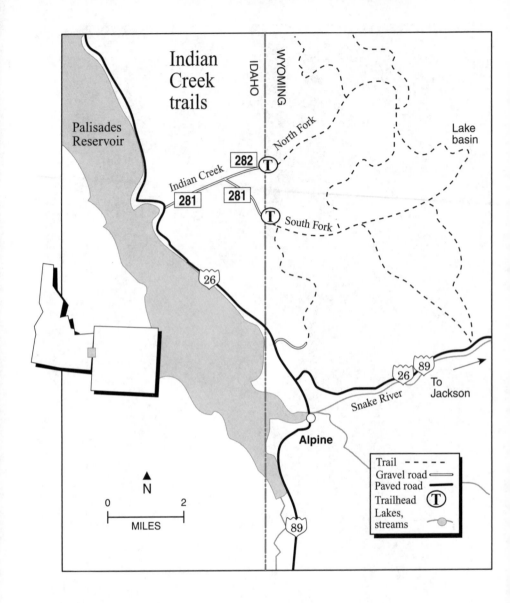

BEST TIME TO GO: Late June to October.

The Indian Creek trail starts out right on the Idaho border and climbs east into some super backcountry.

Indian Creek has two main canyons – north and south – that are heavily forested and deep. Fir, spruce, pine, cottonwood and aspen are thick throughout the lower reaches of the canyon. The trail takes you high into the lower reaches of the Snake River Range. Many of the peaks along the canyon and near the lake basin are close to 10,000 feet high.

If you are on horseback or are a fast hiker, you can connect the two canyons via some passes at the top of the canyons. This area also makes an enjoyable overnight trip. There are some nice campsites in the lake basin or near Deadhorse Canyon. Be aware that the area is visited regularly by hunters in the fall. The trail is open to motorbikes and snowmobiles. Mountain bikers will find the first two to three miles enjoyable, but it gets very tough after that.

The first four miles up the South Fork are very picturesque and mostly easy. The trail is in pretty good shape. About a mile up, there are a couple of stream crossings without a bridge. A walking stick and a couple of handy logs will get you over dry.

Around the sixth mile, the trail comes to the first of three more stream crossings. The last crossing is not a problem. But the other two can be challenges if the water is high. It may be wisest to just take off your boots and wade through. The water is surprisingly deep high in the canyon — especially during wetter years.

On the way up the canyon are a couple of side canyons with two trails leading south and one heading north. The southern trails climb steeply out of the canyon, over the top and down into canyons that intersect near the east-west flowing Snake River and Highway 26-89. The northern trail climbs up to the north rim of the canyon and follows it over to near the lake basin.

After the sixth mile, the trees begin to thin and most of the hillsides are covered in grass and scrub brush with an occasional wind blasted fir tree. About the seventh mile the trail climbs into a lake basin. This last mile up is steep – gaining about 1,000 feet. The lakes are really large, spring-fed ponds tucked in close to the mountain ridges.

Just before the lake basin is a trail junction. The trail heading east goes down Dog Creek Canyon and eventually down to Highway 26-89 near Hoback, Wyo.

From the lake basin, the trail climbs up and over a 9,000-foot-plus ridge and drops into the North Fork canyon of Indian Creek after winding through two more smaller passes. The head of the canyon is a beautiful alpine mountain cirque.

From the top of the North Fork canyon it's about another 6 miles back to the trailhead, but the walk back along the road to complete the loop is almost another 3 miles. The North Fork canyon is narrower than the South Fork Canyon. If you don't like hiking on dirt roads, you might want to stash a mountain bike at the other trailhead and ride the last three miles back to your vehicle.

SOUTH HORSESHOE CREEK

GETTING THERE: From Idaho Falls, take Highway 20 north past Rexburg and take the exit onto Highway 33 heading east. Drive about 27 miles and turn south on the Powerline Road. Drive 4 miles and turn east on Packsaddle Road. Drive 3 miles east and turn south (don't cross the Teton River). Drive 1 mile south and keep on the main road as it turns southwest. After 2.5 miles you will come to a sign indicating Horseshoe Creek. The trailhead is another 2.5 miles up the road.

DISTANCE: About 3 miles to the top of the first main ridge; 4.5 miles to Elk Flat; about 17.5 miles for a loop down North Fork of Mahogany Creek and back to the trailhead.

ELEVATION: The trailhead is at about 6,000 feet; the first ridge hits 8,000 feet.

HOW STRENUOUS: Easy to the beaver dams, moderate to strenuous up to the first ridge.

WHEN TO GO: June through October most years. Snow often lingers on the north-facing slopes above 8,000 feet. The access roads can be a mess following a heavy rain or snow. This area is heavily hunted during the fall.

The Horseshoe Creek trail is one of those "get away from the crowds" type paths. You may see a few vehicles at the trailhead, but chances are you may never see anyone on the trail.

The trail is open to bikers and foot traffic (bikers should see the Horseshoe Canyon trails in the biking section). There is plenty of parking available about 100 yards from the trailhead for horse trailers.

The trail offers different possibilities depending on how far up the trail you travel. After about 1 mile you come to a series of beaver ponds.

In the next 2 miles, the trail climbs up next to a nameless peak at 8,065 feet. The trail climbs over a ridge and comes to Elk Flat after about 4.5 miles. Before Elk Flat the trail intersects with two other trails. One trail heads northwest to a radio station relay tower and the other goes east down the North Fork of Mahogany Creek. Beyond Elk Flat, the trail climbs up Garns Mountain which stands at 9,016 feet. On a clear day expect some inspiring views of the Teton Mountains. Garns Mountain is a bald, round-topped mountain.

If you're looking for an overnight camping spot, head up to Elk Flat. There is also a trail heading south out of Elk Flat that follows much of the Big Hole Mountains' crest for about 12 miles. The trail ends at Pine Creek Pass on U.S. Highway 31 – the road between Swan Valley

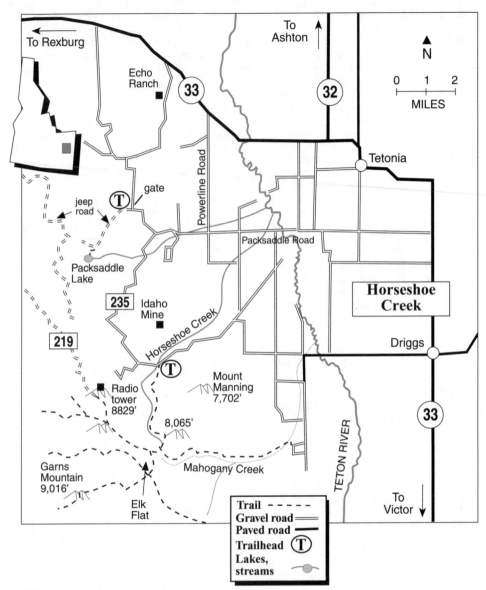

and Victor.

These trails take you through some beautiful rugged mountain country. Expect to find some parts of the trail to be a bit beat up by erosion and clogged with downfall.

CRESS CREEK NATURE TRAIL

GETTING THERE: Take U.S. Highway 26 east out of Idaho Falls, go about 14 miles and turn left, follow the signs to Heise and Kelly Canyon Ski area. Immediately after you cross the bridge over the Snake River, turn left. Go about 1.5 miles to the parking area.

DISTANCE: About 2 miles round-trip.

DIFFICULTY: Mostly easy.

SEASON: April to November.

SPECIAL CONSIDERATIONS: If you time your visit in the evening, you'll be treated to an awesome sunset on clear summer days.

A hiker skips along the paved Cress Creek Nature Trail.

The Cress Creek Nature Trail is like an old friend to many hikers in eastern Idaho.

But like some old friends who have gone off to the city and returned with an uptown personality, the Cress Creek Nature Trail has changed radically in recent years.

In 2003, this trail near Heise has had major improvement work done on it. The parking lot at the trailhead was expanded and now boasts a restroom. The once crumbling banks have been pushed back and shielded with chain-link fence. Perhaps the most major change is the cement sidewalk that gradually climbs the hill making the first half mile of trail wheelchair accessible. Work on Cress Creek Nature Trail continues.

The trail still follows the same general route of the former trail, only it takes its time with gentle switchbacks up the Snake River canyon side. Walkers can shortcut some of the switchbacks via stairs.

Along the first half mile are large metal signs that combine history, geology and natural facts about the surroundings. Pay attention to one sign in particular, there is a serious test later on up the trail.

The higher you climb, the better the views get. At the end of the paved section of trail, the route continues along a gravel road. As the road begins to go downhill, look for a dirt trail on your left. Take this uphill trail. This is part of the old Cress Creek Trail that makes a large loop higher up the hillside and follows along the creek. This loop trail adds another mile onto the entire route. If you continue down the gravel road you'll end up back at the river road that you drove in on.

Most of the area is high-country desert — sage brush, scrubby trees, lava rock and a few cactus — until the trail reaches the creek. Here, you enter lush growth with thick green, leafy foliage. The small stream is clogged with water cress. If you read the signs at the start of the trail, you'll also be able to identify one of the most dangerous denizens of the backcountry: Poison ivy. This nasty plant stands guard near the trail and along the stream area. Make sure the kids know how to identify it.

The trail features nice overlook views of the Snake River valley to the west and some of the Snake River canyon to the south and east. On clear days you can see Big Southern Butte and the mountain ranges to the west.

Perhaps the best time to hike this trail is close to dusk. With the setting sun back lighting the distant mountains and valley you can make out the Lost River and Lemhi mountain ranges.

There is a faint trail off the upper part of the loop trail that leads to the top of the canyon ridge. A radio tower is visible at the ridge top. This route is more of a workout and adds another

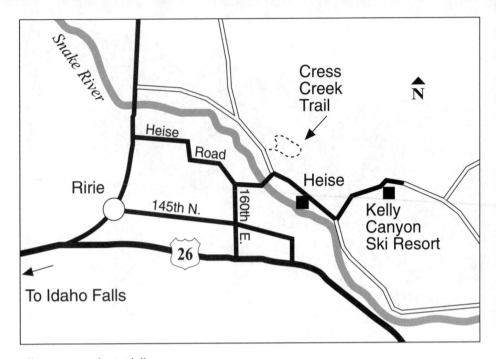

mile or so onto the total distance.

There is a variety of wildlife that inhabits the area. Some include rabbits, ground squirrels, snakes, lizards, deer, eagles, osprey, foxes and several kinds of song birds.

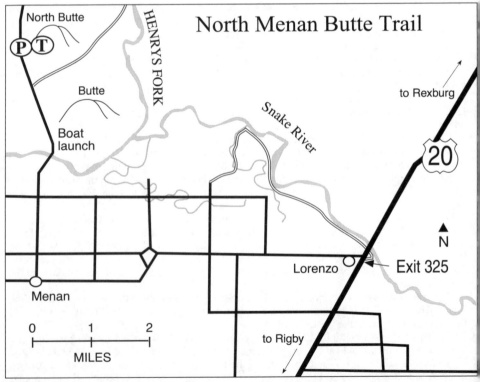

NORTH MENAN BUTTE

GETTING THERE: Drive north on Highway 20 going toward Rexburg. Take the Menan-Roberts Exit. Turn west onto the Menan-Lorenzo Highway and drive west to N. 3600. Turn right (north) on 3600 and drive to the bridge across the Snake River. When the road crosses the river it is called the Twin Butte Road. Drive about a mile and look for the BLM trailhead/parking area on the right at the base of the North Butte's west side.

Menan Butte is a popular trail pretty much year-round. It offers wonderful views of the surrounding Snake River Plain and the view from the top is especially sweet about sunset. Because of its proximity to Idaho Falls and Rexburg, it attracts a lot of dayhikers from both towns.

Menan Butte is basically a small, dead volcano. Its formation about 10,000 thousand years ago changed the course of the nearby rivers. The Henry's Fork and Snake River converge nearby.

The mini-peak also seems to be a magnet for critters. It is common to see deer, coyotes, rapters and rabbits. North Menan Butte is publicly owned and has been designated as a National Natural Landmark and a Research Natural Area by the United States Congress. The Bureau of Land Management has designated the North Butte as an Area of Critical Environmental Concern. Motor vehicles are off-limits. The BLM has built a trailhead, pit toilet and parking lot on the west side of the butte.

The trail up to the top leaves the west side parking area and climbs about 800 feet in elevation, using mostly easy switchbacks on the steeper sections. At the top, you arrive at a huge crater rim. This rim is about 3,000 feet around. A trail leads around the rim and requires a little bit of fun scrambling in places. On the north end of the butte there are a few antenna/radio facilities. The entire route is about 3 miles.

31

From the left, Mount Owens, the Grand Teton and Table Mountain.

Peak bagging

TABLE (ROCK) MOUNTAIN

GETTING THERE: From Victor, Idaho, drive 8 miles north on Highway 33 to Driggs. Turn right (east) at the main intersection, following the signs to Grand Targhee Ski Resort, drive 6 miles, and turn right onto a paved road with a sign for Teton Campground. This road soon becomes gravel. Drive 5 miles to the trailhead/parking lot for North Teton Creek Trail, or continue down the road to the South Teton Creek Trailhead.

DISTANCE: 12.5 miles roundtrip if you take the North Fork trail; 9 miles roundtrip if you take the ridge route from the South Fork parking lot.

HOW STRENUOUS: The trail gains 4,100 feet from trailhead to summit. It's a lot more enjoyable if you're in good shape.

SEASON: Early July most years, to October. March to April as a ski climb.

SPECIAL CONSIDERATIONS: If you don't mind the cold, April can be a good time to climb the peak. Go on mornings when the temperatures are cold enough to keep the snow solid to avoid post holing. The temperatures can be as much as 20 degrees colder on the summit than the valley floor. Bring along a jacket.

Despite being strenuous, this is perhaps the most popular hike on the west side of the Tetons. There are good reasons for this. One is a magnificent payoff at the top. When you scramble those last few yards, you are treated to a view of all the range's big peaks. This hike is also popular because it can give novices a real sense of accomplishment. The trail can be crowded throughout July when area Boy Scout and girls' summer camps send groups up the mountain.

As with any tough hikes, you'll enjoy this one if you are in good condition.

There are two routes up the mountain. The longer, more gradual main route — sometimes called "The Huckleberry Trail" and the shorter ridge trail.

The ridge route trims at least an hour and a half of hiking off the main route, but it is steep and

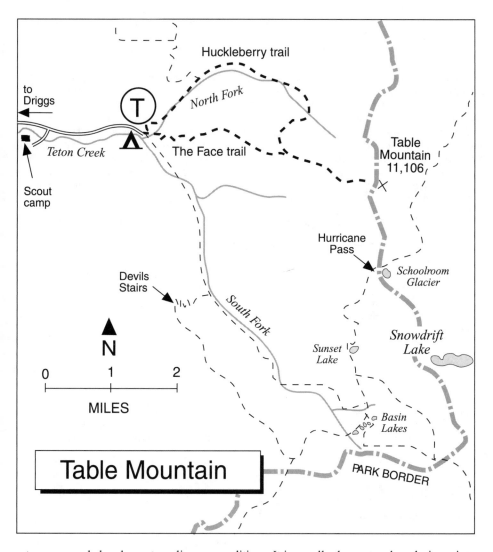

Table Mountain

not recommended under wet or slippery conditions. It is usually the route taken during winter ascents.

To access the ridge route, drive to the South Teton Creek trailhead as if you're going to hike to Alaska Basin. Look for a small trail on the northside of the restroom. This is the ridge trail. Most of the hike's elevation gain comes in the first 2.5 miles. As you gain the top of the canyon, you'll be treated to some nice views of the South Fork Teton canyon. After 2.5 miles, you gain the main ridge leading up to Table Mountain. At three miles, the trail joins the main trail up to the summit block.

The main "Huckleberry" trail follows the North Fork of Teton Creek. To access this trail, park at the trailhead before you cross the creek bridge near the campground. The hike starts out with switchbacks for the first .5 miles until you climb about four hundred feet. After this first initial workout, the trail settles in for a gradual incline following the North Fork of the Teton Creek.

After a few hundred yards, the trail enters the Jedediah Smith Wilderness Area. The Forest Service has limited the maximum number of people in each group on the trails. Check for current regulations. Wildflowers are usually in abundance along this trail during mid-July and early August. Moose are sometimes seen in the willows near the creek.

The trail crosses the creek three times before it begins to climb abruptly again. At about the

3.5-mile mark, the trail begins to switchback up to the mountain's summit ridge. This ridge is at the 9,900-foot level. As you climb to this ridge, the trail enters into the alpine tundra zone. Here, summer is short and few trees survive. Those that are alive are stunted, bent and twisted. You often encounter snowfields across the trail.

Once you are at the top of the ridge, the thin air and lack of barriers to sight play tricks on your perception. It looks like Table Mountain is just up ahead, but in fact you've still got two miles to go and more than 1,000 feet of elevation to gain.

The last mile can be tough on tired legs. Be patient, rest often, snack and drink regularly.

The last hundred yards is a scramble up to the box-shaped summit block and then comes the wonderful reward. The view is breathtaking — and not just because you're out of breath. Remember to pack a camera and/or binoculars. From this vantage point there is so much to see. It's a good place to linger and eat lunch. The flat-topped mountain summit is about as long and wide as a couple of school buses set next to each other. With a pair of binoculars you can pick out climbers picking their way to the top of the Grand Teton just to the east.

FOSSIL MOUNTAIN

GETTING THERE: From Victor, Idaho, drive 5.5 miles north on Highway 33. Turn right (east) onto a paved road. Look for signs at the beginning of the road for Darby Girls Camp. After a mile the road becomes gravel. After another half mile the road forks. Go right and follow this road about 6 miles to its end, where you may park.

DISTANCE: About 6 miles to the top.

DIFFICULTY: Moderately strenuous.

SEASON: July to October.

SPECIAL CONSIDERATIONS: Expect to see tons of fossils on the side of the summit block.

The easiest way to the top of 10,916-foot Fossil Mountain is up the South Fork of Darby Canyon trail. Most people know of this trail as the Wind Cave trail or (in girls camp circles) the Monument Trail. Because of the nearby Darby Girls Camp, this trail probably gets as much use

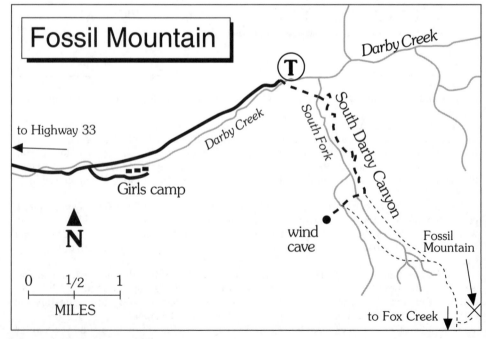

A marmot peaks out from under a boulder in the Tetons.

on some weekdays as it does on weekends.

The trail begins at the end of the Darby Canyon road and crosses the creek on a footbridge. After about a half mile, the trail enters the Jedediah Smith Wilderness Area. From here it gently switchbacks up the South Fork of Darby Canyon.

In midsummer this canyon is filled with wild flowers.

After about 3 miles, the trail crosses to the west side of the canyon and heads for the Wind Cave. There is a faint trail that continues up the canyon toward Fossil Mountain.

The faint trail soon fades away. Don't worry about getting off track. Just set your sights on the pass to the southwest of Fossil Mountain and hike the path of least resistance.

When Fossil Mountain appears in view, its west face is imposing. It's almost straight up, cliffy and loose rock.

Two miles after leaving the main trail, you'll reach the Fossil Mountain pass.

From the pass, there is a faint trail that starts up the ridge to Fossil Mountain. The peak's south end is a steep ramp of broken and loose rock. The hiking up is slow, but not too hard.

Almost at every turn, ancient seabed creatures — clams, coral, seaweed — lie cemented into the broken up rock. There are also geode crystals broken open and on display. What might be an uneventful grunt up the side of a mountain becomes a slog of discovery.

After about a third of a mile, the ramp of scree gives way to the level summit ridge. A few hundred feet north and you're standing next to a cairn with a summit register inside.

The views from the top of Fossil Mountain take in the southern end of the Tetons. You can easily make out the tram on the top of Rendezvous Peak. To the southeast, you can see the tops of the Wind River Range.

Coming down from the mountain can be more taxing than going up. The loose rock occasionally will scoot out from under and bite legs and hands.

On warm summer days, beat the heat by detouring to the Wind Cave on the way back down the canyon. The cave is like a giant, frosty air conditioned room.

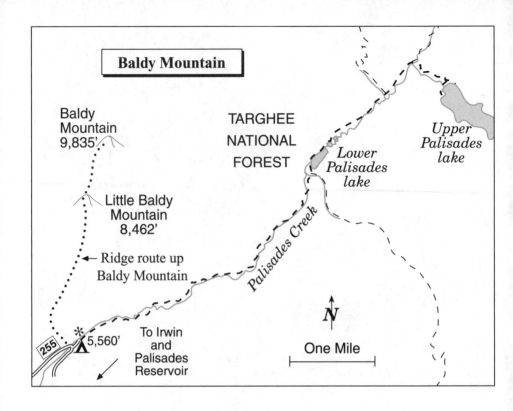

Baldy Mountain

Baldy Mountain 9,835'

TARGHEE NATIONAL FOREST

Upper Palisades lake

Lower Palisades lake

Little Baldy Mountain 8,462'

← Ridge route up Baldy Mountain

Palisades Creek

N

255 ▲5,560'

To Irwin and Palisades Reservoir

One Mile

BALDY PEAK

   GETTING THERE: Drive southeast from Swan Valley on U.S. Highway 26 to Irwin. Turn left on the Palisades Creek Road at the sign for Palisades Creek Campground. Follow this road for 1.5 miles. Just before the campground and a bridge across the creek is a parking area. Park here.
   DISTANCE: About 3 miles round-trip.
   DIFFICULTY: Strenuous.
   SEASON: April and May for skiing/snowboarding. June to November for hiking. Go early in the morning to beat the afternoon heat.
   SPECIAL CONSIDERATIONS: The large summit-to-base gully facing Swan Valley avalanches in late winter/early spring (often in April) — don't be around when it happens. Skiing is safest after the avalanche occurs.

   Don't let Baldy Peak in the Snake River Mountains fool you. Although it looks like a doddering old grandpa of a mountain with bald top and mellow-looking ridges, it takes a bit of muscle and determination to bag this peak.
   With a 4,000-foot elevation gain and steep snow-drifted ridges, this climb can be a rewarding conditioner. The peak appeals to more than just peak baggers seeking nice views overlooking Palisades Reservoir and the Snake River valley. Backcountry skiers and snowboarders often climb the peak in late winter and spring to test their mettle on the long southwest gully or south-facing bowl just below the summit.
   There are two popular routes up Baldy Peak: The long and mellow route from the Rainey Creek trail and the short and grinding ridge from the Palisades Creek trail parking area.
   Most prefer the short route. From the parking lot at Palisades Creek trail, scramble up to the ridge on the other side of the fence that marks the forest boundary. This ridge is the one on your left if you are facing upstream, up the Palisades Creek Canyon.

A herd of mountain goats hang out on the steep slopes of Baldy Mountain.

The steep slog begins immediately. The elevation is about 5,600 feet at the car and 9,835 feet at the summit. The 4,000 feet of vertical are gained in less than 3 miles. Once on the ridge, the climb is fairly straightforward. Stay on the ridge and it will take you all the way to the top. It helps if the day is clear enough to see the summit in the distance.

The ridge is not all uphill, though. About a third of the way up the ridge is a high spot called Little Baldy. There is a waist-high cairn marking the spot. In this area, there are resident moose. Look for moose sign along the ridge for the next half-mile. Also keep your eyes open for mountain goats on the open slopes.

From Little Baldy, the ridge dips slightly before climbing steeply up to some rocky high points. When in doubt, stay as close to the ridgeline as possible.

About two-thirds of the way up, the ridge levels one last time before making a final steep

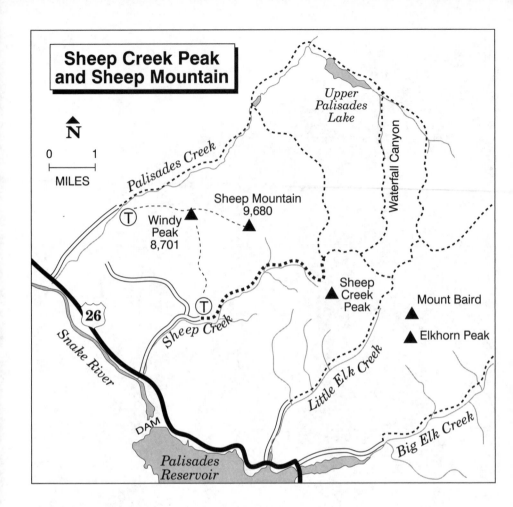

Sheep Creek Peak
and Sheep Mountain

N

0   1
|—————|
MILES

Palisades Creek

Upper
Palisades
Lake

Waterfall Canyon

Sheep Mountain
9,680

Windy
Peak
8,701

Sheep Creek

26

Snake River

DAM

Palisades
Reservoir

Sheep
Creek
Peak

Mount Baird

Elkhorn Peak

Little Elk Creek

Big Elk Creek

ascent to the summit.

The final 200 to 300 yards are steep and loose.

The summit has an old military ammunition can with notes of people who have climbed the peak. On clear days, you'll spot the Tetons to the northeast and the mountains of central Idaho to the west.

Unless you're strapped into skis or a snowboard, the descent off Baldy is a mixed blessing. What took hours to climb, takes only minutes to plunge/ski or hike down. On the downside, your quad muscles pay a price for all that quick descending. It's a good idea to stop every 15 minutes or so and relax.

SHEEP CREEK PEAK

GETTING THERE: From Swan Valley, drive southeast on Highway 26 about 10 miles. About 3/4 mile south of the Gaging Station turn left (north) onto Sheep Creek Road. There is a sign for the road, but it can't be read when heading southeast. Drive 2 miles up Sheep Creek Road. Near the sign for the Mennonite Camp, the road forks. Keep right. The road gets rutted and bumpy for the next mile. The trailhead is at a Forest Service sign next to the road.

This is a trail with quick payoffs and rewards.

The rewards for climbing Sheep Creek Peak (try to say that fast three or four times) are a stun-

38

Summit register on Baldy Peak is an ammunition canister wired to a post.

ning view of eastern Idaho and western Wyoming and the chance to see mountain goats and other wildlife.

Another benefit of hiking this trail is the solitude. While most of eastern Idaho's hikers will be one canyon north of you hiking the Palisades Creek Trail, you'll likely have the Sheep Creek Peak Trail all to yourself.

Sheep Creek Peak, 9,950 feet, is one of those giants you see along the highway as you drive to Palisades Reservoir. The peak is one of a trio of large peaks on the northeast side of the reservoir near the dam. The other two giants are Mount Baird, at 10,025 feet and Elkhorn Peak, at 9,940 feet.

There are two main ways to get to the top of Sheep Creek Peak. The first, and shortest, is to hike up the Sheep Creek Trail. This trail connects into the Waterfall Canyon Trail and is one of the shortest ways to get to the waterfalls — but not necessarily the easiest.

The other approach to Sheep Creek Peak is from the Little Elk Creek Trail. In early summer, the Little Elk Creek approach often has much more snow.

The trail starts at the end of the bumpy Sheep Creek Road. A high-clearance vehicle is recommended for the last half-mile. The road ends at a Forest Service sign which names the trail and says "Waterfall Can. 4." About 3/4 of a mile up the trail another Forest Service sign says "Waterfall Can. 5." Five miles is about right from the trailhead to the top of Waterfall Canyon.

The top of Sheep Creek Peak is about 3.5 miles from the end of the road.

The trail starts out as an old jeep road and slowly narrows into an ATV type trail. The trail becomes a footpath after a little more than a half mile. Elevation gain is a steady uphill almost the entire way. From the trailhead to the base of the peak, the trail gains about 3,000 feet.

One thing to keep in mind is that the Sheep Creek Canyon doesn't have much water in it. Once the snow has melted, the canyon will be dry, especially up high. Bring all your water for day and overnight trips.

After about two miles, the canyon narrows and becomes even steeper.

In early July, the upper parts of the canyon are still covered with large snow patches. In some places, the trail disappears under snow. But you shouldn't get lost if you stick to the main canyon.

At the top of the canyon the trail enters a small basin. Here hikers are treated to the view of the long, crescent-shaped ridge of Sheep Creek Peak. The summit is still about 500 to 600 feet above. Look for mountain goats cooling themselves on lingering snow patches along the summit ridge.

Fresh mountain goat tracks are seen in the snow just below Sheep Creek Peak.

From the base of the ridge there are different ways to the top. The main idea is to get on the summit ridge, then walk it to the summit.

Two good routes to the summit ridge include switchbacking up a low point along the northwest ridge or scrambling up a prominent rocky rib on the northern face.

As soon as you hit the summit ridge, you are treated to one of the best views in the entire Palisades area. All of the reservoir, the north end of the Salt River Range, the Gros Ventre Range, the upper end of the Wind River Range, the Tetons, the Centennial Range and more suddenly jump into view. It's worth doing again for that view.

On the summit is a small cairn. Tucked inside is a small register.

SHEEP MOUNTAIN

GETTING THERE: See text.
DISTANCE: About 3.5 miles one-way.
DIFFICULTY: Strenuous, gains about 4,500 feet.
SPECIAL CONSIDERATIONS: Keep your eyes open for mountain goats. They are often seen below the cliffs near the summit. Bring along binoculars.

The fun of climbing this mountain is the awesome views from the top.

On a clear day, you'll be treated to some nice views of the surrounding Snake River mountains, the Greys River Range to the south and the Tetons to the northeast. Below you is the Snake River valley and the blue waters of Palisades Reservoir.

There are two different main routes to the top of Sheep Mountain. Either route requires some serious uphill hiking.

Route 1: Park at the Palisades Creek trailhead, walk over the bridge and hike to the base of the southeast side of Palisades Creek canyon. Follow a barbed wire fence up the canyon rim for about a quarter of a mile. This route basically climbs and follows the Palisades Creek canyon rim.

The first high point is called Windy Peak (8,701) on the Targhee Forest Service maps. It can be a bit disheartening knowing that you have another mile and another 1,000 feet up to go from here. Stick with it, though, the top is awesome. Follow the ridgeline which turns and heads almost straight east. It's a good idea to occasionally look back the way you have come so that you can find your way back. Some of the side ridges could fool you on the way down.

40

Clouds swirl around the Elk Mountain Lookout in the Wyoming Range.

The final summit push is steep until you arrive on the summit ridge.

One odd thing on this hike is patches of cactus. Look for mountain goats in the large rocky bowl between Sheep Mountain and Windy Peak.

Route 2: This route starts by driving up the road to the Sheep Creek summer home area just before the Palisades Dam. About two miles up the road take a left up Sawmill Canyon. The road ends after a mile or so depending on your vehicle.

From the end of the poor road, you will be about 1.5 miles (as the crow flies) southwest from Windy Peak. Climb the ridge next to the canyon (called Canary Canyon on the Targhee Forest Service map) and go up toward Windy Peak. From the top of Windy Peak, follow the ridgeline to Sheep Mountain.

Remember to save some energy for the return trip. As with most mountains, going down can be a quad-burner.

ELK MOUNTAIN LOOKOUT

DISTANCE: 5 miles roundtrip.
DIFFICULTY: Strenuous.
GETTING THERE: See text.

Just south of Alpine, Wyo., is a beautiful canyon that boasts several trailheads, primitive campsites, a lively river and abundant wildlife.

The Greys River Road leads right out of the town of Alpine and within minutes you'll find yourself in the backcountry. Among the several fun trails is a lookout high on the Elk Mountain ridge. This area is sometimes called the Greys River Range, but it is all part of the Wyoming Range that runs north and south for more than 50 miles south of Hoback, Wyo., and east of Star Valley. The range is separated from the Tetons to the north by the Snake River canyon and boasts several 10,000 footers.

In the fall, half the fun is driving the winding road along the east side of the Palisades Reservoir. The aspens are a bright yellow and present a picture perfect setting. The drive up the Greys River Canyon is just as beautiful.

41

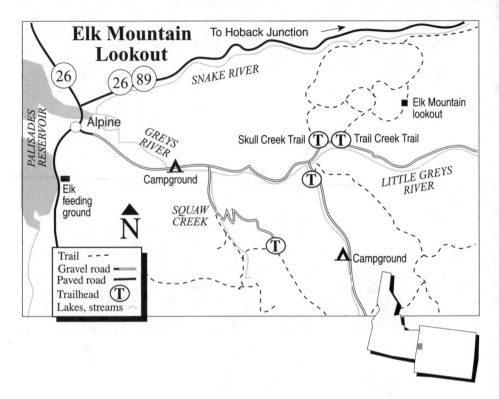

Elk Mountain Lookout

26

26 89

SNAKE RIVER

To Hoback Junction

Alpine

GREYS RIVER

PALISADES RESERVOIR

Elk feeding ground

Campground

SQUAW CREEK

N

■ Elk Mountain lookout

Skull Creek Trail (T)(T) Trail Creek Trail

(T)

LITTLE GREYS RIVER

(T)

(T) Campground

Trail - - -
Gravel road ═
Paved road ━
Trailhead (T)
Lakes, streams ~

Few of the trailheads are marked with signs. To find the trail to the lookout, drive a few miles up the Greys River Road to an intersection with the Little Greys River. Turn left and drive 1.2 miles up this road and turn left on a narrow dirt road. Drive about a quarter of a mile or until the road gets too bumpy for your liking. The road quickly degenerates into an ATV trail after the last campsite.

The Bridger-Teton Forest Service map calls this trail "Trail Creek." It starts out as a mellow ATV trail and gets steeper and steeper. There are a few side trails created by grazing cattle that could possibly confuse hikers. The main idea is to stick to the main route and keep right to climb up to a ridgetop after about two miles. If the trail you are hiking drops down, you're probably off track.

After two miles of uphill, the trail connects with a ridge. Follow the ridge, which will hook south. Eventually, if you sight along the ridge to the south, you will see a small building in the distance. The trail sticks to the ridgeline and takes you to this lookout.

While not the most picturesque of buildings, this small, one-room lookout does get you out of the wind, and it provides a 360-degree panoramic view of most of the range.

Inside the lookout are goofy notes and names scratched and penciled on the walls. Some (if you can believe the dates) are almost 40 years old.

The building has been repaired in recent years. Some of the broken glass panes have been replaced with Plexiglas.

One of the nice things about the view is that it inspires you to explore more canyons and ridges in the Wyoming Range. You can access some of these areas for backcountry skiing. Allow extra time and energy to ski up to the mountains because most of the roads are not plowed in winter, or you can hitch a ride on a snowmobile to reach the slopes. A good source of information on some of the peaks in this area is Tom Turiano's encyclopedic "Select Peaks of Greater Yellowstone."

A deer trots past the scree fields several hundred feet below the summit block of Mount McCaleb in the Lost River Range.

MOUNT MCCALEB

GETTING THERE: From Arco, drive north on Highway 93 about 20 miles to the town of Mackay. Turn right on Main Street and follow the road 1.9 miles and turn left on Lower Cedar Creek Road. Follow this road to near the end at the mouth of the canyon (stay above the creek ravine). About a quarter of a mile before the mouth of the canyon, take a jeep road to the left that heads to the northwest and angles toward the mountain. Drive as close to the foot of the mountain as your vehicle will take you. Pass two jeep roads and take the third if you are driving a high-clearance vehicle with power. There is a very steep jeep trail up the side of the mountain that is only recommended for ATV or powerful four-wheel drive machines. From your parking spot, hike up the prominent gulley between Little Mac and Mount McCaleb. For more information and photos, go to www.idahosummits.com.

DISTANCE: 6 to 9 miles roundtrip depending on how close you can drive to the mountain.

DIFFICULTY: Very strenuous. Gains nearly 5,000 feet in elevation.

Mount McCaleb, at 11,600+ feet, is that picturesque peak to the east of Mackay. It's one of the last of the big brutes on the southern end of the Lost River Range. Like many of the peaks in the range, the top has a huge vertical cliff face – perhaps 300 feet high — that gives the impression that only serious climbers need apply. Fortunately the west ridge of the peak offers a straightforward – albeit, arduous – "dog route" to the summit.

One of the hardest parts about climbing this peak is getting to the base of the mountain. The Lower Cedar Creek Road is accessible with a sedan and careful driving, but a high-clearance vehicle is preferred. You can park near the mouth of the Lower Cedar Creek Canyon and hike northwest along the base of the mountain. With a high-clearance vehicle and the extra time to explore the maze of jeep trails, it is possible to drive closer to the route. If you park at the mouth of Lower Cedar Creek canyon, add about two miles (one way) to the hike.

The trick to finding the easiest route up McCaleb is picking the right starting ridge. It's

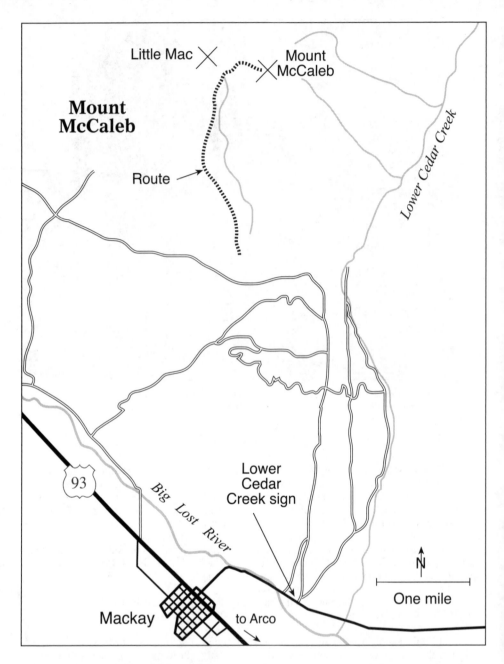

easy to see from the highway near Mackay, but harder once you drive and hike to the base of the mountain. There is an intermitent trail up the ridge that puts you onto the northwest side of the peak. When you pop out of the treeline, you are staring at the huge slope of loose scree. Be forewarned that the top looks closer than it really is. From the treeline to the summit is more than 1,000 feet of elevation gain.

You can hike up an obvious gully that leads to the west ridge or go straight up the southwest line and work around to the west face. Snow often lingers on this face throughout the year.

The summit of Mount McCaleb is a narrow strip that drops off abruptly on the east, south and north sides. There are technical routes up the southwest cliffs of McCaleb in the 5.7 to 5.10

44

difficulty range.

NOTE: If this peak whets your appetite for more exploring and peak-bagging in the Lost River Range, refer to the book "Trails of Eastern Idaho" by Margaret Fuller and Jerry Painter for a guide to all of Idaho's 12,000-foot peaks.

A couple pause to give their dog a drink on the way to the top of Bell Mountain.

BELL MOUNTAIN

Getting there: From Idaho Falls, drive west on Highway 20 and take Highway 33 to Howe. Drive to Howe and head north on the Little Lost River Highway. Stay on this highway until it turns to gravel. Drive .6 miles on gravel and turn right (east) at a yield sign. Follow this dirt road and keep left at a main junction. The road will lead you up Basinger Canyon — the canyon to the north of the west ridge leading to the summit of Bell Canyon. Close gates behind you. The road gets nastier the farther up you go.

Drive north in the Little Lost River Valley toward Bell Mountain and your eyes will be drawn to the long west ridge that starts at the valley floor and climbs all the way to the top of the peak. Just before the summit block is a giant wall that looks nearly impassable for mere hikers.

Bell Mountain is an impressive 11,612-foot peak in the northern end of the Lemhi Range northwest of Idaho Falls. The standard route up the peak is from the Little Lost River Valley north of Howe.

The higher up Basinger Canyon you drive, the nastier the road gets. For the upper end, high clearance and four-wheel-drive vehicles need only apply. You can park your vehicles lower in the canyon at a relatively flat area and hike or pile into the back of a pickup truck and drive the last half-mile up the road.

There is a "pretend" trail near the end of the jeep road that starts up the canyon, but the general idea is to grind your way up onto the top of the west ridge. It's about 3,000 feet of elevation gain to the top of the ridge and the lion's share of the total effort.

Start up the pretend trail, then leave the trail after perhaps a quarter of a mile and zig-zag up the north side of the ridge until you made a rocky chute that goes to the top of the ridge. Once on the west ridge, the way is obvious and the mountain summit — like a giant magnet — pulls you up.

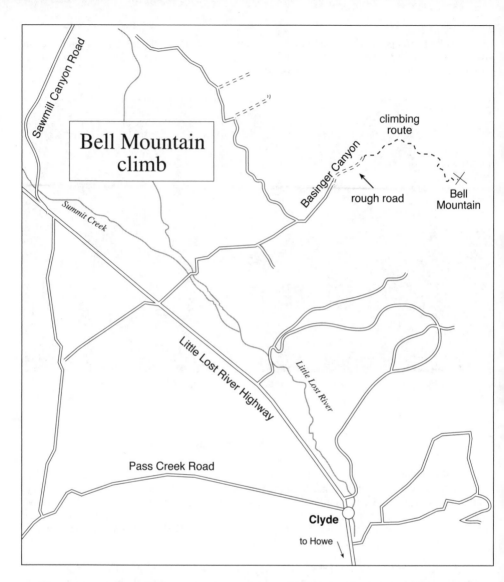

There are two obstacles on your way to the summit block. The first is a large tower that blocks most of the west ridge. Circle around the right side is easiest. The second challenge — the giant wall that can be see from the road as you drive up the Little Lost River Valley — is a piece of cake. There is an easy, albeit steep, hike around on the left side.

Once past these sentinels, the ridge presents a giant ramp up to the rocky summit block. What looks difficult from a distance is mostly easy once you get closer. The summit block represents about 800 or so feet of scrambling to the top. Oddly, the rock was not the petrified ocean-bottom mud often seen on other central Idaho peaks, but a beautiful quartz-type rock.

A good route is to scramble up the main west rib of the broken up summit block and trend to the right (south) when ever things became more challenging. Near the top, leave the rib and scramble into a broad gully. There is evidence of pathways in the gully from previous scramblers.

At the top, look for a small cairn with a register stuffed inside.

Bell Mountain's west ridge is rated a class 3 climb — meaning there's some easy scrambling with very little scary stuff. By comparison, Borah Peak is also rated class 3, but there are some actual class 4 (exposed) moves that cause people to chicken out and turn back. There is little to worry about on this scramble up Bell.

46

A scrambler nears the summit of Bell Mountain on the west side of the Lemhi Range.

If you're looking for bigger challenges, Dean Lords and Brian Wood put up a technical class 5 route on the northwest side of the peak. The east side route up Bell Mountain can also be more challenging.

While you might think Bell Mountain is named for the bell shape of its summit block, it's actually named after Robert Bell, Idaho's first state mining inspector.

47

Bikers pause along the Continental Divide Trail north of Targhee Pass.

49

A biker flies down the popular Palisades Creek Trail in the Snake River Range.

Biking

A note about mountain biking trails. In recent years, mountain biking trails have proliferated like rabbits. Local clubs and organizations have put together favorite rides, built new trails and retrofitted old trails to accommodate bikers, and the effort continues. Areas in the Big Hole Mountains, the Portenuf Range, Snake River Range and Teton Range seem to add trails annually. Rather than attempt to be comprehensive — because any guidebook would quickly become out of date — this book looks at most of the favorites and includes many of the best. This sampling will introduce bikers to areas of trails that should keep them busy for years to come.

TIMBER CREEK TRAIL (LEMHI RANGE)

GETTING THERE: From Howe, 23 miles northeast of Arco on Idaho Highway 22-33, drive north on the road between Howe and Ellis for 38.5 miles to the Sawmill Canyon Road. Only part of the last 9 miles is paved. Turn right (north) on the improved Sawmill Canyon Road, passing the Fairview Guard Station after 46.8 miles. Ignore several side roads and keep to the Timber Creek Road (labeled 101 on the old Forest Service maps) to the 50-mile point. Here, turn left (west) on Road 105 up Timber Creek. This road passes Road 442 that leads to the Timber Creek Campground. Continue on Road 105 (pass a turnoff for Redrock Creek Road.) after 54.5 miles. After another mile, the road splits. Continue on Road 105 to the end. At the end of the road, look for the start of trails 4076 and 4137.

This enchanting area has many trails — they follow creeks and ridges, take you to lakes, mountain tops or over passes. Generally, the area is sparsely used except during big holiday weekends or during hunting season. It's far enough from anywhere to offer amazing night skies.

A good launch point for this outing is the Timber Creek Campground about 50 miles north of Howe in the Little Lost River Valley between the Lost River Range and Lemhi mountain ranges. In midsummer this campground can fill up fast but there is camping on Forest Service land elsewhere. It has 10 sites in a fairly remote setting, a pit toilet, tables, metal fire rings, horse accommodations and water spigots. The price in 2013 was $5 at a self-service kiosk.

The trail begins at the end of the Timber Creek Road and climbs up to Timber Creek Pass on the crest of the Lemhi Range. This trail is about 3 miles up and offers nice views at the top (as well as the chance to see critters along the way). There are actually two paths to the top of Timber Creek Pass — 4076 and 4137. Both are open to ATV, mountain bikes and foot traffic. The west side trail (4137) is steeper and rougher, particularly as it nears the top of the pass -- expect to do some serious hike-a-bike. Some sections are badly eroded. At the top of the trail near the pass, there was a sign warning ATVers that the trail was not for them.

Trail (4076) is about a mile longer (4 miles), but much gentler and offers fun flow and speed coming down. Be aware that ATVs can be on the trail. If you take trail 4076 exclusively, know that it doesn't have any water on it after the first quarter of a mile. Trail 4137 follows streams most of the way up a canyon.

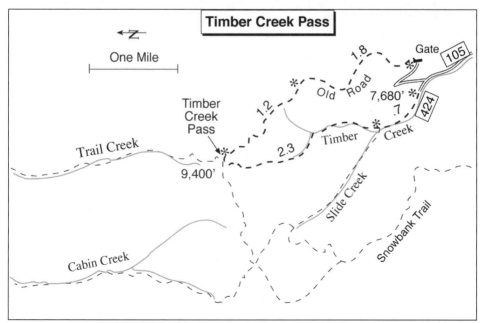

51

Mountain bikers might enjoy the challenge of riding up trail 4076 — it is a bit rocky in some places, though. The trail gains most of its elevation via kind switchbacks. Trail 4137 is not as kind and a tough hike-a-bike on many stretches.

HARRIMAN STATE PARK

GETTING THERE: From Ashton, Idaho, drive north on Highway 20 about 20 miles. The turnoff for the park is before you come to State Road 47. The park headquarters are about .5 miles from the highway. A per-vehicle entrance fee is charged.

Harriman State Park, often considered a fisherman's haven in the summer and a skier's destination in the winter, offers a little something for most riders. If you've been there in the winter to ski, than you're already familiar with the trail system.

While most of the trails are considered mellow biking, you can get some big ups and downs by heading up Thurmon Ridge and you can get some distance by riding along the river to Island

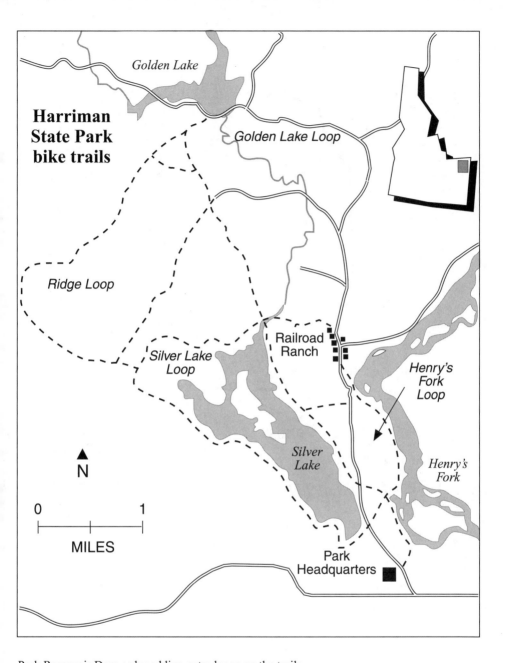

Harriman State Park bike trails

Golden Lake

Golden Lake Loop

Ridge Loop

Silver Lake Loop

Railroad Ranch

Henry's Fork Loop

Henry's Fork

Silver Lake

N

0 — 1

MILES

Park Headquarters

Park Reservoir Dam or by adding extra loops on the trails.

These trails are shared by hikers and horseback riders, but most weekends traffic is minimal. If you're worried about crowds, check at the main office to see which trails are most likely to be packed.

If you've only been to the park in the winter, Harriman can be a treat in the summer. Perhaps the most popular — and scenic — routes are the trails that follow the Henry's Fork River and the loop around Silver Lake. These routes also offer some tree cover to avoid the summer sun. The route out to Golden Lake is less forested.

Because the trails are maintained for skiers and horseback riders, they are also accommodating of bikers. The only trail you may have to duck and dodge tree limbs on is the Thurmon Ridge trail.

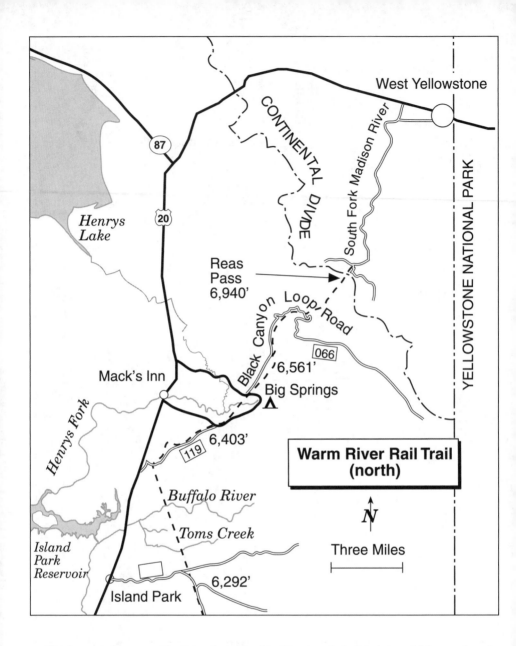

The lower trails are mostly flat and easy to ride. It's a good place to bring children and novice riders.

Just like hiking, it pays to get out of bed early to avoid the heat and possible thunderstorms of the summer afternoons.

In recent years, the park has groomed its winter trails for fat bikes. Most of the same ski trails have been set for biking. It's best to check on grooming, especially after a recent storm, to allow for the best fat biking conditions.

OLD RAILROAD TRAIL (WARM RIVER TRAIL)

MAPS: Caribou-Targhee National Forest

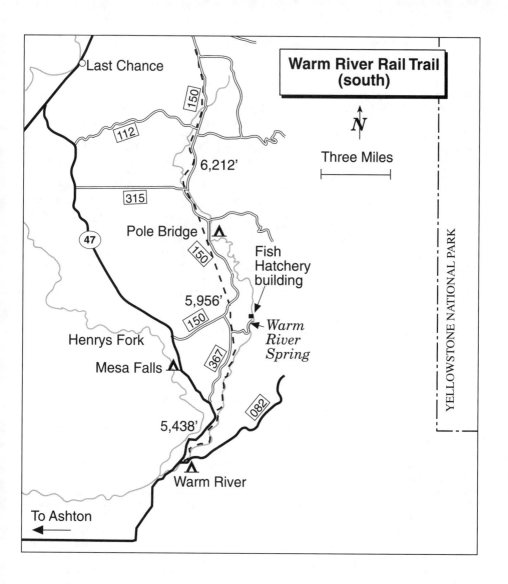

Warm River Rail Trail (south)

Last Chance

150
112
6,212'

N

Three Miles

315

47

Pole Bridge

150

Fish Hatchery building

5,956'

150

◄ *Warm River Spring*

Henrys Fork

367

Mesa Falls

5,438'

082

Warm River

To Ashton

YELLOWSTONE NATIONAL PARK

GETTING THERE: There are several trailheads for the trail. If you want to do the whole trail, probably the best place to start is at Reas Pass near the Idaho-Montana border, so your trip will be all downhill. Although the railroad bed exists from Reas Pass to West Yellowstone, following the trail can be confusing. To begin at Reas Pass, drive on U.S. Highway 20 to a point 2 miles west of West Yellowstone. Here turn south onto the South Fork of the Madison River Road. Passenger cars can drive to Reas Pass, which is about 7 miles from the highway.

Another trailhead is at the Black Canyon Road east of Mack's Inn. To reach it, take U.S. Highway 20 to Mack's Inn, about 33 miles north of Ashton. Turn east at Mack's Inn on Forest Road 059 and follow the signs to Big Springs. At Big Springs, turn north on the Black Canyon Road (Forest Road 066) and drive 6 miles. A sign marks where the road intersects the rail trail. There is parking along the road just before the intersection. From here, you can go to Reas Pass or start south toward Warm River.

The Warm River Campground is at the south end of the trail. To reach it, drive east of Ashton on Idaho Highway 47 and go north on Mesa Falls Road for about 10 miles, following the signs for Warm River.

For more details and a map on this and other hiking and biking trails, consult the guidebook

"Trails of Eastern Idaho" by Jerry Painter and Margaret Fuller. The book on more than 100 area trails is available at area bookstores and sporting goods stores.

This trail goes by several names. The old railroad bed trail from Reas Pass to Warm River is considered by many to be one of the best long mountain biking routes in eastern Idaho, and one of the best in the state. The trail follows the old Yellowstone Special railroad route, which carried tourists from Pocatello and Idaho Falls to Yellowstone National Park's West Entrance during the first half of the century. The old steam engines chugged through the farmland and backcountry for decades until the line was no longer financially sustainable. When the tracks were torn out, the trail that remained was graded, and trestle bridges were refurbished for horseback riders and mountain bikers in summer and snowmobilers and fat bikers in the winter.

Today, the trail is so good that it's like riding a soft sidewalk though the backcountry. About the only time the trail is rough is during the spring and early summer. During this time, trail users face downed trees across the trail and occasional boggy areas that often flood the trail. By mid-summer, most of the water has receded and the downfall has been cleared away.

Because the trail is a railroad grade and gains elevation slowly, it's a great beginner route or a good long-distance trip for those in good shape. The nice thing about this trail is that it's interesting. Just about the time you tire of the endless sea of lodgepole pines, the trail crosses a trestle bridge over a creek, or the forest opens up to reveal a gorgeous view of the Island Park plateau. Places such as Big Springs, Buffalo River and Warm River offer great opportunities for side trips, especially if you want to stop and camp and do some fishing.

Because the route is intersected by side roads, it's easy to break the trail into shorter sections. This works well if you have children along or if you want to do the entire route over a few weekends.

The entire route is about 48 miles long (add another 10 miles if you start from West Yellowstone), which means car shuttles have to be creative. You can start at the intersection of the Black Canyon Road with the trail, or start at Reas Pass on the Idaho-Montana border. The section from Reas Pass to Black Canyon is the toughest part of the whole trail, but experienced mountain bikers will find it pretty easy.

The section from Reas Pass to the Black Canyon Road is part of the Continental Divide Trail. It is 2.5 miles from the Black Canyon Road to Reas Pass.

Continuing south from the Black Canyon Road, the first five miles until Big Springs are scenic. The trail passes though thick forest and deep canyons. A couple of vistas open up, allowing you to see most of the upper end of the Island Park plateau. There is also a glimpse of the distant Teton range. The route descends quickly out of the Henry's Lake Mountains down to the plateau.

Big Springs is a nice side trip for those with some extra time. The springs provide most of the flow for the Henry's Fork of the Snake River until it is joined by the Buffalo River.

Just beyond the springs the trail crosses the Henry's Fork on a long trestle bridge.

A mile past Buffalo River the trail passes through a huge meadow of several square miles.

One highlight, especially for kids, is the railroad tunnel. About three miles out from the Warm River Campground the trail passes though a tunnel in the rock. It is long enough to become fairly dark inside.

The Warm River Campground is the end of the line. Here, paved roads take over the old railroad grade. The trail comes in at the upper end of the campground. There is plenty of parking outside the campground and several nice campsites with restrooms and tables in the campground.

ASHTON TO TETONIA RAIL TRAIL

GETTING THERE: The south end of the trail ends on the west side of the giant grain silos in Tetonia just off Egbert Avenue. Here, there is plenty of parking. On the north end of the trail, drive to North Fremont High School in Ashton and park on the east side. Take the road east out of the parking lot (toward the church), then turn north. After about a hundred yards, you'll come to the beginning of the rail trail. There is also parking and a restroom where the trail crosses Highway 47 (Ashton's Main Street) east of town.

This is sweet, mellow riding on one of the state's most scenic areas. With rolling agricultural land, giant trussle bridges and the backdrop of the Teton Range, you can't go wrong on this rail

Riding along the rail trail between Ashton and Tetonia.

trail.

This 30-mile roadbed is perfect for bikers and horseback riders and wintertime snowmobilers.

If you're doing the entire route, start at North Fremont High School parking lot in Ashton. Take the road east out of the parking lot (toward the church), then turn north. After about a hundred yards, you'll come to the beginning of the rail trail. The trail is part of the state Parks and Recreation Department. Often, your best clue that you're on the right path are signs saying "No Motorized."

The trail is about the width and texture of a jeep road. It takes you past rolling farm- and ranch land and often near farm homes. Some of the area is wild enough to attract weekend campers near the trail .

At first, the trail crosses a few paved roads, but after a few miles, you're out in the boondocks enjoying country only seen by cows and a few farmers. Some of the more exciting sections are the tall, steel trestle bridges. The first big one is over Falls River. These refurbished bridges smell of the creosote-treated timbers used for the bridge decking. If biking over a tall bridge a couple hundred feet above the river canyon makes you nervous, just remember that the bridge once held fully loaded railroad cars a thousand times your weight. The bridge is railed on both sides and you'd have to do some climbing to fall off.

The second half of the ride is popular with bikers starting out from Tetonia or the tiny community of Felt. Most ride up to the tall bridge over Bitch Creek, the return back to their starting point. Besides the ubiquitous horses and cows, look for sheep, sandhill cranes, bald eagles and hawks, ground squirrels, rabbits, song birds, badger holes and only a few people.

While most of the trail is easy to follow, one section, about midway, comes to an abrupt halt

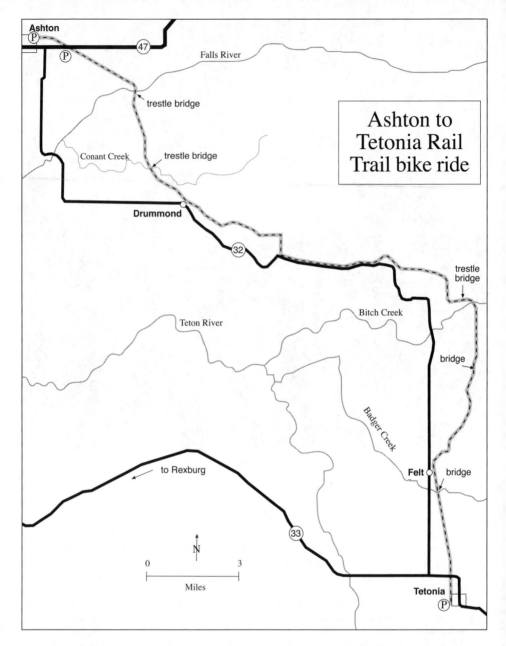

Ashton to Tetonia Rail Trail bike ride

against private property where a landowner refused to let the trail past through his property. A short jog along a steep up-and-down farm road back to Highway 32 after a 1.5-mile detour gets you back on the trail.

Although the grade is generally mellow, some days the prevailing winds can add to the workout. Depending on conditions and how often you stop to take photos, you should arrive in Tetonia in 3 to 4 hours.

The south end of the trail ends on the west side of the giant grain silos in Tetonia just off Egbert Avenue. Here, there is plenty of parking and a kiosk.

For current information and updates on the trail, check the state Parks and Recreation website at https://parksandrecreation.idaho.gov/parks/ashton-tetonia-trail.

One main obstacle to overcome with the ride is transportation. Most people aren't interested

Pausing from a mountain bike ride to soak up the view from the Bitch Creek trestle bridge.)

in riding the trail from one end to the other, then turning around and riding it back -- making for a 60-mile ride (perhaps that would be fine if it were paved). So, most people ride halfway up, turn around and come back to their car. Others leave a car at one end and ride the entire trail to their second vehicle. This involves a lot of driving but is satisfying when you're done.

Another method might be to have two groups start at opposite ends and exchange keys to vehicles when you meet in the middle.

Continental Divide to Mile Creek

This trail starts at Targhee Pass at about 7,000 feet elevation on the Idaho-Montana border on U.S. Highway 20 northeast of Henry's Lake. Before you start, you'll need to leave a shuttle vehicle at the Mile Creek Trailhead or make arraignments for a pick-up.

The trail starts out as a dirt two-track road in a northwesterly direction and climbs up to intersect with the Continental Divide Trail. Several sections of the trail were newly built with fresh-looking signs in recent years.

About the first 7 miles is climbing. Fortunately, there are helpful switchbacks.

After several miles, the trail crosses its first pass around Bald Peak. From near the pass, are nice views of Hebgen Lake to the east.

From the pass around Bald Peak, the trail drops down into a basin between ridges then crosses a mile or so up to the next ridge where the trail intersects with the top of the Targhee Creek Trail north of Henry's Lake.

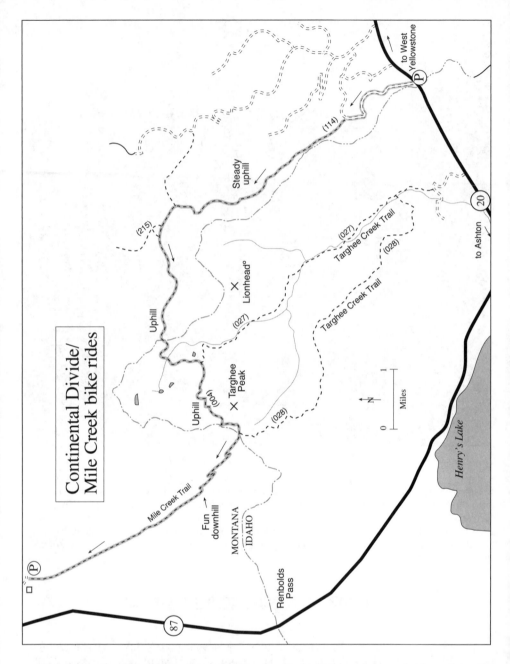

Continental Divide/
Mile Creek bike rides

Ahead, there is a big climb to get around Targhee Peak. At this point you also have the option of going down Targhee Creek and looping back to Targhee Pass -- pedaling up the highway to where you started. Mile Creek is still miles away.

After about a mile of uphill grinding, you hit the hike-a-bike rocky switchbacks to the top of the last pass. This high point was about 10,000 feet.

From this pass, it is fast and fun downhill into Mile Creek canyon on the Montana side. Down in the canyon is sweet rolling single track.

Mile Creek Road connects with state Highway 87 (which goes past the north side of Henry's Lake) and connects to U.S. Highway 20 from the west.

Bike computers peg this route at 22 miles.

A group of bikers pause on a ridge top along the Continental Divide Trail north of Henry's Lake.

Go prepared for some serious uphill grinding (several miles of it) and downhill blasting. Also, bear spray is comforting to have along. This is grizzly country.

Shuttle vehicles are pretty much a necessity unless you get creative with some of the loop possibilities.

CITY CREEK TRAILS (POCATELLO)

DIRECTIONS: See map page 54.

The City Creek Trail system is a fun half-day trip right out of Pocatello into the nearby foothills. These trails attract hikers and mountain bikers throughout the spring, summer and fall.

The system is subject to changes and trail work. They're are additions and reroutes occasionally added. While this guide will not present all of the possible routes, here are a couple of can't-miss options. Bikers would do well to visit the system and try out the several loop and connection possibilities. (See the map for additional trails.)

These trail can get a lot of use, especially on weekends, so an early start can be helpful in avoiding the traffic. Parking is just off of Grant Avenue.

This book features three routes: City Creek, 911 and Over the Top trails.

CITY CREEK

City Creek flows northeast and enters town on the southeast side before joining the Portneuf River. The creek is small and shallow but runs year-round except in severe drought years. It can be jumped in most places. Where the trail crosses the creek, there is usually a foot bridge.

From Grant Avenue, the trail starts out paralleling the south (left) side of the creek and heads up the draw.

Unlike many mountain streams, City Creek doesn't pass through a deep wooded canyon. Instead it flows through a shallow draw. Along the draw is a thick ribbon of maples, aspens and willows. Outside the draw it is practically barren, with only grasses and brush growing on the hillsides.

The trail is mostly a gentle up and down, but it has a steady uphill gain. After the first mile, the trail comes out onto a the City Creek Road. The trail parallels the creek and the road almost its entire distance (about 2.75 miles) until it intersects with other routes providing loop possibilities. Take one of these other routes on your return trip or reverse the trail back.

The potential for head-on collisions with other users is great on these trails. Some sections offer short visibility and blind corners. Be especially cautious when riding downhill and make lots of noise on blind corners.

911

After riding up the City Creek Trail, you can access the top of this fun roller coaster type trail on the way back down. Access this trail after a series of bridges about 1.25 miles up from the start of City Creek Trail or use some of the other connector trails at the top end of the City Creek Trail on the way down the hillside to start at the top of 911. This spur trail is a little less than a mile long and goes through surrounding brushland.

The 911 trail is one-way only (heading down) and is a thrilling blast -- though not for necessarily for beginners.

OVER THE TOP

This trail comes out of the middle of the City Creek Trail and climbs (switchbacks) steeply up to the top of Kinport Peak. This is a trail for those looking for a serious, challenging grinder and aerobic workout. This spur trail is about 3.75 miles. Expect to sweat, but you will get some nice views of the surrounding area and of the city below.

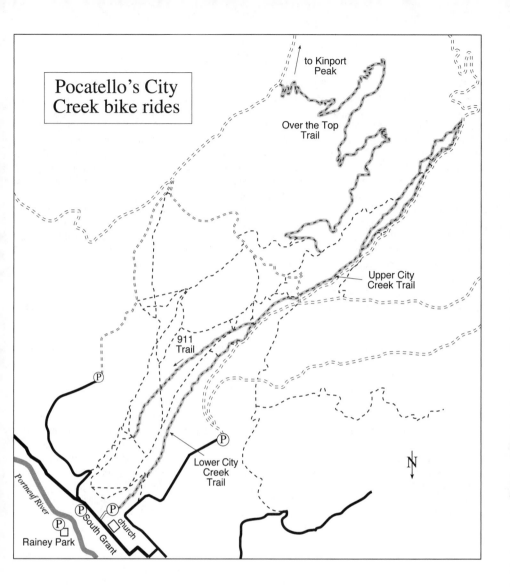

Pocatello's City Creek bike rides

to Kinport Peak

Over the Top Trail

Upper City Creek Trail

911 Trail

Lower City Creek Trail

N

Portneuf River

Rainey Park

South Grant

church

MINK CREEK AREA

GETTING THERE: From Pocatello, drive south on Interstate 15 10 miles and take the exit to Portneuf. Follow the signs to Mink Creek Recreation Area. Drive 5 miles from Portneuf south up the Bannock Highway to Cherry Springs Natural Area. Drive 2 miles south of Cherry Springs and turn left (east) and follow the signs to Scout Mountain Campground and Crestline Trailhead. Drive 4 miles south on Bannock Highway from Cherry Springs to the Valve House Draw and West Mink Creek trailheads. West Mink Creek is on the west side of the road about 50 yards south from the Valve House Draw trailhead which is on the east side. There is no sign that says, West Mink Creek. There is a small Forest Service sign with the number 059. Valve House Draw has a large gate at the trailhead. Its Forest Service number is 5171.

HOW STRENUOUS: West Mink Creek and Valve House Draw are moderate to strenuous depending on your distance. Scout Mountain Campground loop to Crestline is strenuous.

ELEVATIONS: West Mink Creek and Valve House Draw both start out at 5,200 feet and top out at 6,600 feet. Scout Mountain Campground is at 6,500 feet and climbs to 8,350 and back down to 6,000 at the Crestline Trailhead. Add another 700 feet if you take the side trip to the top of Scout Mountain.

DISTANCES: The Scout Mountain Campground to Crestline Trailhead is 13.5 miles. Add 4 miles if you go to the top of Scout Mountain. West Mink Creek to its junction with Gibson Jack is 6 miles. Valve Spring Draw to its junction with the trail south of Scout Mountain is 7.5 miles.

The Mink Creek area is popular with bikers because most of the trails are open to mountain bikes at least part of the year. To help prevent erosion, many of the trails are closed to biking during the winter months. Most open March 15 and close Dec. 30. Two popular, moderately easy trails are West Mink Creek and Valve House Draw.

West Mink Creek trail follows the creek up a canyon forested with fir and aspen. Good foot bridges take care of the three stream crossings. The springs at the upper end of the watershed are used for municipal water. Because of this, dogs are not allowed on this trail. Most of the trail is also a "research natural area." This designation boils down to no motorized vehicles of any kind allowed and no camping. If you want to camp, you'll have to do so outside of the "natural area."

The Valve House Draw trail just north of West Mink Creek is open to hikers, horses, mountain bikers, motorcycles and ATVs that meet certain size restrictions. The first part of the trail was once a jeep trail. The trail follows a spring-fed creek for about 6 miles. After 8 miles the trail joins the trail that goes south out of Scout Mountain Campground. This trail allows dogs, but doesn't open for bike use until mid March. Camping is permitted. The canyon is mostly forested and offers some nice views.

Bikers looking for a loop route can ride south on the South Fork Mink Creek Road and turn east up Box Canyon and continue on until you connect with the trail coming south from Scout Mountain Campground. Head north on this trail until you connect with the Valve House Draw trail. Complete the loop by riding the 1.5 miles back to South Fork Mink Creek Road on the paved Bannock Highway. This loop has the advantage of a mostly gradual climb up Box Canyon and mostly downhill on the Valve House Draw trail.

Bikers looking for a serious workout can take on the Scout Mountain to Crestline loop. Start at the Scout Mountain Campground near the nature trail. The trail heads due south for 2 miles then turns east and circles around the south side of Scout Mountain and starts heading north when you reach a junction with a jeep trail. This jeep trail offers a steep side trip up to the top of Scout Mountain. Add an extra 4 miles to the trip if you wind your way up to the top of the mountain. The trail leaves the jeep trail after .5 miles and heads due north 2.5 miles along a ridge. You will come to a junction. Take the left fork and switchback down two miles to the Crestline trailhead. This 13-mile loop gains and loses close to 2,000 feet.

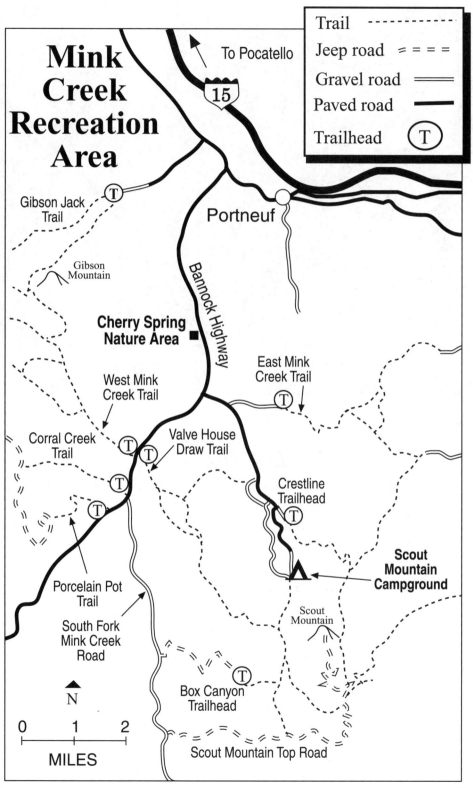

Mink Creek Recreation Area

Trail ---------
Jeep road = = = =
Gravel road =====
Paved road ▬▬▬
Trailhead Ⓣ

To Pocatello
15
Portneuf

Gibson Jack Trail
Gibson Mountain

Bannock Highway

Cherry Spring Nature Area

East Mink Creek Trail

West Mink Creek Trail

Corral Creek Trail

Valve House Draw Trail

Crestline Trailhead

Scout Mountain Campground

Porcelain Pot Trail

South Fork Mink Creek Road

Scout Mountain

N

0   1   2
MILES

Box Canyon Trailhead

Scout Mountain Top Road

Ken Durstine photo
Waterfall along Moody Creek seen from the Waterfall/Webster Dam Loop.

KELLY CANYON AREA

GETTING THERE: From Idaho Falls drive east on Highway 26 for about 16 miles and turn left at the signs for Kelly Canyon Ski Hill and Heise Hot Springs – continue following the signs to the ski hill. At 3 miles, turn right after crossing the Snake River and continue past the hot springs, past the golf course on your right and continue all the way up to Kelly Canyon Ski Hill. The listed trails have individual directions from the ski hill.

SIDEWINDER TRAIL

GETTING THERE: From Idaho Falls, drive east on U.S. Highway 26 toward Ririe. Turn north at the signs to Kelly Canyon Ski Resort/Heise Hot Springs. Continue to follow the signs to Heise Hot Springs. Continue past the resort golf course and the 7N Ranch red barn, then turn right onto the river road. The trailhead is 2 miles from this point. The road becomes gravel past the Kelly Island Campground. Follow the road until you reach a public parking area with a trailhead with a kiosk with signs for Stinking Springs. The left-hand spring-loaded metal gate across the dirt road from the parking area is where the Sidewinder Trail begins. The right-hand trail (open to motorized traffic is Stinking Springs Trail).

This relatively new mountain biking trail on the south side of Kelly Mountain is a winner. Called the Sidewinder Trail, the route is closed to motorized traffic. It starts near the old Stinking Springs motorized trail just across the road from the large parking area off the South Fork Snake River road. To access the new trail, use the metal gate on the farthest left.

66

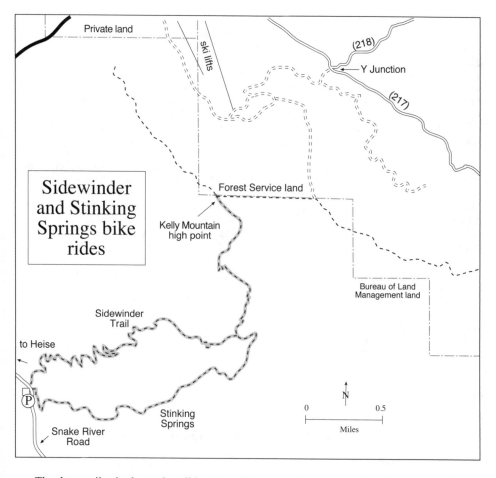

The three-mile single-track trail is open to hikers and horseback riders, but the majority of users are mountain bikers. The trail is on Bureau of Land Management land and was built as a cooperative effort.

The trail is generally moderate in difficulty as it uses long, meandering switchbacks to climb up the lower slopes of Kelly Mountain's southwest side. There are only a few short uphill stretches that force riders to crank harder. Usually, the uphills are followed by some flat or even downhill sections for a quick recovery.

At the top of the trail it connects into the Stinking Springs route and continues to the top of Kelly Mountain. The Stinking Springs trail is a bit rougher and rockier. The Stinking Springs trail climbs to the top of Kelly Mountain. From there, you can take the ski resort service road/ cat track down the other side, or if you're more adventurous, other more exciting downhill routes off the north side of the hill. The return back down the Sidewinder Trail is a fun downhill blast. The hairpin turns are banked just enough for fast turns.

Because this side of the mountain gets a heavy dose of the summer sun, it's often best to ride this trail during the morning hours or later in the evening.

Some bikers looking for a longer outing can ride up the paved road to the Kelly Canyon Ski Resort, up the service road to the top of the hill and down the Stinking Springs motorized trail to the top of the Sidewinder Trail.

This side of Kelly Mountain is usually closed to human entrance in winter until after April to protect deer herds.

STINKING SPRINGS

GETTING THERE: From Idaho Falls, drive east on U.S. Highway 26 toward Ririe. Turn north at the signs to Kelly Canyon Ski Resort/Heise Hot Springs. Continue to follow the signs to Heise Hot Springs. Continue past the resort golf course and the 7N Ranch red barn, then turn right onto the river road. The road becomes gravel past the Kelly Island Campground. Follow the road until you reach a public parking area with a trailhead with a kiosk with signs for Stinking Springs. The left-hand spring-loaded metal gate across the dirt road from the parking area is where the Sidewinder Trail begins. The Stinking Springs Trail is the right-hand trail.

If you like long climbs that are rewarded with steep and technical downhills then this trail is for you. Although usually done as a loop ride, some riders prefer the shuttle method and eliminate almost all of the climbing. To just do the downhill ride of Stinking Springs, leave your shuttle vehicle at the Stinking Spring trailhead. Pedal back down the river road toward 7N Ranch and at 2 miles turn right onto the paved ski hill road and get ready for the long climb. At about 4.25 miles the road turns to gravel and the ski hill is to the right. Continue on to the Y-junction then take a hard right. At about 5.70 miles the cat track for the ski hill is to the right – pass through the gate and follow the cat track as it winds its way up the east boundary of the ski hill. The last portion of the cat track is the steepest so save some juice for this part. At about 6.8 miles the track begins to level off – take a left, ride the two-track for a bit and then stay left as the track splits. A brief climb to the radio tower on the ridge ends the climbing at 7.4 miles; it's all downhill from here. Drop down the gravel road heading east and pass through the gate on the right at the trailhead for Stinking Springs. At about 8.25 miles take a left onto a rocky portion of the trail and hang on as the descent becomes loose and steep for a little while – just keep in mind that the trail really does get better as it descends toward the river. After passing a cattle trough the trail widens and becomes very enjoyable. At 11.5 miles the trail ends at the river road and the parking area.
You can take this same route to the top of Kelly Mountain and instead of going down the Stinking Springs Trail, head down the Sidewinder Trail. Or go up one and down the other.

WATERFALL/WEBSTER DAM LOOP

GETTING THERE: A word of caution: This trail intersects with so many other trails and roads that you can expect to get sidetracked and off track more than a few times. Unless you have a serious sense of adventure, it's probably best to ride it with someone who is familiar with the route. Many of the intersections are not marked. It can be helpful to have a GPS unit and a compass. To get there, drive to the Kelly Canyon Ski Resort and continue past the resort to the Y Junction. Turn left at the Y Junction on Forest Road 218. Drive .8 miles to Morgan Summit (top of the hill) and continue another .8 miles to a junction with FR 887. Turn left (west) on FR 887 and drive about .25 miles and park at a smallish parking area (N43° 39.18′ W111° 35.53′). The ride starts here and goes north on trail 290 (Lyons Creek).

This popular trail is a mixture of single track, ATV/two track, and dirt roads and makes a 12-mile loop. It crosses dozens of side tracks and roads and it is extremely easy to get off track. To add to the confusion, cows add new trails each year to many areas. The riding is moderately challenging with hills both up and down. Some of the downhill sections are rocky and technical.
From the start, go north about .25 miles where the trail crosses the boundary between Forest Service land and state land. Continue north a few hundred yards to a fence. This is the beginning of the loop — usually done counter clockwise. Cross the fence and keep right. The trail continues northeast. After a few hundred yards, you'll pass a trail on the left. Ignore it and continue northeast. After another .25 miles you intersect with two track — ignore the right turn and continue north. The trail crosses a main road in another .25 miles (your GPS should read N43° 38.62′ W111° 35.34′). After another half mile, the track intersects with another wide track. Continue left going in a mainly north direction. Continue on this track in a north-northeast direction for about a mile (ignore a left hand path). The track comes to a road. Turn right on this road and ride for about 100 yards and take a left on a wide track (going northeast). This trail follows State Creek for the next 1.5 miles — the creek is on your left. After about 1.5 miles you come to the Forest

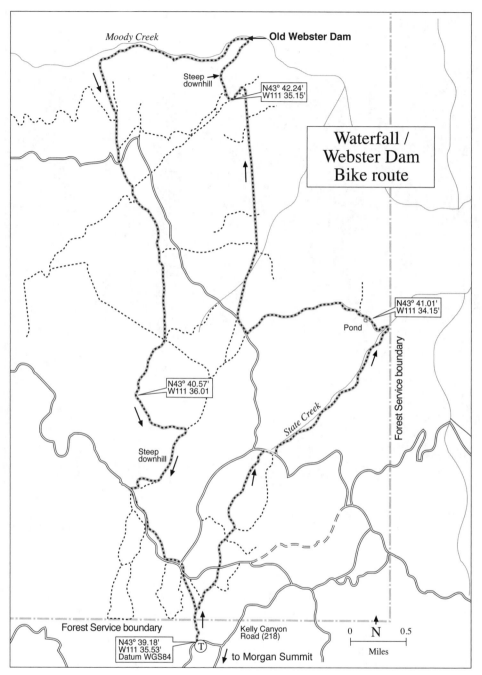

Moody Creek

Old Webster Dam

Steep
downhill

N43° 42.24'
W111 35.15'

Waterfall /
Webster Dam
Bike route

N43° 41.01'
W111 34.15'

Pond

N43° 40.57'
W111 36.01

State Creek

Forest Service boundary

Steep
downhill

Forest Service boundary

N43° 39.18'
W111 35.53'
Datum WGS84

T

Kelly Canyon
Road (218)

to Morgan Summit

0   N   0.5

Miles

Service boundary and a gate. Here, you cross the creek on your left and go a short ways (1/8 of a mile) back up the creek following a narrower trail. This trail turns in a westerly direction following a smaller stream. Shortly, it comes to a small dam/pond at N43° 41.01' W111 34.15'. Here the trail forks. Keep left and continue west. For the next mile, the trail follows this small creek, crossing it a few times. The trail swings southwest and intersects with a road at N43° 40.93' W111 36.11'. Turn right onto the road going north northwest for 1/8 mile until you come to an intersection with a smaller two-track. At this intersect, one road heads northeast and one north. Take the track going north. Stay on this track going due north for the next nearly

Ken Durstine photo
Trail along the Waterfall/Webster Dam Loop.

2 miles. Ignore other trails along the way. When the trail ends at a T, take a left and go a few hundred yards to a set of intersecting trails at N43° 42.24′ W111° 35.25′. Turn right and head north again. Keep right at the next intersection in a few hundred feet. Continue down a steep hill going north for about .5 miles to the bottom of Moody Creek canyon and the old Webster Dam. From here, you turn left and follow fun trail along Moody Creek (on your right) for the next 1.25 miles going west, after that distance the trail turns south following a small side stream. This trail climbs for about .75 miles where it intersects with a road at N43° 41.86′ W111° 36.14′. Cross the road and continue in a south southeast direction, following a tiny stream uphill. After about .2 miles, you'll pass under powerlines. a few hundred feet after you come to an intersection at N43° 41.68′ W111° 36.01′. Keep left at this intersection and continue in a southeast direction for the next mile continuing to climb. The trail comes to a fence and gate at N43° 40.89′ W111° 35.77′. Go through the gate and head south with still more uphill. After about .3 miles you'll come to another intersection at N43° 40.57′ W111° 36.01′. Take a left and ride for another .3 miles. At the next intersection, turn right and head steeply downhill for close to .5 miles (keep right at any forks). The next intersection at N43° 40.05′ W111° 36.04′ comes to a road. Turn left onto the

road and follow the road for about a .3 mile. The road comes to a gate. At the gate, leave the road and follow a trail on the northeast (left) side of a creek. This trail roughly parallels the road for another .4 miles before it rejoins the road where the road intersects with another road. A few hundred feet past this road intersection (going south) the road is intersected with some wide trails on the right (southwest). There is a gate here at N43° 39.58′ W111 35.63′. Take the trail on the left which beelines south (a bit uphill) to a fence in about .3 miles. At the fence, the loop ride is complete. From the fence, head south another .25 miles back to your car.

MOODY SWAMP/THOUSAND SPRINGS

GETTING THERE: From the end of the pavement at Kelly Canyon Ski Resort, drive 11.4 miles on Road 218. At 11.4 miles turn right on FR 651. Drive to the end of the road (about 1.5 miles) and park at the Moody Swamp trailhead. From here, follow trail 077 to Thousand Springs.

Starting at the Moody Swamp Trailhead about 11 miles from Kelly Canyon Ski Resort in the Big Hole Mountains, this trail is essentially a dirt bike/ATV trail. It's restricted to machines 50 inches wide or less. Of course, there are no rules against hiking or mountain biking the trail, should you prefer muscle power. The trail offers some excellent mountain biking opportunities. Just beware that you will run into your motorized brothers, especially on the weekends. Stepping out of the way on foot or bike is not a problem.

Most of the trail is forested — a blessing on hot summer days. Biting bugs are present.

From the trailhead, it's a little more than a mile to the first junction. At this junction, you can continue on trail 077 or take trail 121. If you want some views, go left on 077 and up 121. Trail 121 climbs steadily up to the top of a ridge after another 1.5 miles (this is hike-a-bike terrain or ditch the bike for the short jaunt up to the top of the ridge called Red Butte).

At the top are some nice views of the Big Hole mountains and the Grand Teton in the distance.

Trail 121 intersects with trail 068 — this trail becomes the Burns Creek Trail — a right turn

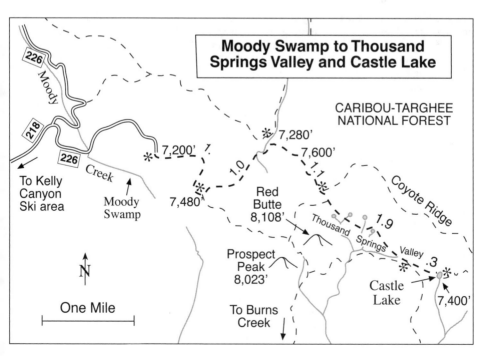

Moody Swamp to Thousand Springs Valley and Castle Lake

After years of drought, Castle Lake has shrunk somewhat.

takes you down Burns Creek and a left goes to Thousand Springs canyon in about 1.25 miles. There is a "trail" that drops off the ridge (very steeply) from trail 121 and follows a crappy sheep trail down to Thousand Springs. There was a Forest Service sign indicating that the trail was not for motorized traffic. It is not recommended for anything but hikers or mountain goats — it has grades up to 40 percent and goes straight down.

Instead, take trail 068 down to Thousand Springs canyon.

The Caribou-Targhee Forest Service map shows that there is a Castle Lake up the Thousand Springs Trail. From the intersection of the Thousand Springs Trail (077) and the Burns Creek trail (068), take trail 076 to Castle Lake — about another .6 mile or so.

Don't expect much at Castle Lake — it's more of a pond these days. It's very shallow and grass fills most of its former glory.

From here, head back down Thousand Springs (trail 077) and continued on this trail back to the Moody Swamp trailhead.

This route is about 10.5 miles. There are some rocky sections to contend with, but there are also some nice flow sections that should leave a smile on your face.

BUCKSKIN MORGAN RIDGE/FENCELINE/HAWLEY GULCH LOOP

From the ski hill, continue driving on the gravel road for about 1 mile and park at the "Y-junction" where the road splits 3 ways. The ride starts up the left fork in the road (FR 218), and ascends switchbacks before topping out on Morgan Summit at about .9 miles. The Buck-skin trail starts from here off the left side of the road.

Follow the single track as it climbs a short, steep section before leveling out for a fantastic

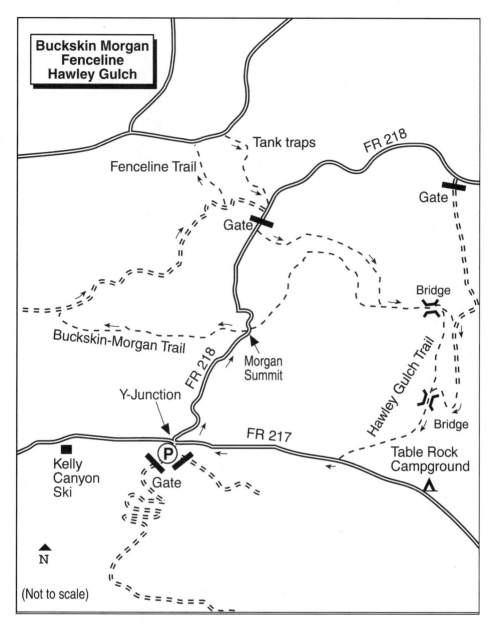

Buckskin Morgan
Fenceline
Hawley Gulch

Tank traps

FR 218

Fenceline Trail

Gate

Gate

Bridge

Buckskin-Morgan Trail

FR 218

Morgan
Summit

Hawley Gulch Trail

Bridge

Y-Junction

FR 217

Table Rock
Campground

Kelly
Canyon
Ski

Gate

N

(Not to scale)

ride that winds through the forested ridgeline. At 2.6 miles the single track ends and merges with a 2-track road. Take a hard right and follow the 2-track as it dips, climbs and winds its way along the forested ridge. The dirt gives way to a rocky two-track as it crests and drops for a fantastic descent with two hairpin corners. At about 4.8 miles try not to miss a remnant of a road on the left. Take this turn and climb briefly before dropping down on a faded track – there is a fenceline on the right that parallels the trail as it climbs gently again through the trees before dropping down and through a gate at 5.4 miles. Pass through the gate and take a right. At 5.45 miles make a right on an old road that has "tank traps" and usually stagnant pond-like water in it. Pass the traps and open it up on the descent as the road gives way to a single track with a stout little kicker near the end. Ride or step through the small creek and join up with FR 218 at 6.08 miles. Make a right and head up the road passing over a cattle guard and at 6.3 miles take the faint trail on the left. Ascend through thick growth, descend,

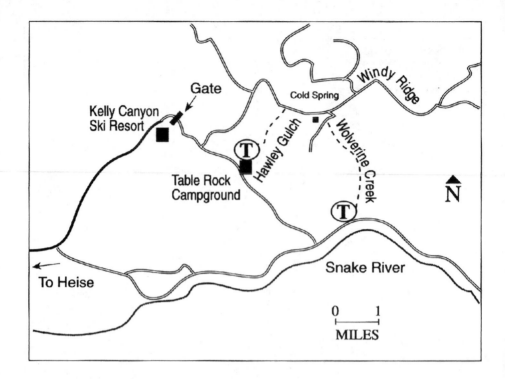

make a left and head for the two-track at 6.46 miles. From here go right and at 6.66 miles make another right onto a single track. Follow this as it weaves its way through the forest and drops steeply and merges with another single track at 6.95 miles, from here make a left. At 7.23 miles cross a bridge over Hawley Creek and climb the short steep hillside to connect with a dirt road. Follow this road downstream as it gives way to a single track before merging with the old Hawley Gulch trail and bridge at 8.3 miles. Navigate the loose scree and pass the Poison Flats trail before enjoying the descent into Table Rock Campground. CAUTION: Please be courteous of uphill travel through this section of trail. This portion of the trail sees heavy use during the weekends. Connect with FR 217 at 9.12 miles and take a right climbing the road back to the parking area at about 10.4 miles.

HAWLEY GULCH/WOLVERINE CREEK LOOP

An all-time favorite, Wolverine Creek ranks the highest with local bikers who have ridden here for years. This trail is most enjoyable as a downhill/loop ride but hard-core cyclists are known to do it as an up-and-back. From the ski hill, drive up the gravel road to the "Y-junction" and take the middle fork in the road that descends to Table Rock Campground; park here.

Pedal from the campground back up the dirt road and take a right at about .52 miles into the Poison Flats parking area. Ride through the loose gravel and start up the wide trail. Follow the single track as it weaves its way through the trees and eventually joins up with the Hawley Gulch trail at .96 miles. Turn left onto the Hawley Gulch trail and continue climbing upstream. Turn right at the foot bridge and pedal up the short switchbacks. Continue on the wide flat trail as it passes over a cattle guard, takes a sharp left and flattens out again before joining FR218 at 2.64 miles. From here turn right and follow the main dirt road as it climbs briefly, then flattens out before climbing again to top out on Windy Ridge. From here it's mostly downhill! As the road descends, look to the right at about 4.46 miles for road 883; take this two-track. Where the two-track/road takes a sharp left, drop down off the track angling left and look for the start of another less defined two-track. Follow the trail as it descends through the trees and switchbacks before opening up in a flat meadow. Climb up a short incline before descending again

Cranking along the Wolverine Creek trail at Kelly Canyon.

and passing through Wolverine Creek and the final section before the trail empties out on the river road at about 9.39 miles. Turn right and follow the road as it climbs back up to Table Rock Campground at 13.10 miles.

SOUTH FORK OF THE SNAKE RIVER

This trail begins at the end of the Snake River Road several miles from the pavement near Heise Hot Springs. Although a long drive, it can be part of the fun, offering some nice scenery. This road is passable with a sedan, but expect rocks and occasional ruts.

At Black Canyon, look for a Forest Service kiosk about 50 yards up the canyon from the trailhead. Here, is the start of the South Fork Trail. This trail roughly parallels the north side of the Snake River and winds east to end at Dry Canyon near Swan Valley after about 5 miles. This section of trail follows a roadless section of the river.

In spring, the trail is green and beautiful. It offers expansive views of deep rock cliffs and forested canyon sides with fir and aspen. Large islands in the river have mature cottonwood stands. Wildflowers also put on a nice show.

Be prepared for some hard peddling. There are several ups and downs as the trail follows the contours of the side canyons. The steeper sections are often littered with loose rock, causing long sections of hike-a-bike. There are also some enjoyable sections of mostly flat trail that offer nice views of the river.

This trail is popular with the motorbike crowd. If you want to avoid most of the motorbikes, and possibly see more wildlife, start your bike at dawn.

Most people do this trail as an out and back, but it is possible to leave a shuttle vehicle at either end (though it may take as much time to drive back and forth as to just ride back.

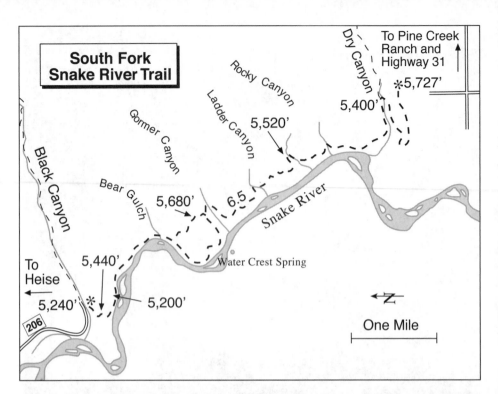

South Fork
Snake River Trail

Black Canyon

Gormer Canyon

Bear Gulch

Ladder Canyon

Rocky Canyon

Dry Canyon

To Pine Creek
Ranch and
Highway 31

*5,727'

5,400'

5,520'

5,680'

6.5

Snake River

5,440'

Water Crest Spring

To
Heise

5,240' *

5,200'

206

N

One Mile

*A dilapidated sign along the South Fork of the Snake River gives distances to Black Canyon
and Dry Canyon.*

PALISADES CREEK TRAIL

GETTING THERE: Drive southeast from Swan Valley on U.S. Highway 26 to Irwin. Turn left on the Palisades Creek Road at the sign for Palisades Creek Campground. Follow this road for 1.5 miles. Across the creek before the campground is a parking area for stock/horse users. Above the campground on the north side of the creek is a parking area for hikers. A footbridge gives access to the trail from there and bypasses the campground.

The non-motorized trail up to the Palisades Lakes may be the most popular in eastern Idaho. There are several reason for this. The lakes offer excellent fishing, gorgeous mountain scenery, great wildlife viewing, easy hiking and a Forest Service campground at the mouth of the canyon. In addition, bridges across the creek make the route easier for bikers, hikers and horseback riders. On any summer weekend scores of people make the trek up the canyon. To avoid crowds, try to go during the week, or in spring or early fall before hunting season.

Both lakes were formed ages ago when giant landslides came down the canyon and blocked the creek. The canyon is thickly forested with fir, as well as some aspen and willow. If you scan the mountain walls you may see mountain goats.

It is 4 miles to the lower end of the lower lake. The first mile of trail is moderate biking, then the trail begins to throw some lung-busting uphills at you. The trail also has a few rocky sections, especially about .5 miles before the first lake. The trail mellows a bit between the first lake and the last main bridge across the creek before heading steeply, and roughly up to the upper lake. Expect some hike-a-bike sections.

The upper lake is at 6.2 miles. If you're looking for a longer trip, the trail to Upper Palisades Lake continues up Waterfall Canyon (at times very steep and eroded) and connects with the trail down Little Elk Creek. This extension is not recommended for bikers.

You can also continue up Palisades Creek past the turnoff for the upper lake at 5.7 miles. The bridge across Palisades Creek at this turnoff is a beaut — built for horses to cross. There aren't any bridges beyond this turnoff, so the several crossings of Palisades Creek make this

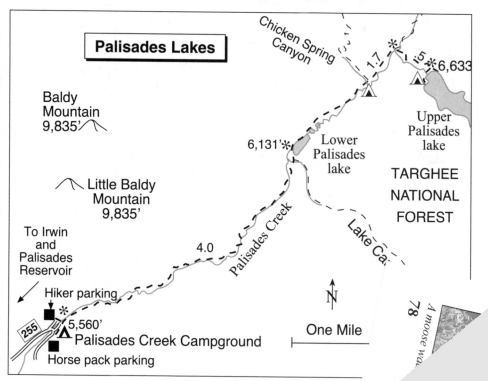

Palisades Lakes

Chicken Spring Canyon

6,633

Baldy Mountain 9,835'

Upper Palisades lake

6,131'

Lower Palisades lake

TARGHEE NATIONAL FOREST

Little Baldy Mountain 9,835'

To Irwin and Palisades Reservoir

4.0

Palisades Creek

Lake Ca.

Hiker parking

255

5,560'

Palisades Creek Campground

Horse pack parking

N

One Mile

77

A moose wa

...es in the water above the Lower Palisades Lake just off the trail.

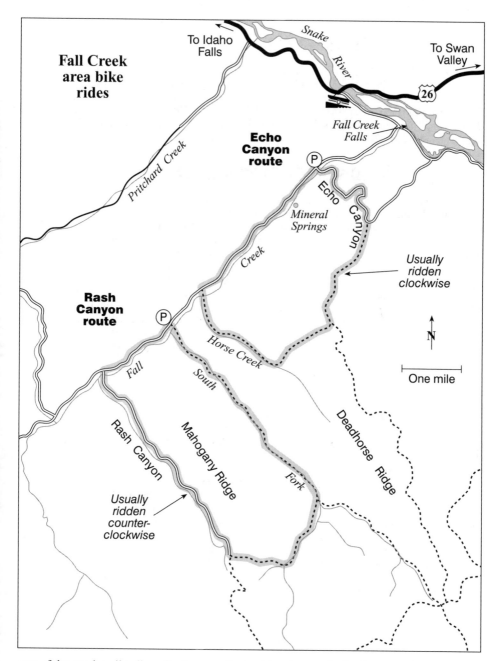

Fall Creek area bike rides

To Idaho Falls

Snake River

To Swan Valley

26

Fall Creek Falls

Echo Canyon route

Pritchard Creek

Echo Canyon

Mineral Springs

Creek

Usually ridden clockwise

Rash Canyon route

Horse Creek

N

One mile

Fall

South

Rash Canyon

Mahogany Ridge

Fork

Deadhorse Ridge

Usually ridden counter-clockwise

part of the creek trail tedious for those on foot or bicycle — only for the most diehard bikers. It's best to tackle this stretch after mid- to late summer when the creek is lower. It is a great way to lose the crowds, though, because few people continue beyond the lakes. If you do continue up Palisades Creek you will reach the Mosquito Creek trail, which leads into Jackson Hole.

Perhaps the best reason to ride all the way up to either lake, is the blast back down. Some sections require some technical riding skills, while others offer a nice flow. Be sure to make noise on blind corners because the trail often has large groups of hikers and horse back riders.

The Caribou-Targhee National Forest, Palisades Ranger District map is a good reference map.

FALL CREEK CANYON AREA BY SWAN VALLEY

GETTING THERE: From Idaho Falls, take Highway 26 east past the Kelly Canyon turn-off and continue on to Swan Valley. Just before Swan Valley, the highway crosses the Snake River – turn right onto the Snake River Road (FR 076) before crossing the highway bridge, and follow for about 1.5 miles to the intersection with Fall Creek Road (FR 077). Turn right and continue up the canyon. The Echo Canyon parking area is about 1.5 miles up the road on the left. The South Fork parking area is further up the road at about 4 miles.

ECHO CANYON TO HORSE CREEK LOOP

This suggested loop is for the serious hill climber who likes to grind it out in granny gear – to be rewarded with a fun and sweeping downhill on uncrowded singletrack. This ride also works well as an out-and-back ride if you eliminate Horse Creek from the loop.

From the large parking area at Echo Canyon trailhead, ride up through the gate and climb briefly up the gravel road and take a right onto the start of the actual trail. The climbing kicks in as the trail ascends through forested ridgelines and open draws. At about 3.2 miles pass the sign for Deadhorse Ridge and stay right as the trail keeps climbing and tops out on a brief ridge. Pass through the gate as the trial descends and keep following the sign to Deadhorse Ridge. Climbing once again, the trail finally tops out before a steep and loose descent through a poorly positioned gate. After passing through the gate the trail intersects with Horse Creek on the right. Pass through this gate and descend the next 3 miles of fun singletrack that ends at a creek crossing before joining up with the main dirt road. Be aware that this creek crossing can be deep and swift in the early summer. Once on the dirt road turn right and pedal back to the Echo Canyon trailhead at about 7.9 miles.

RASH CANYON TO SOUTH FORK LOOP

This Fall River Canyon ride is another classic of the region. With almost all of the climbing in the first half of the ride, it's a great warmup climb with a very fun descent that won't leave you white-knuckled and gripped.

Park at the south fork of Fall Creek right off the main road. Ride up the main road, (FR 077), for 1.5 miles Rash Canyon is on the left with a bridge over the creek; turn left and cross the bridge. Follow the two-track (FR 170), as it climbs Rash Canyon for 4 miles with the last .5 miles being a bit of a lung-burner. At the intersection at about 5.5 miles, continue straight over the top and drop onto another two-track that gives way to a singletrack at about 6.75 miles. Another intersection will be found at 8 miles – turn left and follow the trail as it turns into a two-track and descends down through the south fork of Fall Creek. There are at least three creek crossings before the trail empties out onto the main road – the last one being Fall Creek itself. End the ride at your vehicle at about 12 miles.

HORSESHOE CANYON

GETTING THERE: From Driggs, turn west off of Highway 33 at the main street light (this is going opposite of the road leading to Grand Targhee). Follow this road west out of town. After six miles, the road turns north (right) – this is 700 West. When in doubt, stay on the paved road. Go one mile north and turn west (left). After about a half mile, turn left again and follow the road to the end of the pavement and park on the left.

From the parking area, you'll do some uphill grinding on FR 235 for 3.2 miles. After 3 miles, look for an unmarked intersection that drops down into a meadow on your right. On the other side of the clearing is a marked trail (070). From here, the trail climbs for about a half mile. At

...iding one of the many trails in the Horseshoe Canyon area with the Tetons in the background.

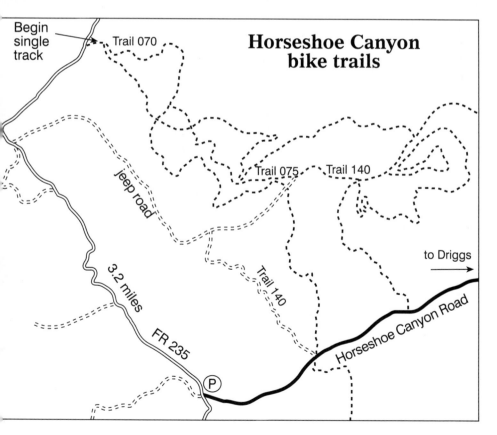

times you might ask yourself if you're taking the trail in the wrong direction.

At the next intersection, you'll have options. If you go straight, you'll finally enjoy some fun downhill runs before having to do some more climbing.

There are enough trails winding back and forth in this area to keep a biker busy most of the day. After exploring many of these trails (some with ramps for jumping), you can blast down a trail that drops back onto the paved Horseshoe Canyon Road about a mile east of the parking area.

The several intersecting trails can be confusing, even with a map, and may take a few visits to work out the lay of the land in your head.

If you get totally lost, find a trail heading east toward the Tetons and it will eventually drop you back onto the Horseshoe Creek Road.

DARBY CANYON (ASPEN BIKE TRAIL)

GETTING THERE: From Victor, drive 5.5 miles north on Highway 33. Turn right (east) onto a paved road. Look for signs at the beginning of the raod for Darby Girls Camp. After a mile the road becomes gravel. After another .5-mile the road forks. Go right and follow the road for about another .5 mile. Look for the parking area/kiosk on your left. This Forest Service trail is 034. Stick to the main trail heading north for biking. A side trail heading east leads to the climbing crag.

DISTANCE: 4.5 miles one way.

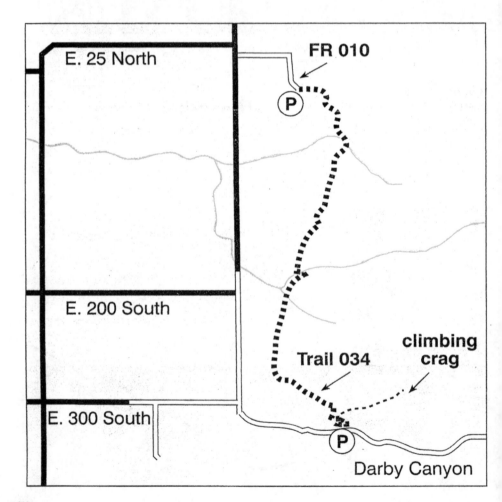

Levi Painter blasts through a small stream along the Aspen Trail north of Darby Canyon.

This is a sweet single track mountain biking trail that starts (or ends, depending on your direction) from the canyon and goes north, following the foothills of the west side of the Teton range for about 4.5 miles.

The Teton Valley Trails and Pathways organization has made improvements to the trail in recent years, particularly to the beginning at the south end, adding switchbacks to save some energy on the hill climb avoid some erosion.

If you're so inclined, you can combine a strength workout with an aerobic workout. Both the trail to the rock climbing cliff and the biking trail start in the same spot.

Bikers call this the Aspen Trail. The Forest Service calls it Trail 034. This trail is all single track and open only to nonmotorized traffic.

At first, some sections of the trail are a bit rocky and may force you off your bike – pushing instead of pedaling. But after about a quarter of a mile of uphill, the trail levels out and becomes a fun and mostly mellow ride. Some of the downhill sections are a blast.

It is important to keep an eye out for other traffic, especially on the fast downhill sections because you can expect to pass other trail users. Some will be coming from the north to south direction. On a given weekend you might encounter trail runners, horseback riders and, of course, other bikers.

Because horses use the trail, having a front fender on your bike is a useful accessory to keep flying manure out of your face.

Most of the trail passes through forested country, which makes the ride a bit cooler on hot, sunny days. Occasionally, the trail opens up to some nice views of Teton Valley.

Another word of advice: The mosquitoes are often present in late spring and early summer.

Many people ride the trail from north to south because there's a large, accommodating parking area at the trail's north end. If you wish to ride it both ways, riding it from north to south, then south to north back to your vehicle is probably preferable. The south to north direction offers plenty of fun downhill. You can also ride back to your starting point via mostly paved roads if you are so inclined.

GRAND TARGHEE RESORT

Grand Targhee Resort is a favorite powder skiing destination in the winter for eastern Idahoans, but the resort is building a solid reputation as a premiere mountain biking venue in the summer months. With miles of beginner to expert trails, plus lift-assisted access, there is something for most mountain bikers to explore.

The resort operates on National Forest land on the west side of the Tetons east of Driggs. It offers about a dozen trails for bikers looking for a trail ride and don't require lift assistance — just park and head off on one of the trails. There is also access from the parking area to Mill Creek and Cold Creek trails leading into Teton Canyon to the south.

The lift-assisted trails (requiring a summer lift ticket) offer serious downhill/free riding – and a bike and rider and body armor up to the task. These downhill rides are general black diamond or double black diamond trails. The resort also rents all necessary gear and bikes should you need them.

If you have your own gear, and just want to ride, this is a top-notch destination.

Here are three recommendations for trails to try:

• RICK'S BASIN/QUAKIE RIDGE LOOPS: These trails are over the resort's cross-country ski trails. The riding is generally intermediate and fun with some nice views of the surrounding mountains. In early summer, the wildflowers are awesome.

From the parking lot, walk your bike to the base of the Shoshone lift. Get on the cattrack behind the lift. Go up and northeast. After about .5 miles you will climb up to a bench where the Rick's Basin trails take off. There are two main loops you can ride -- the Rick's Basin Loop and Quakie Ridge Loop. These trails can see minor changes over time, but are usually marked to keep you from getting lost. Depending on your route, distances are between 3 to 7 miles. This is pleasant, fun riding and it can be done in any direction.

• CHUTES AND LADDERS/OTTER SLIDE: Access these bike park-style trails near the base of Dreamcatcher ski lift. The Otter Slide trail winds up and intersects with Chutes and Ladders. Pay attention to traffic direction. These trails are all about fun terrain and roller coaster fun.

Julie Geng photo
A biker poses along the 38 Special Trail at Grand Targhee Resort.

• ANDY'S TRAIL: This trail also starts near the base of the Dreamcatcher ski lift and heads in a southern direction along the western slopes of Peaked Mountain. This moderate to challenging route takes a couple of miles to arrive on the southwest side of the peak. This is a good trail to access the Mill Creek Trail that drops down into Teton Canyon.

MILL CREEK

GETTING THERE: From Driggs, drive east on Main Street following the signs to Grand Targhee Resort about 6 miles, turn right onto the Teton Canyon Road (there should be a sign for the Teton Canyon Campground). Drive about a half mile to the winter parking area with a gate and kiosk. From here, ride your bike back to the paved road and go up the hill to the ski resort.

The Mill Creek Trail makes a good loop. Starting from the same gravel winter parking lot near the mouth of Teton Canyon, you can see the sign for Mill Creek Trail. The south end of this trail has been rerouted in recent years to end at the parking lot.

The two general ways to access the trail is to pedal up it (a serious aerobic workout) or

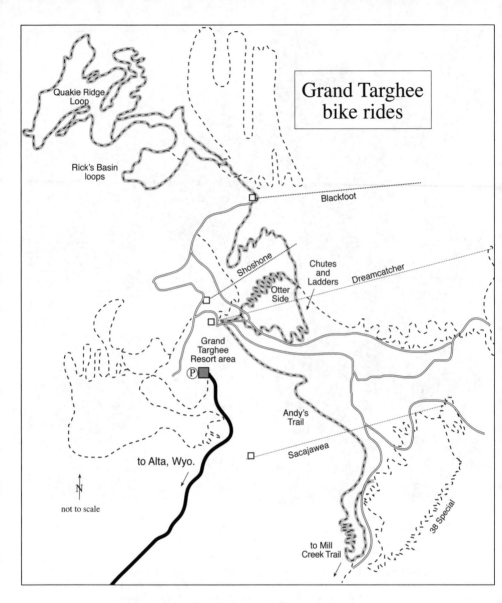

Grand Targhee
bike rides

Quakie Ridge Loop

Rick's Basin loops

Blackfoot

Shoshone

Chutes and Ladders

Dreamcatcher

Otter Side

Grand Targhee Resort area

P

Andy's Trail

Sacajawea

to Alta, Wyo.

N

not to scale

38 Special

to Mill Creek Trail

to pedal up the paved road to the Grand Targhee Ski Resort and zoom down from the top end. Most people start at the top of the trail accessed from Grand Targhee Resort service road (off the Sacagawea Ski run) and blast down the trail. After about a mile on the service road, take a single track trail that heads south downhill. This trail connects with a two-track road that forks. Take the left hand two-track road that heads steeply down a canyon. After about 3/4 of a mile, the two track becomes a single track and the serious fun begins.

This single track is fast, with only a few occasional flat or slightly uphill sections.

Most of the trail is well cleared and straightforward. There are a few rocky spots to slow down for and a few water bars to bounce over. It is steep enough to get going fast enough to give yourself a scare now and then. This is a good trail to take on warm days because the lower section is mostly forested. In the fall, the trail passes through some colorful aspen groves turning gold.

At the bottom, the trail spits you out on the Teton Canyon Road and next to your car (if you parked at the winter parking lot area).

The entire loop takes about two to three hours.

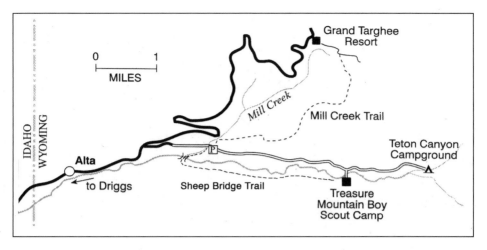

A couple of caveats, if the trail is wet, wait for things to dry out. This avoids damage that might occur to the wet trail.

The second proviso is to check with Grand Targhee Resort (307-353-2300) before going to see if access is open at the top end of the trail. The resort sometimes does construction work on the ski hill near the trail involving heavy equipment and some blasting. The resort occasionally has other activities, such as road rallies and trail runs that could also preclude a bike ride.

TETON CANYON BIKE TRAIL (SHEEP BRIDGE TRAIL)

GETTING THERE: From Driggs, follow the signs on Main Street to Grand Targhee Resort. Drive six miles and turn right onto a dirt road with a sign for Teton Campground. Drive about .3 miles to a dirt parking area on the right side of the road. The trail leaves the parking area on the southeast end.

This short trail begins from the same winter parking area on the Teton Canyon Road about a half-mile from the pavement as the Mill Creek Trail. Some folks call this the Sheep Bridge Trail.

The trail leaves the parking area and heads south on a dirt road. After about 100 yards, the road turns west, but a trail continues south over a nice footbridge, then follows the south side of Teton Creek upstream (east).

This trail is easy going and in good condition. The route is mostly flat or only slightly inclined. A few holes and ruts are evident from grazing cattle.

This trail passes through mostly forested terrain. A few sections go through brush and open land.

After a little more than two miles, the trail turns into the creek and ends. Here there is a shaky, slippery log bridge over the creek. If you cross the creek, you will find yourself at the west end of the Treasure Mountain Boy Scout Camp.

The return trip is much faster with the added help of a slight decline.

This is a good trail for beginning bikers, families, tag-along dogs or quick outings. You can also add this short route onto another quick outing to fill out your day.

Spooky Trail to Rocky Peak Trail

This trail is in the Pine Creek Pass area on the southern end of the Big Hole Mountains west of Victor.

The best part of the trail is the last third, which features nice downhill riding through open

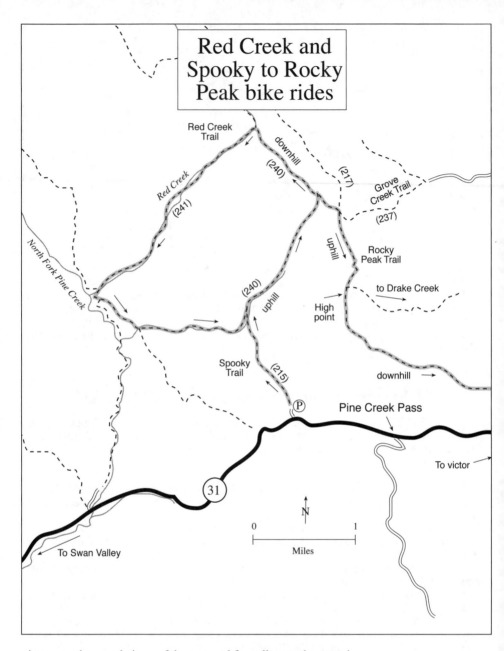

Red Creek and Spooky to Rocky Peak bike rides

Red Creek Trail

downhill

(240)

(217)

Red Creek

(241)

Grove Creek Trail

(237)

North Fork Pine Creek

uphill

Rocky Peak Trail

(240)

uphill

to Drake Creek

High point

Spooky Trail

(215)

downhill

P

Pine Creek Pass

To victor

31

To Swan Valley

N

0   1

Miles

vistas, meadows and views of the near and far valleys and mountains.

GETTING THERE: Drive 2 miles east on Highway 31 from Pine Creek Pass and park at a large parking area on the left (south) side of the road. Take note of your surroundings and where the trail (on the opposite side of the road comes in. This is the end point of the ride.

From here, pedal back up the highway (west) to the pass (be careful of the sometimes crazy traffic and narrow shoulder) and continue down the other side 1 mile. Take the right turn down a short, bumpy road to the Spooky/Red Creek Trail (No. 215) start.

This is where the work begins. The trail climbs steadily for the next 1.5 miles to a junction. At the junction, keep right on Corral Creek Trail (No. 240). From here, continue 1.3 miles. Some sections are steep, as well as some creek crossings and require some hike-a-bike. The next intersection marks the start of the Red Creek Trail (if you go left). Turn right, and climb a steep section (prepare to hike) for about .3 miles. Cross a cattle guard and take a right at the next intersection. This trail is the southern section of the Big Hold Crest Trail (not signed). The trail that continues straight is the Grove Creek Trail.

Continue on the Big Hole Crest Trail in a southeasterly direction, mostly uphill for the next .7 miles. Expect a bunch of bike pushing. After a bit of huffing and puffing, you'll pass the Drake Creek Trail on your left. Continue past it to the high point of this ride – stop here and soak up the views and catch your breath. From here, continue down the Rock Peak Trail (No. 230), generally downhill, for the next 2.7 miles back to the highway and the car park. There are some nice views along the way and a few sections of rocky trail to get your attention. The entire ride is almost 10 miles. The trail spits abruptly out on the highway, so pay attention to the ending.

RED CREEK, RUSH, CREEK TRAILS

GETTING THERE: (see Spooky Trail directions)

The Red Creek Trail starts 1 mile west of Pine Creek Pass on the north side of Highway 31. This is called Spooky Trail No. 215. This trailhead offers access into the southern end of the Big Hole Range with several options for long and short hikes or rides.

Ride 1.4 miles north on the Spooky Trail, then take a counter-clockwise loop back to the Spooky Trail to return to the trailhead. Total miles are about 9.5.

This route starts with 1.5 miles of uphill riding, then you come to a junction. This is the beginning of the loop and in an hour or so, you'll return to this junction.

About a mile later of more uphill and some level riding, you'll pass some meadows. Some seasons this area has sheep camps with shepherds from far away South American countries. Don't be surprised to run into thousands of sheep crowding the trails and hillsides.

Another third of a mile down the trail is a signed junction with Grove Creek Trail. Take a left here. The trail eventually crosses a bridge and heads downhill. This section of downhill is fast and furious and fun as heck.

The next junction is shortly after this. If you go right, the trail leads north deeper into the Big Hole Range and offers more trails for those interested in an all-day ride. Left continues along the Red Creek Trail. This interesting trail has a few ups and downs and a lot of creek crossings. Some of the creek crossings can be blasted across without dismounting. But others hold rocky traps and are better hiked across. There are about six creek crossings.

Most of this ride is thick forest of fir and some aspen trees.

After about 2.5 miles, the trail meets a jeep road. Hang a left at the road and climb a steep hill to the top of a ridge. At the top of this dirt road, the route descends down some fast, flowing up-and-down whoop-di-doos. After about two-thirds of a mile, take a left on trail No. 240 (Corral Creek Trail). This trail does a bit of climbing back to the first junction with the Spooky Trail in about 1.2 miles. Here, you turn right and fly downhill back to the start.

This trail is not a beginner trail. There are some fast, technical sections with some rocks and root obstacles and some serious workouts on the uphills. A few short sections are hike-a-bike. This is a great introduction to the fun trails for hiking or biking in the Big Hole Range.

CALAMITY CREEK

GETTING THERE: The trail is accessed by first driving to Green Canyon Hot Springs resort. From Idaho Falls, drive to Rexburg. From Rexburg, drive north on Highway 20 and take the exit for Highway 33 going east to Driggs and Grand Targhee Resort. At about mile marker 116, turn south (right) at a tiny sign for Green Canyon Hot Springs. This is just after crossing a large bridge over Canyon Creek. After making this turn, set your trip odometer on your car to 0. From here, it is about 12.5 miles to the start of the ride. This Canyon Creek Road starts out paved, then becomes good gravel, then dirt. In a few places there are ruts to avoid, but it is doable in a passenger sedan unless muddy. There is one tricky fork in the road that comes at mile 8.5. Take the left fork, or you may end up in the middle of a cattle drive with cowboys

89

Sign on the Calamity Creek Trail

giving you dirty looks. At mile 12.5, look for the signs for a single-track trail 060. This trail comes from both the right and left sides of the road. Continue a little ways up the road to a small pullout on the left and park.

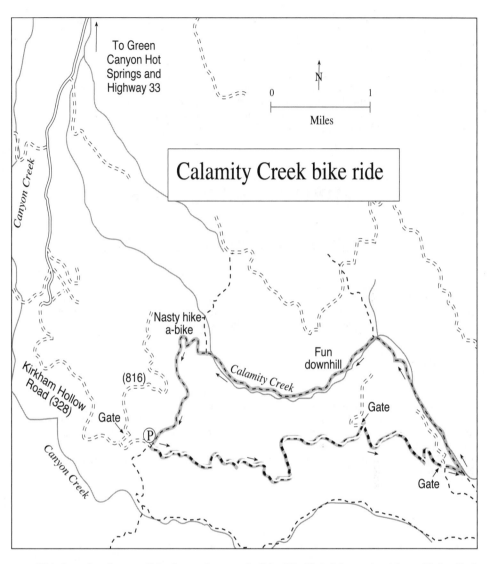

This is a giant loop trail in the northern end of the Big Hole Mountains (about 11.5 miles) and the first 5 miles are gentle uphill and the next 3 or 4 miles are single-track downhill. You might think you've struck gold. But then the shine comes off quickly with some of the toughest hike-a-bike trail in the Big Hole Range. More like wrestle-a-bike.

Fortunately, the nasty uphill bike hauling is only about half a mile or so.

This trail takes you deep into the wild country of the Big Hole Mountains.

From the point where you park, bike up the road for about 5 miles. The road climbs continuously but gradually. The road is surrounded on both sides with thick forest most of the way. You may pass vehicles off the road camping for the weekend.

After a little more than 5 miles of pedaling up the road (it helps to have an odometer on your bike), look for a trail sign on your right — No. 233. Take this trail and almost immediately (about 20 yards) the trail connects with Trail 224. At this junction, take a left and follow this trail. Take another left to go down Calamity Creek Canyon for the next several miles.

The trail starts out fast and flowing. After about 1.5 miles, the trail hits a nasty downhill "rooty" section with some sharp switchbacks. These ruts and roots can be a bit scary — use caution. Beyond the eroded root section, the trail crosses the creek a few times and enters a long, flowing side hill section. The trail is usually in good shape and is enjoyable to ride.

91

After a few miles of riding high above the canyon bottom, the trail drops down to cross the creek. Here is where you payback for all that fun downhill. The trail crosses the creek and comes to a junction with trail 060. Take a left turn and prepare for awful uphill. This section could use some switchbacks. Instead, it goes straight up the side of the canyon. Serious erosion has caused huge drops, waist-deep ruts and exposed rocks and roots. After about a half-mile of this, the trail begins to improve, but there are still some steep sections of hike-a-bike. Eventually, the trail throws some downhill in to take the bad taste out of your mouth.

This trail returns to the road you drove in on near your vehicle.
These trails are open to foot traffic, bikes and motorbikes, but not ATVs.

TETON PASS AREA TRAILS

TRAIL CREEK TRAIL (RUSH HOUR TRAIL)

GETTING THERE: Driver to Victor and down the Teton Pass road (Highway 33) going east. Park near the entrance to the Mike Harris Campground or take a road just across from the Mike Harris Campground on the north side of the highway and drive 50 yards down this paved road and park at near the trailhead (trailhead is on the right). You can also start from the east end of the trail at a large parking/pullout area at the Idaho-Wyoming state line on Highway 33.

This is one of the funnest mountain bike rides anywhere. While many of the area trails are like meat-and-potatoes, the Trail Creek Trail (also known as Rush Hour Trail) is like a bowl of ice cream.

From the west end, the trail climbs up into the forest with a series of switchbacks for a few hundred yards before leveling off. This trail then roughly parallels the highway heading east until it ends at the Idaho-Wyoming state line. It features fast sections with banked curves and fancy wooden bridges across gullies and streams. The trail is almost free of rocks and gotchas, making it a great ride for novices. Too bad it's only a little more than 2 miles long one way. If you only do it one way, the east to west (state line back to Mike Harris) is the best. This ride should put a grin on your face.

MAIL CABIN CREEK

GETTING THERE: From Victor, drive east on Highway 33 toward Teton Pass. Look for the Coal Creek Trailhead/parking lot on your left. Just after the Coal Creek Trailhead, turn right and drive a few hundred yards down a short road -- this is Mail Cabin Creek -- and park at the end. The trail leaves from here. If you plan on a shuttle, leave a vehicle at the Mike Harris Campground on the way up. Or you can leave your vehicle at the Mike Harris Campground and ride up the highway to Mail Cabin Creek. If you do this, be careful of the sometimes heavy traffic.

This is another trail that has benefitted from work done by the Teton Valley Trails and Pathways organization. Some of the steeper sections have had switchbacks added to cut down on the required energy to get up. But you can still expect some hike-a-bike hills after the first 2.5 miles of easier gradual uphill. After about a half-mile of walking, things ease up a bit and you reach a junction with the Mosquito Creek Trail that connects into the Palisades Creek drainage. This ridge is at about 8,500 feet and offers nice views of the surrounding mountains. This area attracts backcountry skiers in the wintertime.

Take a right on the ridge and follow this ridge for 4 miles. There is a exposed drop off on the left (southwest) side of the ridge that requires bikers to pay close attention. After 7 miles, you come to the junction with Pole Canyon. Continue right and downhill. This section is fun and challenging with rocky and rooty sections — be careful. Things ease up technically and

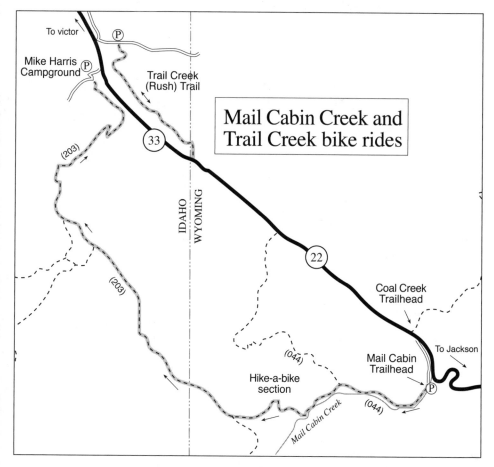

it's all mostly fun the rest of the way. After close to 10 miles, you come to the Mike Harris Campground road and back to your vehicle (if that's where you left it).

BLACK CANYON AND LITHIUM TRAILS

GETTING THERE: From Victor, drive about 10 miles to the top of Teton Pass. Continue down the pass to the town of Wilson, Wyo. From Wilson take the Old Pass Road on the south side of Highway 22 and the west end of town. Follow this road to the parking lot at the end. Leave a shuttle vehicle here, then drive back to the top of Teton Pass to begin the bike ride.

Black Canyon Trail is one of the more popular rides from the top of Teton Pass. On the west side of the parking area at the top of the pass, access a dirt road heading south. Near the radio towers follow a single track trail uphill for about 1.25 miles. This part of the trail gains about 800 feet before dropping. Along the way, you will pass the Lithium Trail heading left (east) and dropping off the ridge.

About a fourth of a mile past the Lithium Trail near the top, Black Canyon Trail heads left (east) off the ridge. The trail begins with short switchbacks and turns down into the beautiful canyon below. Expect some rocky, technical sections. But most of the riding should be enjoyable to intermediate and above bikers. There are some fun sections, especially toward the bottom of the canyon. Expect a few stream crossings in the canyon. This trail can be muddy in the early season or after a storm. After 6 miles, the trail intersects with the Old Pass Road

93

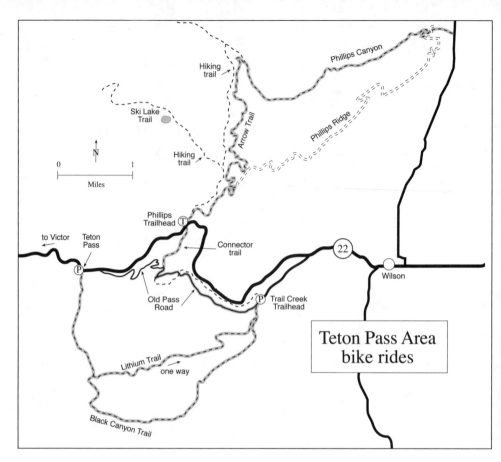

Teton Pass Area
bike rides

at Trail Creek Trailhead. There is a nearby parking area for a shuttle vehicle. If you're up for a serious grunt, you can peddle back up to Teton Pass via the Old Pass Road.

If you're up for a serious, advanced ride, you can take on the Lithium Trail -- one of the area's test pieces for mountain bikers. This trail has lots of rocky areas and loose sections with jumps over gaps. Don't underestimate this ride. Expect a long hard downhill. This route is about 4.75 miles to the Trail Creek Trailhead from Teton Pass.

PHILLIPS CANYON TRAIL

GETTING THERE: (see directions below)

This trail is a popular loop ride or a one direction route if you use a shuttle vehicle.

If you do the loop, you'll cover two-track, single track and paved sections.

Start this ride at the Trail Creek Trailhead off of the Old Pass Road southwest of Wilson. From the trailhead, ride 2 miles up the Old Pass Road and look for an old single track trail on the right at the elbow of a right switchback on the road. This single track leads to Highway 22 (Teton Pass road) after about a mile. From here, cut across the highway to the Phillips Canyon Road on the north side of the highway. Ride up this Forest Service road (gravel/dirt) passing a sign for Ski Lake on your left. Keep right. Continue uphill and cross a small creek or two (if it's wet). This section of trail is also called the Arrow Trail, though it is not at all straight. This trail contours below the Phillips Pass Trail (open only to horses and hikers) for nearly 5 miles. At the end of the Arrow Trail, it joins the Phillips Canyon trail and goes down. The trail heads downhill from here through some technical terrain, at times rocky and rooted. After about 4.5

Julie Geng photo
Lunch along the Phillips Ridge Trail

miles, the trail ends at the Fish Creek Road where it is 3 miles back to Wilson. From Wilson, ride through town to Old Pass Road and back to your car.

Another popular option is to ride the Phillips Ridge Trail that leaves off of the Arrow Trail a bit more than a mile in. This trail is avoids some of the technical downhill of the canyon trail.

You can avoid some of the uphill workout from the Trail Creek Trailhead by leaving a shuttle vehicle in Wilson and driving up to the start of the Phillips Canyon Road just off Highway 22. Expect to put in close to 20 miles if you ride the entire loop.

Deer cross the Timber Creek Trail in the Lemhi Range. See directions, Page 51.

97

Kelly Canyon's Y Junction winter signs before the Forest Service kiosk was updated.

SKIING

KELLY CANYON SKI TRAILS

GETTING THERE: From Idaho Falls drive east on Highway 26 for about 16 miles and turn left at the signs for Kelly Canyon Ski Hill and Heise Hot Springs – continue following the signs to the ski hill. At 3 miles, turn right after crossing the Snake River and continue past the hot springs, past the golf course on your right and continue all the way up to Kelly Canyon Ski Hill. About 100 yards before the main entrance to the resort is a parking area on the right for Nordic skiers.

If you're just getting started with cross-country skiing or you're an old hand and want a place nearby, the Kelly Canyon area has a lot to offer.

Winter transforms the summertime hiking and mountain biking trails throughout the Kelly Mountain area into some of the best ski trails in the area – and it's all within a half-hour's drive of Idaho Falls. The area is just east of Heise Hot Springs resort off Highway 26 in the Targhee National Forest.

Most of the 20-plus miles of trails start near the "Y Junction" 1.25 miles up the hill from the Kelly Canyon Ski Lodge. In recent years, parking at or near the ski resort has become problematic with the resort wanting to charge an exorbitant fee to cross-country skiers and snowshoers. Hopefully this mess will get sorted out in the future. Skiing up the hill to the Y Junction can be a bit daunting for beginners, but experienced skiers usually find this section to be a good warm up.

At the junction, you have the immediate option of one of four trails: Tyro Loop, the logging road to the warming hut, Kelly Mountain or the Buckskin-Morgan Loop. A little farther away are three other main routes: Hawley Gulch Overlook, Hawley Gulch Loop and Hawley Gulch Upper Trail.

The Kelly Canyon trails aren't a place for solitude, at least not on the weekends. But you should have the trails mostly to yourself after about the second or third mile. This area is well-forested with fir and aspen. Keep a lookout for deer, moose, occasional songbirds and small mammals. Deer are often seen not far from the ski resort. Moose hang out not far from the Y Junction.

Here's a summary of the trails shown on the map:

Tyro Loop

This is a one-mile route that starts just behind the sign at the top of Y Junction. This trail is rated easy, but it is often not groomed.

Kelly Mountain Area

This area follows a jeep trail to the top of Kelly Mountain. The route switchbacks up the mountainside and tops out near the No. 4 chair lift and continues east along the mountain ridge. This area is not marked and rarely patrolled. It is popular with telemark skiers looking for some nice downhill slopes. This trail is rated most difficult.

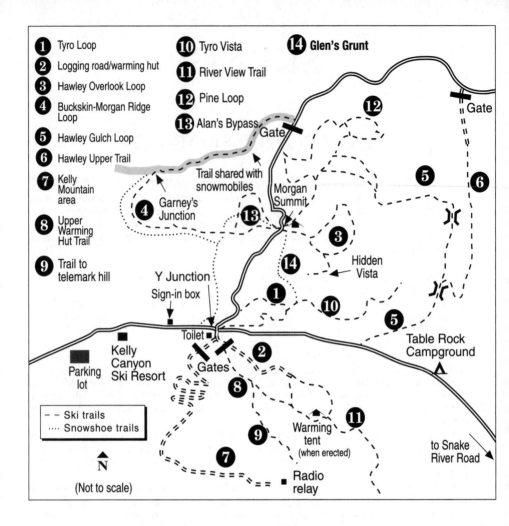

1 Tyro Loop

2 Logging road/warming hut

3 Hawley Overlook Loop

4 Buckskin-Morgan Ridge Loop

5 Hawley Gulch Loop

6 Hawley Upper Trail

7 Kelly Mountain area

8 Upper Warming Hut Trail

9 Trail to telemark hill

10 Tyro Vista

11 River View Trail

12 Pine Loop

13 Alan's Bypass

14 Glen's Grunt

Trail shared with snowmobiles

Garney's Junction

Morgan Summit

Gate

Gate

Hidden Vista

Y Junction

Sign-in box

Toilet

Kelly Canyon Ski Resort

Parking lot

Gates

Table Rock Campground

Warming tent (when erected)

Radio relay

to Snake River Road

– – Ski trails
···· Snowshoe trails

N

(Not to scale)

BUCKSKIN-MORGAN RIDGE

This 5-mile route heads up from the Y Junction to Morgan Summit. Most people head up the steep section of the trail to the ridge and return via the north loop in clockwise fashion. The northern section of the loop sees some snowmobile activity. This trail is rated more difficult. Some years a warming hut is erected at Morgan Summit off the road and through the gate.

HAWLEY GULCH LOOP

This 5-mile route takes you through some nice backcountry that receives less use. Head down the road from the Y Junction toward Table Rock Campground. Less than a mile down the road you will see the Hawley Gulch trailhead on the left. This trail eventually leads into a steep-sided canyon (the gulch) that circles around to Morgan Summit.

Be aware that small avalanches can be present in the gulch. More expert skiers may enjoy taking this trail in the other direction. From this direction the trail is a wild, downhill blast on skinny skis. It is not advisable to take this trail on hard, icy snow. This trail is rated most difficult.

HAWLEY UPPER TRAIL

This route is really a longer, kinder, gentler alternative to the Hawley Gulch Loop that avoids

Sam Painter heads out across unbroken snow.

the steep canyon route. The trail is rated more difficult.

HAWLEY OVERLOOK

This is a short side loop that is mostly level at the top of Morgan Summit. The trail takes you to the rim of Hawley Gulch and offers some very nice views of the surrounding country. This trail is rated easy to moderate.

HUT TRAILS

These relatively easy trails loop to the warming hut. In recent years, the warming hut h not been set up. In the past, the hut was a favorite with youth groups and families as an o' night stay. To the south of the warming hut is a popular slope — Norm's Hill — for tele sI

RIVER VIEW TRAIL

This trail contours around the west end of Kelly Mountain for some nice views of River and Antelope Flats beyond. It can also be used to get above the tele ski hill.

For information on snow and trail conditions, contact the Eastern Idaho Visif 523-1010 or Kelly Canyon Ski Resort at 538-6261 or access the Idaho Falls Ski C

Swans are a common sight along the ski trails at Harriman State Park.

HARRIMAN STATE PARK

GETTING THERE: From Ashton, Idaho, drive north on Highway 20 about 20 miles. The turnoff for the park is before you come to State Road 47. The park headquarters is about .5 miles from the highway. A per-vehicle entrance fee is charged and a grooming fee is charged per skier.

DISTANCE: Loop trails range from 2.5 miles to 12 miles.

ELEVATION: About 6,100 feet at the park headquarters; a bit more than 6,500 feet along ˙idge Loop Trail.

⌐ICULTY: Most trails are easy, except for distances. The Ridge Loop trail is rated "most ˙ the park.

ˊkiing: From late November to early April depending on the snow. Most of the ˙ummer use by Memorial Day.

ˊs a class act when it comes to providing quality Nordic skiing and sum-ˉrk, Idaho.

ˇier or biker or horseback rider can make several trips to the park ˇer. Harriman's trails take you along the Henry's Fork of the ˇilver Lake and through forested ridges and into the Harriman

ˌand owned by several officials of the Oregon Shortline Railroad. The

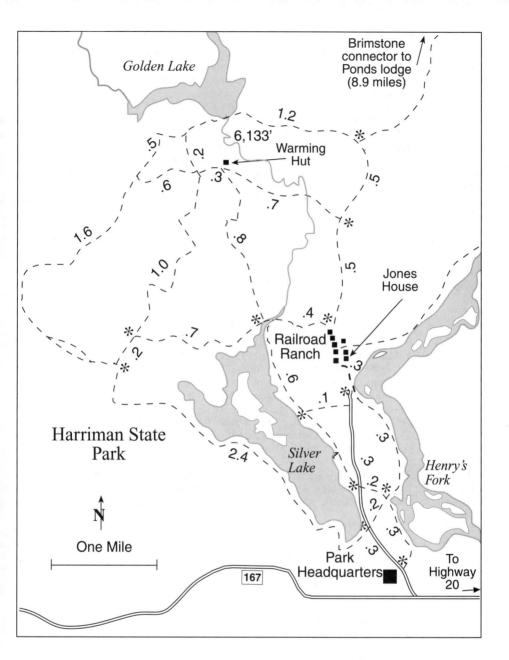

property was the private retreat of such wealthy families as the Harrimans of Union Pacific Railroad and the Guggenheims, who were prominent copper mine holders. For 75 years, the private land holdings were maintained as a healthy hunting reserve and working cattle ranch. Today, 27 of the original railroad ranch buildings, from the cookhouse to the horse barn, are still intact, furnished, and carefully maintained.

Activities include excellent fishing along the Henry's Fork for cutthroat trout and superior wildlife viewing along the lakes, creeks and river bottom. Harriman is one of the prime wintering sites in North America for endangered trumpeter swans. Also look for Canada geese, ducks, eagles, elk, deer and coyotes. Bring along a pair of binoculars.

The park is day-use only unless you make prior arrangements to rent one of the cabins at the Railroad Ranch. The park also has two yurts for overnight rental. The park begins taking reservations Oct. 1 for the following year.

In the winter, cross-country ski trails begin at the park's headquarters building and from a parking area near the railroad ranch area. On weekends, a warming hut is open at the railroad ranch area. Coffee and hot chocolate are served. Snow in the Harriman area during mid-winter (January) averages around 3 feet deep.

A variety of difficulties are offered among the park's seven loop trails. Most are fairly flat, except for the Ridge Loop trail which gains 400 feet in its 7 miles. The Ridge Loop trail offers the best views and the best chance at solitude on weekends. But the Ridge Loop is not always groomed. All trails are marked at intersections with signs to keep you on track.

Of the several possible routes to try out, don't pass up the trail along the Henry's Fork. The Thurmon Creek Loop is also enjoyable. It passes through ups and downs and in and out of patches of forest. The dominant tree at Harriman is lodgepole pine.

In recent years, the park has groomed its trails for fat bike use. The trails can be challenging for biking after a recent snowfall, but generally set up nicely after a few days.

During the summer months, the same trails used for skiing are used for hiking, biking and horseback riding. This is a wonderful area to visit during the fall. The park has some patches of aspens, willows and cottonwoods that add splashes of color to the evergreens. Because many of the pines have been killed by a beetle infestation during the 1970s, wildflowers are abundant along the forest floor during the summer months.

BRIMSTONE TRAIL (POND'S LODGE)

GETTING THERE: From Rexburg, drive north on Highway 20. Continue north past Ashton. At Last Chance drive 4 miles north and look for the Island Park Ranger Station on the right. The Brimstone Trail is about .5 miles north of the ranger station; turn left immediately past the bridge over the Buffalo River. There is a plowed out area for parking about a dozen vehicles. More parking is available at the nearby Pond's Lodge. A trailhead sign can be seen near the parking area.

DISTANCES: The entire Brimstone Trail system is 9 miles long. Moose Loop is 3 miles around; The Eagle Trail is a little less than a mile; Thurmon Ridge Loop is 2.5 miles; Tank Trap Trail is about .3 miles; The Box Canyon Trail is about 1 mile; Boggy Springs is .6 miles; and the Antelope Park Loop is 1.6 miles long.

DIFFICULTY: All the trails are well-marked and usually groomed with the exception of the steep downhill off Thurmon Ridge. Most of the trails fall in the easy category with a few up and down sections. Caution: When the snow is icy and hard, downhill sections can become very fast. Distance can be a factor.

SPECIAL CONSIDERATIONS: Island Park Ranger Station (208) 558-7301. For current conditions and grooming schedules, contact the ranger station. Another excellent map – Winter Recreation Trails – produced by Fremont County is also available at most gas stations and at Pond's Lodge. This color map covers all the ski and snowmobile trails from St. Anthony to well north of West Yellowstone. The Brimstone Trail is a Park 'N' Ski area requiring a sticker to be displayed on your vehicle's windshield.

When most people think of cross-country skiing in the Island Park area, Harriman State Park is probably what first comes to mind.

The Brimstone trail offers the same scenic and wildlife opportunities, but often without the crowds that flock to Harriman. But like Harriman, all of the trail junctions have helpful signs with maps to tell you where you are and where you can go.

Expect to see several species of waterfowl, including an occasional rare trumpeter swan. Sometimes moose are seen in this area.

The Brimstone trail is a series of loop trails along the Buffalo and Henry's Fork rivers. The trailhead is immediately north of the bridge over the Buffalo River on Highway 20 and immediately south of Pond's Lodge. If you pass Pond's Lodge, you've gone too far.

With all the loops available on the Brimstone trail, it is possible to ski most of the trail with very little overlap.

The first loop on the Brimstone trail is the Moose Loop. This mostly flat trail takes you over to the Island Park Reservoir dam.

At the dam site you could meet up with a few snowmobiles. Many people come out here to

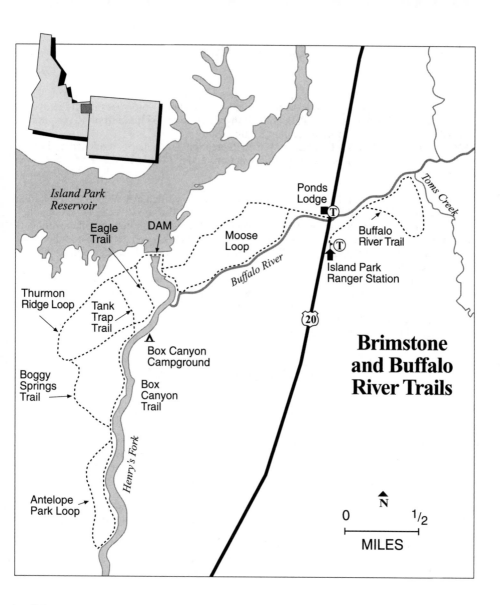

Island Park
Reservoir

Ponds
Lodge

Buffalo
River Trail

Eagle
Trail

DAM

Moose
Loop

Island Park
Ranger Station

Thurmon
Ridge Loop

Tank
Trap
Trail

Box Canyon
Campground

Box
Canyon
Trail

**Brimstone
and Buffalo
River Trails**

Boggy
Springs
Trail

Henry's Fork

Buffalo River

Antelope
Park Loop

0   1/2

N

MILES

ice fish.

Just beyond the dam crossing, there is a plowed out parking area for those who wish to skip the Moose Loop and the ski across the road above the dam. The trail from the plowed parking area comes quickly to the junction with Thurmon Ridge and Eagle Trail.

The Thurmon Ridge route climbs a few hundred feet to the top of the ridge before dropping south. At the top of the ridge the groomed trail vanishes. Beyond the groomed trail a sign warns skiers that the 200-foot plunge off the ridge is steep and difficult. This section is often full of deep powder that can swallow up people on skinny tour skis. If you're game for this steep section, you might try mellow, easy traverses down the hill.

The trail to Boggy Springs Trail is mostly gentle. The Boggy Springs section is nearly flat.

At the intersection of Boggy Springs and Box Canyon keep an eye out for bald eagles flying along the Henry's Fork.

It is possible to continue south from the Antelope Park trail and connect into the Harriman State Park trails. The connection is about 7 miles, but the trail is sometimes not groomed.

BUFFALO RIVER

GETTING THERE: From Ashton, drive north on Highway 20. At Last Chance drive 4 miles north and look for the Island Park Ranger Station on the right. If you cross the bridge over the Buffalo River, you've gone too far. Park at the Ranger Station to ski the Buffalo River Trail.

DISTANCE: The Buffalo River Trail is 2.6 miles long.

SPECIAL CONSIDERATIONS: A Winter Recreation Trails map – produced by Fremont County — is available at most Island Park gas stations and at Pond's Lodge. This is a Park 'N' Ski trail.

If you want to take advantage of the huge amounts of snow often available in the Island Park area, but want some place different than Harriman State Park, Buffalo River is a great option.

The Buffalo River trail offers the same scenic and wildlife opportunities, but often without the crowds that flock to Harriman. The trail is usually groomed weekly and perfect for rookie skiers.

The Buffalo River Trail leaves the Island Park Ranger Station and travels north to the river. Parking is at the ranger station.

The trail goes upstream along the south side of the river then loops back at Tom's Creek. The trail passes through lodgepole pine forest – the tree that dominates the forests of Island Park.

Expect to see several species of waterfowl, including an occasional trumpeter swan. Sometimes moose are seen in this area.

This trail is basically flat the entire way.

BEAR GULCH-MESA FALLS

GETTING THERE: Drive 13 miles north of St. Anthony on U.S. Highway 20 to Ashton. At Ashton, turn right (east) and drive 5 miles. This is State Highway 47. The road swings left (north). After 4 miles you will pass the Warm River Campground. Continue up Highway 47 another 3.3 miles to the parking area on your left. This is a Park 'N' Ski trail.

DISTANCE: It's 5.8 miles if you do the entire loop trail to the Lower Falls. If you just stick to the rim up and back, it's longer, about 7.5 miles. Add another 3.5 miles if you ski to the Upper Falls.

The main reason for skiing Bear Gulch is the great views. Besides the river canyon below, there's the dramatic view of Mesa Falls.

The trail starts at a pullout off State Highway 47 near the old Bear Gulch ski area. During the summer, Highway 47 is the popular route to view Mesa Falls. During the winter, the road is plowed only as far as the pullout. The parking area is large enough to accommodate several cars and trucks with trailers. There is a toilet here.

Just to the west of the parking area is the old Bear Gulch ski resort. The ski resort closed down in the '70s.

The ski trail starts at the north end of the parking area. From here the route parallels the road for about 200 yards then shares .4 miles of uphill trail with the snowmobilers to the top of the Henry's Fork River canyon rim. The first half mile of trail is the steepest and gains 200 feet before settling into mostly gentle terrain.

Once at the top of the canyon rim, the skier and snowmobile routes separate. The ski trail is clearly marked by a sign on the left side of the road.

The trail follows along the edge of the canyon rim and presents regular wonderful views of the gorge below. The trail is marked with blue diamonds and Forest Service symbols of skiers or bikers. The route is fairly easy to follow, even when tracks are missing.

Most of the trail passes through thick forest, but there are regular openings that allow views of the canyon on your left (west).

If you continue to follow the rim trail, you will come to Grandview Overlook and a Forest Service campground. The overlook is one of the payoffs for taking this trail. It offers great views of the 65 foot high Lower Mesa Falls.

A skier takes in the Upper Mesa Falls after skiing up from Bear Gulch.

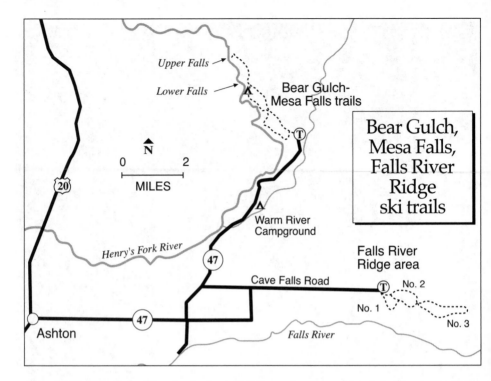

Bear Gulch,
Mesa Falls,
Falls River
Ridge
ski trails

Beyond the Grandview Overlook, the trail follows the rim another 1.8 miles to the Upper Mesa Falls. There are two ways to get there. You can ski along side of the road (shorter) or follow a skiers-only trail that starts next to a large Mesa Falls sign on the east side of the road. This trail gets skiers away from the snowmobile traffic and loops back to the road near the side road leading down to the Upper Falls. Skiers are forced back onto the road down to the Upper Falls visitors center/lodge. This .25-mile side road drops down a few hundred feet and feels much longer when you ski back up it. The extra distance and effort to see the Upper Falls is worth it. This impressive falls is 114 feet high.

Return back to Bear Gulch the way you skied in.

Keep this trail in mind during the summer months as a short mountain biking route.

FALLS RIVER RIDGE

GETTING THERE: Drive 13 miles north of St. Anthony on U.S. Highway 20 to Ashton. At Ashton, turn right (east) and drive 5 miles. This is State Highway 47. The road swings left (north). After one mile, look for a sign on your right for the Cave Falls Road. Turn right on the Cave Falls Road and drive east five miles to the parking area. Where the road enters the forest boundaries, it is no longer plowed. The trailhead is on the south side of the road. This is a Park 'N' Ski trail.

DISTANCES: The first loop is 2 miles around; the second loop is 3.1 miles around; the third loop is 3 miles around. Loops 2 and 3 are 6.1 miles, and loops 1 and 2 are 3.6 miles for the outer edges.

The Falls River Ridge ski trail is just off the Cave Falls Road 10 miles east of Ashton, just inside the forest boundary.

A large sign announces the trails, and a map is posted next to the parking area. Three loop trails for skiers are groomed about once a week.

Most of these trails are easy to moderately difficult skiing. The uphills shouldn't slow determined beginners too much. The first part of the trail takes you through open terrain, then goes through a mix of aspen and lodgepole pine forest. The trail at times winds through a narrow path cut through thick forest. There are enough trails here to keep you busy for most of a day.

Sheep Falls on the Henry's Fork in Island Park.

SHEEP FALLS

GETTING THERE: Drive 8 miles north of Ashton on Highway 20 and turn right (east) onto a dirt road. Look for a sign on the highway that says "Sheep Falls."

DISTANCE: It's 3 miles from the pavement to the Sheep Falls Trailhead and another .75 miles on the footpath to the falls.

DIFFICULTY: Mostly easy. The trail is tough to bike, though.

In the summertime, Sheep Falls is a great half-day trip or picnic destination, especially if you like to fish or mountain bike. But in winter, the road and trail to the falls makes a nice short day-trip on skis or snowshoes.

Most people driving north from Ashton zoom right past the "Sheep Falls Road," sign on Highway 20. If you're one of those who have wondered if it would be worth your time to slow down and take a right turn, then read on.

The Sheep Falls Road, like many of the roads in the Island Park area, can be used year 'round.

During the summer, mountain bikers will want to pull off the highway, park and ride the 2.5 miles to the Sheep Falls Trailhead. The half-mile footpath down to the falls can be negotiated by expert mountain bikers, but I would recommend ditching your bikes at the trailhead and walking down to the river. The trail drops quickly and is narrow. There is often deadfall scattered along the way.

Sheep Falls Road, Forest Road 163, is mostly flat and easily driven by the family sedan in summer. The going gets rougher, though, when you arrive at the sign "Sheep Falls Trail" with an arrow pointing down a rutted jeep trail. Some winter days, the road entrance is plowed shut and requires parking on a nearby highway pullout. With care you can drive the next quarter mile to the trailhead in a low-clearance car. At the trailhead is a small turnaround and parking for about four or five vehicles.

The trail down to the river is mostly easy. It descends through a thick forest of lodgepole.

In the winter, the tricky part is finding safe parking off the highway. Often the road entrance is plowed shut. If that is the case, you may need to park at the "historical marker" sign pullout eight tenths of a mile south of the Sheep Falls Road. The next challenge will be following the road to Sheep Falls while it's hidden under three feet of snow. Visiting in the summer first may help.

Once you get to the trailhead for the foot path, you may want to kick off your skis and strap on snowshoes to negotiate the steeper sections. Expect the six-mile round trip to take a few hours.

Because this route is not groomed as a regular ski trail, no Park N' Ski sticker is required for skiers.

Sheep Falls offers two main attractions: Beauty and fishing. The Henry's Fork River makes two big drops – about 10 to 15 feet – around 100 yards apart. The water tumbles over huge lava rocks and continues down a narrow canyon with deep vertical walls. The water is loud and exhilarating. There are some nice perches to stand on to view the two falls and eat lunch.

Between the two drops are some inviting pools and slack water for fishing. Above the first fall are some nice straight runs of water worth trying also. Below the second fall is nothing but impassable vertical walls. If you hike downstream far enough, you will eventually come to some other approachable sections of river. Upstream is more immediately accessible.

This area, like most of Island Park, has abundant wildlife. If you're the first ones down to the river, expect to spook up waterfowl. There is also moose, deer, elk and small mammals.

CALDERA RIM TRAIL

GETTING THERE: Drive 60 miles north on Highway 20 to a large pullout on the left (west) side of the road. You'll know you've come to the right spot if you see yellow snowshoe trail markers posted at the beginning. The trail is intended to be done in a counter-clockwise direction. A map and directions are available at the Idaho Falls Ski Club's website: www.ifskiclub.com.

One could say the Caldera Rim Trail has been a million years in the making. It was about that long ago — give or take a few 100,000 years — when the caldera that Yellowstone National Park

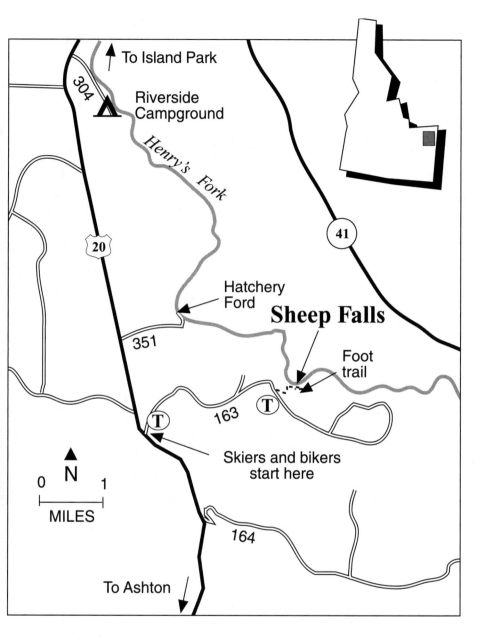

To Island Park

Riverside Campground

Henry's Fork

304

20

41

Hatchery Ford

Sheep Falls

Foot trail

351

163

T

T

Skiers and bikers start here

0 N 1

MILES

164

To Ashton

sits on formed.

The southwestern rim of the caldera a few miles north of Ashton, on the west side of Highway 20, offers a great place for a wintertime day trip. The Caldera Rim Trail, like most winter trails, is at its best after a recent snowstorm. This trail is intended and created for snowshoers. But if you have climbing skins for your cross-country skis, you will do fine on it. The trail is marked with snowshoe symbols — a yellow marker with crossed snowshoes on it. In one section of the trail there's a long downhill that can be a blast on skis.

One nice thing about the Caldera Rim Trail is that it starts basically right outside the car door. As you drive north on Highway 20 from Ashton, look for the first pullout on your left after the highway levels out on top of the hill. It comes up without warning, so be careful not to be going too fast.

If you're going against the prevailing recreational flow and skiing instead of snowshoeing,

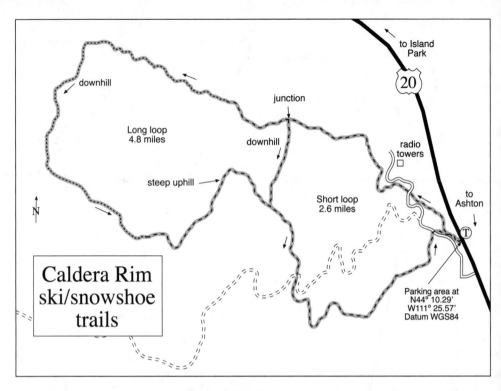

Caldera Rim
ski/snowshoe
trails

you'll find a few challenging uphills (one right at the start) to negotiate in the first half-mile. You can try to side step up and sneak around these hills without putting on skins or breakdown and put them on. Once past the first half-mile, you'll have mostly flat going for the next mile or so. About the first mile, look for nice views where the trees thin a bit on the north side of the ridge you are following. To the north, you can see out over the Island Park area and the Continental Divide beyond.

After about 1 mile, you come to a junction. The Caldera Rim Trail is a large loop with a shorter cutoff loop. This longer trail drops off the ridge after another mile and continues for another 2.5 miles, eventually looping back to the start. Total distance of the longer loop is 4.8 miles, while the shortcut loop is 2.6 miles.

If the snow is deep and powdery, snowshoers may want to think twice before committing to the longer route. If you do take the longer route, it's nice to have partners to trade off trail break-ing duties.

When the trail first drops off the ridge, there is a 200- or 300-yard downhill run before level-ing off again. If the snow was more solid and icy, it could be dicey. Snowshoers, of course, have nothing to fear from a few ups and downs.

About three-fourths of the way around the loop, the trail begins to climb sharply back up to the ridge. Time for skiers to put on climbing skins. Leave the skins on the skis for about the next mile because the terrain will throw a steep uphill at least every quarter of a mile. This trail will probably be very difficult for skiers without skins.

Eventually the trail leads back to Rattlesnake Road which accesses a radio antenna tower. The trail follows this road for a few hundred feet then leaves the road to connect back onto the snowshoe trail near the parking area. You know you're getting close because you can hear high-way traffic.

WEST YELLOWSTONE

The first stop to make when arriving in West Yellowstone, Mont., is the town's visitor center.

112

A sign along the Caldera Rim Trail indicating the Short Cut route.

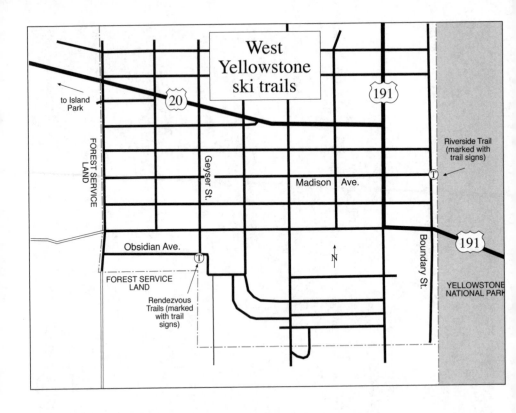

Here you can get information on latest trail conditions and a handy trail map showing all of the area trails. Friendly folks can also tell you good places to eat and sleep. In winter, West Yellowstone boils down to three main activities: Snowmobiling, Nordic skiing and snow coaches. Unlike the summer, when the town is a hive of activity, in winter half the town is shut down. Ski gear is available to rent at a couple of the outdoor shops in town.

MADISON RIVERSIDE TRAILS

GETTING THERE: The Riverside Trailhead is on the east edge of town near the intersection of Madison Street and Boundary Street and heads east into Yellowstone National Park.

The first section of the trail makes a beeline straight through a lodgepole forest down to the Madison River in about 1.5 miles. Near the river, this trail leaves some of the thick forest and intersects with two loop trails. The southern trail (1.5 miles) closely parallels the river for about a third of its loop, and has a few ups and downs where it drops or climbs in and out of the deep river banks (hillsides).

The northern loop is almost 4 miles and is a bigger version of the southern route. These fun trails are may remind you of skiing along the Henry's Fork at Harriman State Park, only this is Yellowstone and fells wilder. The only buildings are a couple of tiny gauging stations along the river about the size of outhouses.

It's also cool skiing into the national park without being hassled to pay an entrance fee. Occasionally, elk and other critters hang out near the river. It's common to see swans, wood ducks and eagles here.

The skiing is generally easy, except for a few short climbs up the tall banks of the Madison River. Parts of the trail is often groomed in midwinter.

114

Skiing along the Madison River just east of West Yellowstone, Mont., inside Yellowstone National Park.

Rendezvous Trails

GETTING THERE: As you coming into West Yellowstone, Mont., driving east on Highway 20, turn right (south) on Geyser Street and drive to its end.

West Yellowstone is famous for its Rendezvous Trails in the Gallatin National Forest south of town. These trails are built on summertime dirt roads and groomed to perfection for classic and skate skiers. There is also a biathlon course and shooting range in the system.

Access to the trails costs $8 a day or $40 per season or $75 for a family season pass (in 2016). You can pay at the trailhead or pick up passes at local shops.

The Rendezvous Ski Trails boast one of the largest biathlon training sites in the U.S. with 24 shooting lanes. The range has hosted national championships, North American cup events and Olympic team trials. The trails are often the practice area for the U.S. Olympic Nordic Ski team. If you don't mind having people fly past you while you plod along, you'll enjoy it.

There are between 22 and 31 miles of ski trails, depending on what has been groomed — enough to keep most people happy all season. With several loop options to choose from, you can stick to a regular loop or patch together different routes. There's a children's play hill and also a local telemark hill as part of the system.

A good introductory route is the Rendezvous Loop though the heart of the system, offering about 4 miles of moderate skiing. This trail has enough ups, downs and flats to keep things interesting. There are several junctions through the system, but signs with attached maps are posted to keep skiers on track.

There is a warming hut/lodge at the trailhead with chairs and tables to seat a few families. It's a good place to eat a snack or regroup before going out again.

Teton Canyon

GETTING THERE: Take the main street heading east from Driggs (follow the signs to Grand Targhee Ski Resort) and stay on that road for about 5 miles. Look for the Teton Canyon Campground sign and turn right onto the gravel road going up the canyon. The fun starts when you leave the pavement. This road is plowed for about .5 miles to a parking area.

In recent years, the road into Teton Canyon east of Driggs up to the Teton Creek Trailhead has been groomed for skate skiing and classic skiing.

Teton Canyon offers safe and scenic miles of skiing. Another excuse for skiing up Teton Canyon is ice climbing. The canyon walls boast some challenging frozen waterfalls for climbers to lead and top rope.

From the winter parking area, the canyon is wide and the views are super. On a clear day you can see the Grand Teton and some of its neighbors above the canyon to the east. On the north side of the canyon, brush and aspens dominate the slopes. On the south side slopes, the canyon is green with a thick fir forest.

Moose are plentiful along the north slopes from the parking area to the end of the road.

The ski trail up Teton Canyon follows the road. If you arrive after a recent snowfall, you may be breaking your own trail, but groomers are quick to set track for skaters and classic skiers. In recent years, fat bikers are also using the groomed road. From the parking area to the mouth of the canyon is about 4.5 miles. But the route is fairly flat and quick for skiers.

If you've visited this canyon in the summer months on hiking or camping trips you might not recognize it during the winter. The canyon changes personality. The blanket of white will have you seeing everything anew.

At the mouth of the canyon the road ends and trails enter the Jedediah Smith Wilderness. This is the beginning of the Table (Rock) Mountain Trail and the trail to Alaska Basin. Most people turn back here. The canyon narrows and features several side chutes for the next 10 miles. Many of these chutes avalanche regularly during the winter.

About a mile past the Treasure Mountain Boy Scout Camp on the south side of the canyon is a series of frozen waterfalls popular with ice climbers. There are also a few frozen falls on the north side of the canyon about a third of a mile from the trailhead restroom.

Skiing into Alaska Basin on the west side of the Teton Range.

MOOSE CREEK

GETTING THERE: From Victor, Idaho, drive 3 miles southeast on Highway 33 and turn left on the Moose Creek Road; drive .3 miles and turn right (east) and drive to the end of the road and park.

DISTANCE: 4.4 miles up to Moose Meadows; 5.8 miles to the falls; 8 miles to Moose Lake.

Moose Creek is a popular summertime trail and has a loyal following among the Nordic crowd, too.

There are two main users of this trail: The hard-core backcountry skiers who go all the way up to Taylor Mountain (to or from the Coal Creek Trailhead) and the mellower cross-country skiers out for a few miles.

The trailhead is 2.5 miles past Victor off Highway 38. Turn left onto the Moose Creek Road and drive to the end of the plowed section. The road is plowed only to the Moose Creek ranch. During the summer this ranch rents horses for a popular trip up the canyon into the Jedediah Smith Wilderness Area.

Park along the road and begin skiing up the unplowed road. After about a mile the road ends and the trail section begins. The trail forks, with the right-hand trail going up the difficult route to Taylor Mountain (7 miles). Climbing skins for your skis are advisable. This trail eventually connects with the Coal Creek Trail.

Many skiers stay to the left and continue along the creek. The trail forks again after a couple hundred yards. The right trail follows the summer hiking trail and can be steep in places.

117

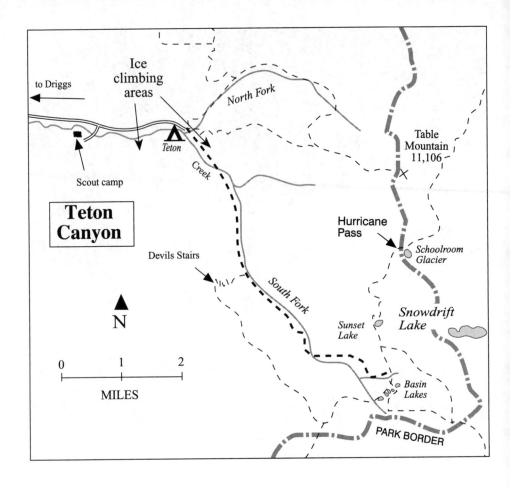

This route mainly appeals to snowshoers. The left-hand trail crosses the creek on a wide log and winds through a patch of willows to come out on the north side of the canyon. The trail then heads up into a side canyon called Sherman Canyon. Because these trails are all self-groomed, the trail distances can vary depending on who was there last or how far you want to go. The canyon gains most of its elevation gradually but is an uphill workout. It tops out after about 2.5 miles and a gain of 1,600 feet.

The return trip back down this side canyon is a blast.

If you're unfamiliar with the area, a good map to take along is the Jedediah Smith Wilderness Area map (available in plastic).

MAIL CABIN CREEK

GETTING THERE: From Victor, Idaho, drive about 9 miles southeast on Highway 33. The Coal Creek Trailhead is on the left (north) side of the highway. The trail to Mail Cabin Creek is on the right (south) side of the highway.

DISTANCE: It's about 1.5 miles to the fork in the trail. It's another 3 miles from the fork to Mosquito Pass. From the fork to Burbank Creek is 2 miles. The trail down Burbank Creek to the highway is 1.5 miles.

DIFFICULTY: Mostly easy for the first 1.5 miles. Trail gets tougher beyond the forks. This is not a beginner ski trail, but appeals to backcountry skiers looking for good runs.

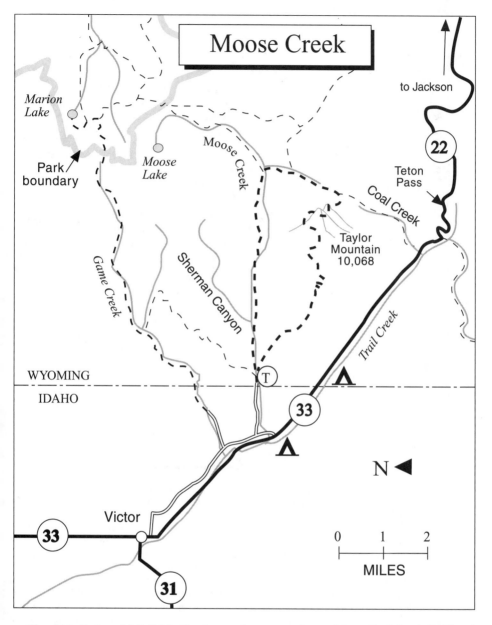

Moose Creek

to Jackson

Marion Lake

Park boundary

Moose Lake

Moose Creek

22

Teton Pass

Coal Creek

Taylor Mountain 10,068

Game Creek

Sherman Canyon

Trail Creek

WYOMING

IDAHO

T

33

N ◀

Victor

33

0   1   2

MILES

31

The ski trail along Mail Cabin Creek starts just across the road from Coal Creek Trailhead, about 2.5 miles west of Teton Pass. There are signs for both Coal Creek and Mail Cabin Creek on the highway. Coal Creek Trailhead is kept plowed out during the winter and is often packed with more than a dozen vehicles on weekends.

The trail along Mail Cabin Creek is not groomed except by skiers themselves. Because the trail receives a steady supply of users, the trail is usually in great shape and easy to follow. This may not always be the case, especially if you arrive on the trail right after a recent snowstorm.

For the first mile and a half, the trail follows the creek closely and is mostly easy going. The country is heavily wooded — most of the brush is safely buried under snow.

After about 1.5 miles, the trail forks. The left (southern) fork continues to follow the small stream of water up a canyon which continues to narrow. After about two-thirds of a mile, the trail becomes too steep for fun tour skiing. Climbing skins are needed beyond this point.

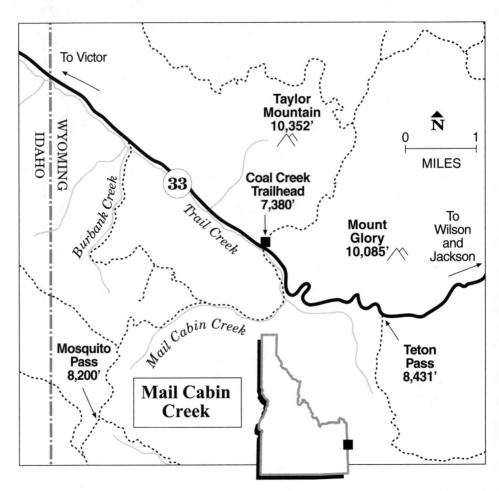

If you continued to follow this trail, it would eventually lead to Mosquito Pass. This pass is technically on the crest of the Snake River Range. This area is where the Teton Range and the Snake River Range come together.

The west fork trail continues to gain elevation but does so smoothly for about a half mile. After a half mile, the trail begins to climb more steeply and even has a few switchbacks. A quarter-mile farther is the destination of many of the backcountry skiers. The trail splits again and leads to some open knobs and rises that offer nice downhill runs.

Theoretically, the trail continues on and drops to the top of Burbank Creek and follows that creek down to the highway. Don't count on this trail being broken in and easy to follow, though.

If you wanted a loop route, you could take the trail all the way to Burbank Creek, then ski back along the highway to Coal Creek, but the route along the highway is not very exciting and is clogged with willow brush along the creek. The best time for this route is under a deep blanket of snow. You would probably have to break trail most of the way. One option is to just hitch a ride back to your car.

Keep these trails in mind for summer visits. Mail Cabin Creek starts out as a short jeep road then quickly becomes a footpath/single track. If you climb all the way up to the top of Mosquito Pass, expect some nice views of the surrounding mountain ranges.

SKI LAKE

GETTING THERE: From Victor, take Highway 33 (it becomes Highway 22 when you

A moose hangs out along Mail Cabin Creek near the ski trail.

enter Wyoming) and drive to the top of Teton Pass. From the pass, continue down the highway about two more miles. Look for a sign indicating Phillips Canyon on your left. Park on a plowed parking area about 100 yards down hill on the right. From here, you'll walk across the road and ski back uphill to the Phillips Canyon Road.

DISTANCE: 4.6 miles roundtrip from the highway parking area.

The Ski Lake trail is on the east side of the Tetons a couple of miles down from Teton Pass. The trail starts at the beginning of Phillips Canyon Road. After following the road for about a quarter of a mile, the trail leaves the road and heads up a hill. The trail continues north for the next two miles.

Ski Lake is a good trail to keep in mind for early season and late-season outings because it tends to get its snow earlier than other trails and the snow lingers longer.

When the parking lot at Teton Pass is packed to over flowing, the parking lot for Phillips Canyon Road often has a few open slots. This trail attracts several skiers with dogs – so much so that there is now a doggy poopy bag dispenser next to the Forest Service kiosk sign at the start of the road. If you bring your dog, it's a good idea to bring a leash at least to cross the often busy Teton Pass road from the Phillips Road parking lot.

The trail is also used by snowmobilers. They generally stick to the Phillips Canyon Road, but occasionally will ride up to Ski Lake.

The trail is poorly marked and also self-groomed. This can be problematic if you've never been there before and after a recent snowfall. You may start following routes that lead to dead-ends made by people out for a few hillside runs.

Perhaps the best way to get there your first time is to follow others from the parking lot. Don't underestimate the ski up. The biggest challenge is usually the last quarter mile of uphill before arriving at the lake bowl. With a bit of determination and zig-zag traversing, you can make it. To make things easier, bring along some climbing skins to slap onto your skis for the last steep section.

Ski Lake is not much to look at, especially in the winter. It's a flat area a couple of acres wide at the bottom of a steep bowl. Years of drought has reduced its size considerably.

For those looking for a big day, you can grind your way up to the top of the ridge another 800 or so feet higher and ski back down some monster slopes. Perhaps the more popular way, though, for backcountry skiers is to hike up from Teton Pass, ski north along the ridge and

121

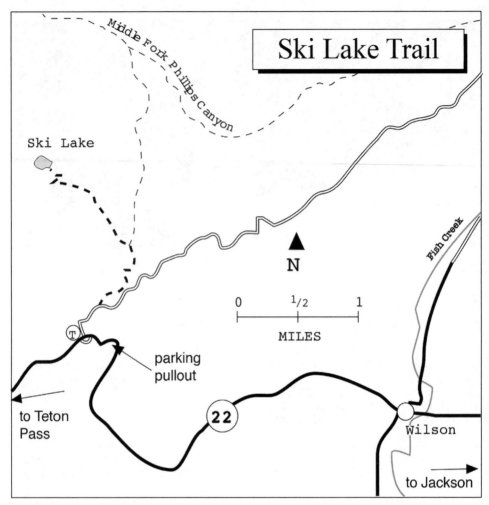

drop off to the east and come down to Phillips Canyon Road and out to the highway. Here you will need to hitch-hike back up to Teton Pass or have a shuttle car parked at the Phillips Canyon parking area.

MINK CREEK

GETTING THERE: From Pocatello, drive south on Interstate 15 for 10 miles and take the exit to Portneuf. Follow the signs to Mink Creek Recreation Area. Drive 5 miles from Portneuf south up the Bannock Highway to Cherry Springs Natural Area. Drive 2 miles south of Cherry Springs and turn left (east) and follow the signs to Scout Mountain Campground and Crestline Trailhead. Drive 4 miles south on Bannock Highway from Cherry Springs to the Valve House Draw and West Mink Creek trailheads. West Mink Creek is on the west side of the road about 50 yards south from the Valve House Draw trailhead which is on the east side. There is no sign that says, West Mink Creek. There is a small Forest Service sign with the number 059. Valve House Draw has a large gate at the trailhead. Its Forest Service number is 5171.

DISTANCES: The Scout Mountain Campground to Crestline Trailhead is 13.5 miles. Add 4 miles if you go to the top of Scout Mountain. West Mink Creek to its junction with Gibson Jack is 6 miles. Valve Spring Draw to its junction with the trail south of Scout Mountain is 7.5 miles.

Ski backpacking near Ski Lake in the Tetons.

Just south of Pocatello off Interstate 15 near Portneuf is the Mink Creek Recreation Area. This area features year-round attractions, including: camping, hiking, biking, horseback riding, skiing, snowmobiling and other outdoor activities. If you like the outdoors, this area is worth checking out.

The Mink Creek Recreation Area boasts several trailheads and the Scout Mountain Forest Service campground. There are also two self-guided short nature trails at the Cherry Springs Natural Area and one near the Scout Mountain amphitheater.

The Mink Creek area is a Park 'n' Ski area which requires you to display the Park 'n' Ski sticker on your vehicle when you park at trailheads. You can purchase them at most sporting goods stores.

The area has six snowmobile and ski trailheads. The trails are well marked to keep machines and skiers apart as much as possible. With its close proximity to Pocatello, you can expect to share the trail with other skiers. As expected, the area sees more use on the weekends. If you start out fairly early in the morning you can get a jump on the crowds and reach farther into the backcountry.

A challenging all-day loop trail is from East Mink Creek trailhead up to Scout Mountain Campground over some ridges and back down Valve House Draw. Expect the going to be easy to moderate until you get past the campground.

If you're looking for some easier routes, try the West Mink Creek trail or the Valve House Draw trail. Both routes have some uphill climbs, but the routes offer some mellower skiing. Keep in mind that these routes can become tougher and scarier when the snow ices up.

Before you go, get a copy of the Caribou Forest Service Pocatello District map to see which trails are shared with snowmobiles. The map also has a helpful rating system for what level of difficulty to expect on the various trails.

OTHER AREA SKI TRAILS NEAR MINK CREEK

GIBSON JACK

Drive toward the Mink Creek/Scout Mountain Area on the Bannock Highway. Just across from the entrance to the Pocatello Country Club about 4 miles from town, turn right on Gibson

Jack Road. Drive to the end of the plowed road.

This trail stays on the road and follows the north side of Gibson Jack Creek. The skiing is generally easy to moderate until the road ends and becomes a trail. The trail follows the creek and begins to climb and become more moderate skiing. This route eventually climbs to a saddle and drops into the West Fork of Mink Creek.

If you have another vehicle parked at the West Fork of Mink Creek trailhead, you can pull off a relatively short shuttle on the Bannock Highway. Take along a topo map and compass (occasionally people do get confused in this area). A possible extra hour or so side trip when the conditions are good is to switchback up to the summit of Gibson Jack Mountain. This summit offers nice views of the Portneuf Valley and Mountains — and, of course, there's the zoom back down to the trail.

WEST FORK MINK CREEK

This trailhead (a Park and Ski trail) is near the turnoff to the Scout Mountain Road. Look for a large plowed parking area on the right side of the road as you drive up the Bannock Highway. This trail is popular with skiers in the winter and hikers and bikers in the summer. The trail starts on the West Fork Road, but turns into a trail after passing a gate about 100 yards up. After about 2.5 miles of forested area, the trail passes through a meadow with beaver dams and ponds. From here, some skiers head south into the Elk Meadow area or continue to follow the West Fork creek over the divide and into the Gibson Jack drainage. If you plan on making connections with the Gibson Jack Trail, it's a good idea to bring along a map and compass.

This trail can become icy, particularly in the late season. This trail does not allow dogs.

VALVE HOUSE DRAW

Park at the West Fork Mink Creek Trailhead (a Park and Ski trail) and walk across the Bannock Highway to the east side of the road.

This trail follows the Valve House Draw drainage for a couple of miles. The terrain is easy to moderate depending on conditions. If things are icy, expect fast and scary descents.

For those looking for a longer ski, this trail can be connected to the East Fork of Mink Creek Road or with the South Fork of Mink Creek. If you plan to ski some of these extensions, take along a topo map and compass.

EAST FORK MINK CREEK NORDIC SKI AREA

Pocatello Parks and Recreation maintains a groomed Nordic ski area a couple of miles up the Scout Mountain Road. There are several miles of skate and classic routes groomed. It will cost you to play here — $6 for adults, but the trails are well-maintained and there is a warming shelter and toilets. Occasionally through the winter, races and other events are held here. There are plans to add to this trail system. To get there, drive south on the Bannock Highway from Pocatello and turn left on the Scout Mountain Road. Drive to the end of the plowed portion of the road. Park 'n Ski Passes are also required.

CRYSTAL SUMMIT

For experienced novices or intermediate and above cross-country skiers, the Crystal Mountain area offers a variety of skiing opportunities that will keep you busy for several winter trips.

Crystal Summit is the highest point on the Bannock Highway (the road that connects I-15 to Arbon Valley). Crystal Summit forms the divide between Arbon Valley and Mink Creek. Parking for winter play is in the plowed areas on both sides of the road. These lots are plowed with snowmobile funds but skiers and sledders with a current Park 'N' Ski sticker have also paid their dues and are welcome.

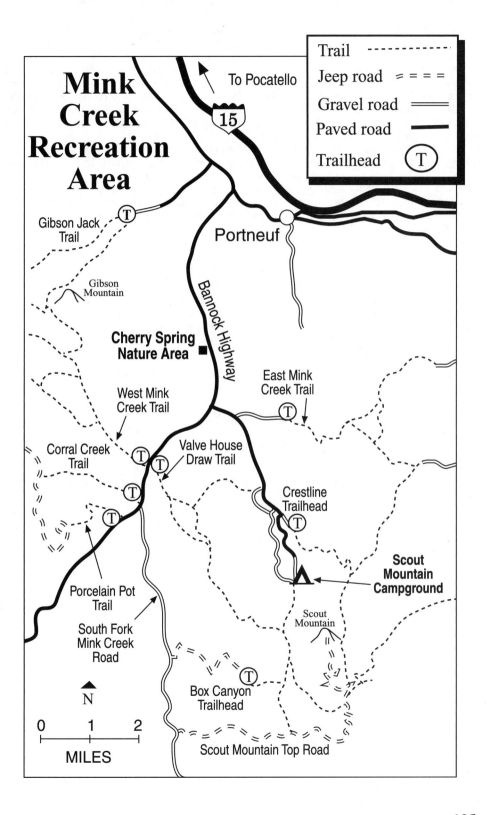

Mink Creek Recreation Area

Legend:
- Trail - - - - - -
- Jeep road = = = =
- Gravel road =
- Paved road ▬
- Trailhead (T)

To Pocatello

15

Portneuf

Gibson Jack Trail

Gibson Mountain

Bannock Highway

Cherry Spring Nature Area ■

West Mink Creek Trail

East Mink Creek Trail (T)

Corral Creek Trail (T) (T)

Valve House Draw Trail

(T)

Crestline Trailhead (T)

Scout Mountain Campground

Porcelain Pot Trail

South Fork Mink Creek Road

Scout Mountain

Box Canyon Trailhead (T)

N

0   1   2
MILES

Scout Mountain Top Road

Crystal Summit offers a little of everything: pleasant trail skiing, telemarking and ridge tour workouts with nice views. Snowmobiles also use the area. If you're looking to avoid the motor crowd, the Caribou Forest Service has set aside the Parody Trail just for skiers.

From the parking area, follow the marked ski trail. If you head north you will connect into the Porcelain Pot Trails. Most skiers follow the trail leading farther into the Crystal area. The trail climbs around an open hill called Corral Point. Within 3/4 of a mile from the parking area, the trail descends into a forested area. It then gradually climbs for about a mile and breaks out on a broad ridge with views of Scout Mountain. Telemark skiers can leave the trail at several points to make short downhill trips on the open slopes.

The Crystal trail links up with the top of the Corral Creek ski trail. At this junction you have a few options. You can tele ski on the nearby hillsides, follow the Corral Creek Trail downhill to a shuttle vehicle or hook up with the snowmobile trail which goes to Elk Meadows.

If you don't care about following trails, you can head through the backcountry looking for hillsides to tele ski or just for the views. This may not be such a good idea on days of low visibility. It is easy to get lost when one hill looks like the next. Pay attention to your surroundings whenever you leave the trail.

SOUTH FORK MINK CREEK

About a mile beyond the parking lot for the West Fork of Mink Creek on the Bannock Highway you'll come to the South Fork Road. This road is a groomed snowmobile trail but both skiers and snowmobilers use the same trail. If you wish to ski this road, a good place to park is in the plowed area at the Corral Creek Trailhead (a Park'N' Ski site).

This is one of those ski routes suitable for beginners. The route sticks to the road and is easy to follow. Probably the best time to go to avoid snowmobile traffic is early in the morning.

CORRAL CREEK

The Corral Creek parking area is up the Bannock Highway about one mile past the West Fork of Mink Creek on the right side of the road (across the road from the South Fork Road). Drive out the Bannock Highway.

The Corral Creek Trail heads west into the woods and is fairly mellow in the first section. The upper end of the trail becomes steep and usually requires some switchbacking to get to the crest. At the top of the crest you can connect into trails that lead to the Crystal Summit-Parody Trail system or just seek out some slopes for telemarking.

126

A moose retreats from a skier in the Snake River Range east of Palisades Reservoir.

127

Dan Sanders on Yellow Man 5.11b, The Discovery Wall, The Fins. Photo by Nathan Smith.

Climbing

Eastern Idaho is home to many diverse gems when it comes to rock climbing. With the ongoing development of new climbing areas, this side of the Gem State has something for everyone: If poking pockets on world-class limestone calls to you, trek to The Fins. If you're craving for seriously steep and powerful routes, head out to Crank Cave and climb on the steepest routes you'll find in eastern Idaho. If climbing in absolute seclusion on stellar limestone attracts you, head to Cedar Creek. If slabby, thin and technical is your game Box Canyon or the Grand Wall will keep you on your toes. Or maybe you're looking for a family-friendly crag like Heise Rock or Ross Park. Like pulling down on an endless sea of fun basalt? Travel to Massacre Rocks and take your pick of over 760 sport routes.

Since the last edition of Sweet Spots, nine additional climbing areas have been added to the new version of the guidebook, making for a total of 13 climbing areas. Most are newer crags that have been developed since the last edition. This may be seen as testament to the fact that perhaps eastern Idaho isn't "tapped out" yet when it comes to development of new climbing areas. Only time will tell.

The climbing season in the area runs from spring to late fall with the exception of the south facing crags composed of basalt (Massacre Rocks, Pointless Crag, South Park, The Playground, Ross Park Sunny Side) These areas are actually more enjoyable during the cold-to-cooler times of the year.

Climbers should consider these climbing areas as local treasures to be cared for and preserved. If we are vigilant in picking up trash, practicing safe climbing and using good manners with landowners, wildlife and each other, the local crags should stay open to all current and future climbers.

Note: the authors use a star rating system only to indicate which climbs they and the general consensus enjoy, prefer or downright dislike. Climbers have such a wide array of preference to style that by no means can one person dictate what is a "good" or "bad" climb. You just have to find out for yourself, but the authors feel like the rating system may help.

No star = marginal   * = worth doing   ** = good climb   * = excellent!**

www.metoliusclimbing.com

Jonathan Siegrist on Better Living Through Chemistry (5.14b/c) Photo: Mike Williams

Bravo Quickdraws

Troy Neu on "56" with The Honing Stone, Solstice Wall and Jet A Wall, respectively, in the background.

The Fins

Located in the extreme southern tip of the Lost River Range just southwest of Howe lie The Fins. Highlighted by world class vertical to slightly overhung limestone that is riddled with pockets and edges, The Fins is truly a unique climbing area to eastern Idaho.

GEOLOGY: A thick sequence of carbonate rocks (limestone and dolomite) are present in most of the mountains of eastern Idaho. Carbonate sediments were deposited in a warm, shallow marine environment, forming broad carbonate platforms in the early Paleozoic period, about 530-300 million years ago. At present, these rocks can be observed as thick, pale gray massive outcrops.

East Idaho is located in a thrust belt which means that horizontal compressive stress forces deform and uplift rocks over time and cause older rocks to be pushed up and over younger rocks. The limestone we see at The Fins (originally deposited as horizontal carbonate bank beds) were uplifted by thrust faulting and formed the flat, steep vertical cliffs that make for such awesome climbing. The ultimate appearances of "fins" is due to erosional forces disintegrating and re-

moving softer sedimentary layers of the carbonate beds.

Fossils of Mississippian age (360-323 million years) can be found embedded in rocks at the climbing area. These fossils may include brachiopods, bryozoans, crinoids, foraminifers, corals, and trilobites.

CLIMBING: Chuck Denure first discovered The Fins in the early-mid 1990's and established a handful of routes on The Headwall and The Honing Stone (aka "The Warm Up Wall). In 1998, on an airplane recon trip with his father, Marc Hanselman came across these same impressive limestone cliffs. He quickly returned with his drill, and was surprised to find routes already on The Headwall. After seeing only a handful of routes in a sea of enormous potential, he recruited Alex McMeekin and the two quickly went to work.

Over the years, word slowly spread and more climbers began to visit. Along with them, other local route developers added their own contributions to the area. These folks include: Peter Heekin, Jeremy Scherer, Matt TeNgaio, Dave Bingham, Mike Benson, Tom Smartt, and Ian Cavanaugh. With grades mainly in the 5.11-5.13

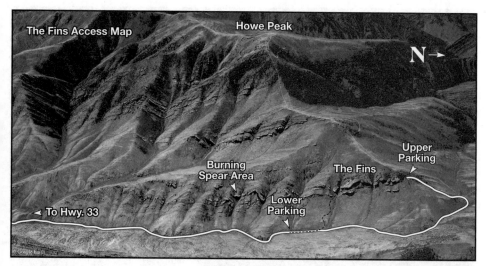

The Fins Access Map

Howe Peak

N→

Upper Parking

Burning Spear Area

The Fins

Lower Parking

To Hwy. 33

range, locals knew The Fins had potential for much harder routes.

Upon first visiting The Fins in 2010, Jonathan Siegrist too saw the area's potential. In 2012 he returned with hardware and a drill with plans to stay for about 10 days – he ended up residing there for almost a month, eagerly upping the ante by adding The Fins first 5.14, "The Catalyst", .14b; one of three mixed routes, "Enter the Dragon", .14; a couple of impressive .13's; and the kingline, "Algorithm", Idaho's first .14d and hardest route to date. Siegrist returned during the subsequent seasons to add even more hard lines, (another .14d among them), and has layed the groundwork for another milestone to add to The Fins' already impressive collection of routes.

The main concentration of climbing sits at the head of Eightmile Canyon and extends southward following the descending ridgeline. Sitting at about 7,600 feet this is a great summer area. However, the morning sun on the east facing walls can be brutal as there is no shade until about 1 p.m. The rock is sharp in nature but offers great texture. The climbing is vertical/slightly overhanging, somewhat powerful, yet technical and sustained! With the exception of a few noted routes, a 60m rope will suffice.

NOTE: Climbers camping at the Upper Parking area has become a common practice. With that, disposal of human waste has become a concern. Please pack out your own waste to help keep this area pristine so others may enjoy it as well.

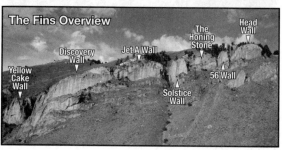

The Fins Overview

The Honing Stone

Head Wall

Discovery Wall

Jet A Wall

Yellow Cake Wall

56 Wall

Solstice Wall

GETTING THERE: From Idaho Falls, head west on Hwy. 20 towards Arco for about 57 miles. About 10 miles before Arco, turn right on Highway 33 and drive north towards Howe. At about 9 miles turn left, west, at a gravel pit onto an unmarked dirt road entering Eightmile Canyon. At about .5 mile down the dirt road, turn right through a gate and at another .5 mile veer right as the road descends down a short hillside. At about 3.6 miles from the highway the lower parking area is found on the left side of the road. The parking area accommodates about four cars. Two-wheel drive vehicles will want to park here. Four-wheel drive cars may continue up the steep road for another 1.5 miles to the saddle, however, this road can be very loose and it is quite steep in some sections. From there, turn left up a two-track road that climbs to a grove of pine trees and an awesome camping spot. Park near the trees and follow the short trail to the Head Wall.

All walls see morning sun, afternoon shade

131

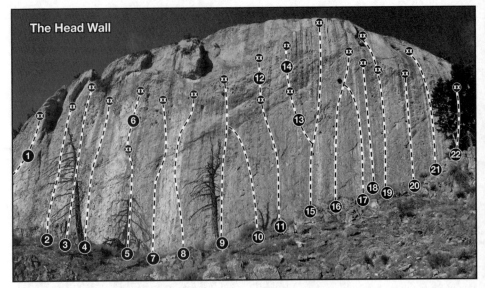

The Head Wall

5.12 is the name of the game at this wall. First wall to be developed at the Fins. 2 minute approach from upper parking area or 60 minute approach from lower parking area. Routes are listed from left to right when facing wall.

1. S-Curves* .12a/b
Left-most route on the wall. Climbs fun pocketed face for 3 bolts, takes a hard right for 5 bolts then straight up for 3 more bolts. 11 bolts. *FA: Peter Heekin.*

Troy Neu dishing it up on Al's Diner, .13a.

2. Virgins of Howe*** .11c/d
Starts on chossy section to great pockets on white limestone to 1st set of anchors. 6 bolts. *FA: Chuck Denure.*

3. Two Hitter Quitter** .12c
Great route with crux at the 4th bolt. Ends on fun jugs. 8 bolts. *FA: Bill Ohran.*

4. Ghost in the Shell*** .12a
More pocket pulling on good stone. Stout for the grade. 6 bolts. *FA: Marc Hanselman.*

5. Stems and Seeds* .11a
Starts by fallen tree. Decent warm up route on somewhat sharp stone. 6 bolts. *FA: Chuck Denure.*

6. Bad Ass Weed** .12a
Climbs past Stems and Seeds anchors into a crux followed by fun jug hauling that's somewhat runout. 10 bolts. *FA: Chuck Denure.*

7. Seven Arrows** .12a
Climbs to the left of the first few bolts then angles right to bulge. 6 bolts. *FA: Marc Hanselman.*

8. Al's Diner*** .13a
2 cruxes. Great route. Named in honor of Alex McMeekin who bolted the route but never got a chance to send due to ankle injury. 8 bolts. *FA: Eric Liedecker.*

Ben Rodes finds the cure for The Munchies, .12c.

9. Bean Fiddler*** .12c
Starts near tree stump. Goes through shallow pod at top of route to ring anchors. 7 bolts. *FA: Jeremy Scherer.*

10. Time Will Tell** .12b
Veers left at 6-7th bolt and joins Bean Fiddler. 7 bolts. *FA: Peter Heekin.*

11. Koona** .12a
Route veers left at the top to anchors. 5 bolts. *FA: Marc Hanselman.*

12. Koona Kahuna** .12a/b
A 3 bolt extension from Koona allowing for more mileage but not really any more difficulty. 9 bolts. *FA: Tom Smartt.*

13. Middle Man* .12b
Starts on Bong then veers left after 4th bolt. Sport anchors. 7 bolts. *FA: Marc Hanselman.*

14. The Munchies** .12c
3 bolt extension to Middle Man. *FA: Tom Smartt.*

15. Clips From the Bong*** .12b
Longest route on the wall. Pull on pockets for 10 bolts then negotiate slab ending on small holds. General consensus downgraded this from original rating of .12c. 13 bolts. *FA: Chuck Denure.*

16. Yukon Gold* .12b
Straight up then right to big pod. Sport anchors. 7 bolts. *FA: Peter Heekin.*

17. White Rhino** .12a/b
Follows white streak then veer left to big pod and merge with Yukon. Sport anchors. 6 bolts. *FA: Peter Heekin.*

18. The Thunder Rolls** .13a
Enjoy the warm up on the first few bolts before the slap-down crux near the top. Tan camoed hangers. 6 bolts. *FA: Ian Cavanaugh.*

19. When Vegans Attack** .11c
Fun route except for last 2 bolts. Anchors were finally added at the 8th bolt making this route much more appealing. To the first set of anchors is .11b. 10 bolts. *FA: Chuck Denure.*

20. Hydroponics** .11a
The easier of the first two. 8 bolts. *FA: Chuck Denure.*

21. Drunk As A Skunk* .11b
Slab ending at chain anchors. 7 bolts. *FA: Chuck Denure.*

22. Little Black Spot* .11d
Right-most route on the wall. Rap ring anchors. 6 bolts. *FA: Dave Bingham.*

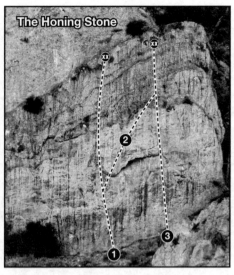

56 Wall

Located between the Head Wall and The Honing Stone. 5 minute approach from upper parking area or 50 minutes from lower parking area.

1. Escape From Choss Angeles**   .11c
Dirty climbing past first bolt to good stone. Follow the diagonal rail then head left to crack. Finishing holds can be found around the left side of the blunt arete. 7 bolts. *FA: Tom Smartt.*

2. Wascally Wabbit**   .12d
Mellow climing leads to hard moves on bomber stone. Enjoy the breadloaf sloper hold. 9 bolts. *FA: Tom Smartt.*

3. 56***   .11b
Climbs the right-trending diagonal seam, then straight up the upper face. A redpoint crux guards the anchors. 10 bolts. *FA: Dave Bingham.*

The Honing Stone

After recent contact with the first ascensionist, the authors realized that this wall was improperly named "Warmup Wall" for years.

10 minute approach from upper parking area or 50 minutes from lower parking area. Less than vertical rock. Easiest routes at the Fins. Routes are listed from left to right when facing wall.

1. The Ginsu**   .7
Long slabby route. 11 bolts. *FA: Chuck Denure.*

2. The Ginsu Variation*   .9
Starts on #1 then veer right after 3rd bolt. Shares bolts and anchors with Cicada. 8 bolts. *FA: Chuck Denure.*

3. Cicada**   .10a
Direct start to #2. Vertical climbing leads to easy slab finish on big holds. 7 bolts. *FA: Matt TeNgaio, Mike Benson.*

Sunrise over The Fins.

Meghan Twohig floats bees? BEES!, .11b. Photo by Tom Smartt.

Tom Smartt on the FA of Escape From Choss Angeles, .11c.

Jonathan Siegrist firing the FA of Enter the Dragon, .14a. Photo by Ian Cavanaugh.

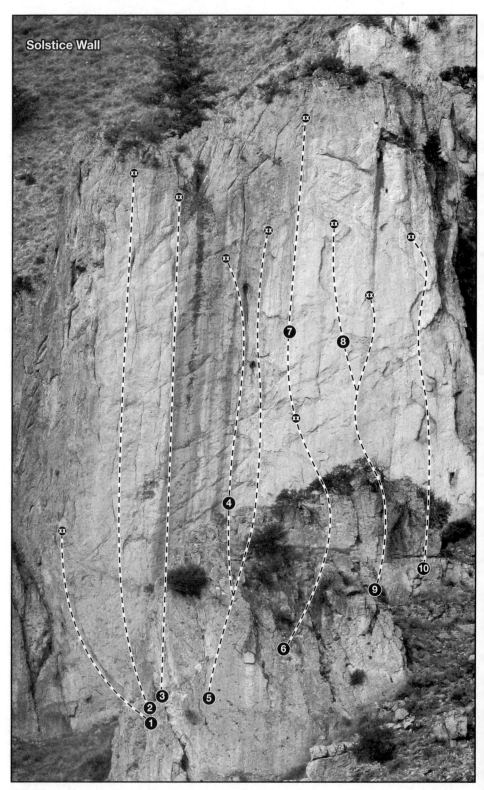

Solstice Wall

Solstice Wall

Nice tall formation to the left of The Honing Stone. The rock quality is much better than it looks. In the summer of 2012, this wall saw a handful of new routes. 10 minute approach from upper parking area or 45 minute approach from lower parking area. Routes are listed from left to right when facing wall.

1. The Blue Tape Route*   .10c
Located on the far left side o f the wall. Follows the flake for 2 bolts then straight up. Staying slightly right of the 4th bolt following the pockets flows better. 5 bolts. *FA: Matt TeNgaio, Mike Benson.*

2. Enter the Dragon***   .14aR
Clip the bolts then follow the impressive crack clear to the top of the wall. Rack up to 1 inch doubles and up to an Orange Metolius. A 70m rope is needed. Chain anchors. 4 bolts/gear. *FA: Jonathan Siegrist.*

3. Year of the Ox***   .13dR
Low 5.13 climbing leads to the cracks above. Purple TCU's. 3 bolts/gear. *FA: Jonathan Siegrist.*

4. The Haka   Project
Shares first 2 bolts with Wings, then breaks left for the business. Joins Wings again at the

rest ledge then climbs the left side of the pods. *Equipped: Matt TeNgaio.*

5. Wings for Mary**   .12b
In loving memory. A tall line in the middle of the wall that climbs through the right side of the pods up high. Stick clipping the first high bolt is recommended. 12 bolts. *FA: Matt TeNgaio.*

6. Huck You**   .11b
Arcs right and then back left to ending "Huck" move. A bit harder for shorter folk. 6 bolts. *FA: Matt TeNgaio, Tom Smartt.*

7. Mind Your Manors***   .14b
6 bolt extension to Huck You. "Power-endurance dynamic crimping". 13 bolts. *FA: Jonathan Siegrist.*

8. Weather Maker   Project
Shares first 6 bolts with Fire, then follows black hangers through crux to big jug below big right-facing flake. *Equipped: Matt TeNgaio.*

9. High on Fire***   .12d
After the 2nd bolt, the rock and movement get better. Has a few nasty biter crimps after the crux. 9 bolts. *FA: Matt TeNgaio.*

10. Solstice***   5.12b
Located on the far right side of the wall. Fun climbing on a variety of holds. 10 bolts. *FA: Matt TeNgaio.*

Jonathan Siegrist FA of Mind Your Manors, .14b. Photo by Ian Cavanaugh.

Jet A Wall

This wall saw a flurry of new routes during the 2015 season. 15 minute approach from upper parking area or 45 minute approach from lower parking area. Routes are listed from left to right when facing wall.

1. Slabotomy* .12d/.13a
Burly route with thin slab climbing. It ain't over 'til it's over. 7 bolts. *FA: Tom Smartt.*

2. The Curse Of Mumm-Ra** .12a
Climb through a couple of horizotntal rails through fun moves at mid route. Finishes left of the anchors.7 bolts. *FA: Ian Cavanaugh.*

3. Rise of Cobra* .12a
Located around the corner to the left of BEES! Climbs to the right of the last bolt. 5 bolts. *FA: Mike Benson.*

4. bees? BEES!!!*** .11b
The upper-most route of the three that are located to the left of G.I. Joe. The name comes from an accident that occured on the highway near the entrance to The Fins in June 2015 that invloved 20 million bees and an overturned semi truck. Most of the bees perished yet, many managed to indiscriminately harrass the Fins for several days. "Luckily, there was enough of a reprieve to bolt the route". 5 bolts. *FA: Tom Smartt.*

Matt TeNgaio FA of High on Fire, .12d. Photo by Mike Benson.

5. Atomic Potato**   .12b
Located uphill just left of Longarm. Sharp, prickly start leads to technical pocketed section. Look for the pocket out right near the top. 6 bolts. *FA: Bill Ohran.*

6. Mr. Longarm***   .12c
Start of the route is a bit of a squeeze job but opens up after 3rd bolt. The name is derived from the reachy moves up top. 8 bolts. *FA: Matt TeNgaio.*

7. Bunny Massacre**   .13c
Climbs up past small bush on good holds. Hard, technical slab climbing awaits. Somewhat similar to Big Bouncy but a bit easier. 9 bolts. *FA: Tom Smartt.*

8. G.I. Joe Bouncy Tank**   .12a
Follows flake to pockets. Crux is at the top of the route. 6 bolts. *FA: Peter Heekin.*

9. The Big Bouncy***   .13d
8 bolt extension from Bouncy Tank. Climbs to G.I. Joe's 5th bolt then veers right and up to where the business starts. 13 bolts. *FA: Tom Smartt.*

10. Jet A***   .12a/b
Starts on pockets and crimps then follows the crack straight up to sport anchors. A must do. 7 bolts. *FA: Marc Hanselman.*

11. Wind Tunnel (aka Speed Boat)**.12d
The route was partially equipped years ago by Marc Hanselman and sat dormant for some time. Tom Smartt finished equipping it and renamed it. Hard start leaving the tombstone block, then delicate climbings leads up to the runnel, followed by very technical slab climbing. 10 bolts. *FA: Tom Smartt.*

12. Throttle Gift**   .12d
Easy start to a blank section below a small roof to well defined crux, then sustained crimping to the top. Bolts. *Equipped: Marc Hanselman. FA: Tom Smartt.*

13. Ol' Blue   Project
Equipped: Tom Smartt.

14. ¡Viva Mantequilla!***   .13b
A short route that packs a punch. Height-dependent sequencing with a windmill move thrown in there just for kicks. 5 bolts. *FA: Tom Smartt.*

15. Water from Stone**   .11b
Located about 100 yards right of route 4. Follows seam. 7 bolts. *FA: Marc Hanselman.*

16. Gastric Warfare*   .12d
Manky start leads to better climbing after 3rd bolt. Follows water streak. Thin slab crux. 8 bolts. *FA: Matt TeNgaio.*

17. Outnumbered But Not Outgunned***   .13a
A fun route that climbs to the left of the small cave up high. Main crux is near the 6th bolt. Previously named "Room with a View" before it was fully equipped. 8 bolts. *FA: Ian Cavanaugh.*

Tom Smartt on the FA of The Big Bouncy, .13d.

139

Inge Perkins firing The Manhattan Project, .14a. Photo by Erik Christensen.

The Discovery Wall

Revered by many, the high quality routes on the Discovery Wall receive a lot of attention – and for good reason. Nearly all the routes on this wall fall under the 2-3 star quality rating and vary in length. This wall saw a lot of new route action during the 2012 and 2013 seasons.

20 minute approach from upper parking area or 40 minute approach from lower parking area. Routes are listed from left to right when facing wall.

Brad Brookes on Hazmat, .12a/b.

The Discovey Wall (Lower Section)

1. Decon*   .12b/c
Left-most route on the wall. Climbs up to crack, finishes on sharp slab. Still a bit dirty as of press time. 7 bolts. *FA: Mike Williams.*

2. Hazmat**   .12a/b
Techy pocket pulling leads to crack, then up to sharp slab and chert jugs at the anchors. 6 bolts. *FA: Mike Williams.*

3. Chapstick***   .12a
Great route with pockets, crimps, and slab. 10 bolts. *FA: Dave Bingham.*

4. Pure Rock Fury**   .13a
If you can make it to the 4th bolt, then it's in the bag. Sport anchors. 9 bolts. *FA: Matt TeNgaio.*

5. Beefeater***   .12d
Stick clip the very high first bolt and climb chossy ledge to start route. A crux start leads to fun, endurance pocket pulling with a 2nd, but easier, crux up high. 9 bolts. *FA: Matt TeNgaio.*

6. The Dinner Roll***   .12c
Bouldery start leads to big moves on good pockets. An 11th bolt and new anchors were added making the original traverse to Shaken's anchors obsolete. 11 bolts. *FA: Jeremy Scherer.*

7. Shaken Not Stirred***   .12a
Fun technical crux low on route leads to pumpy finish. Likely THE best .12a at the Fins. *FA: Marc Hanselman.*

8. Make It A Double***   .13a
3 bolt extension from Shaken. Good air time! Note: Be careful lowering on a 60m rope, it may not get you down all the way. 12 bolts. *FA: Jonathan Siegrist.*

9. Yellowman***   .11a
Starts on chossy flake/ledge. Great route on excellent pockets. A bit sporty and worth every minute. Shares anchors with Shaken. 6 bolts. *FA: Marc Hanselman.*

10. Martini***   .12a
Another excellent 5.12 that ends at the "Martini" flake. 8 bolts. *FA: Brandon Anderson.*

11. Vesper***   .14a
Climbs Martini just shy of the anchors. Veer right after 8th bolt of Martini and get ready for the business for 5 more bolts to the top. Expect some runouts. 80m rope required. 14 bolts. *FA: Jonathan Siegrist.*

12. Manhattan Project**   .14a
Climbs Martini to 6th bolt, then up and right for 5 more bolts. 11 bolts. *FA: Jonathan Siegrist.*

13. EBR-1**   .11a
Tricky start to big pockets. Rap ring anchors. 6 bolts. *FA: Peter Heekin.*

141

Chad Moore on Son of Discovery, .13a.
Photo by Meghan Twohig.

14. Fallout*** .13d
Fun start to hard crux over blank bulge and second crux below the anchors. 9 bolts. *FA: Jonathan Siegrist.*

15. Son of Discovery*** .13a
The name of this route comes from the original name of the project route it started on, Route of Discovery. Anchors were added to make an enjoyable hard route on the bottom 1/3 of what was at the time an open project. Stick clip 1st bolt. Continuous technical climbing that dosen't let up until the end. Chain anchors. 4 bolts. *FA: Tom Smartt.*

Stephanie Carter powers through the monos on Pure Rock Fury, .13a.
Photo by Ian Cavanaugh.

16. Algorithm*** .14d
The king line at The Fins. Begins on Son of Discovery, traverses right and then keeps going to the top! Idaho's first .14d. The route was previously named "Route of Discovery" that ended at the pod at bolt 10, after the original crux traverse. It was equipped by Marc Hanselman and Alex McMeekin and sat as an open project for years. It was also the first route to be bolted on the massive wall, hence the name, It wasn't until 2012 when Jonathan Siegrist added more bolts and took it to the very top and renamed the line. 80m rope is needed. 15 bolts. *FA: Jonathan Siegrist.*

17. Mala Leche** .14d
Get ready for multiple V13 moves. Burly from the get-go. 5 bolts. 1 bolt anchor. *FA: Jonathan Siegrist.*

18. The Catalyst*** .14b
The Fins first 5.14. Was previously an open project named "Beginners Mind". 8 bolts. *FA: Jonathan Siegrist.*

19. The Excerciser open project
3 bolt extension of Catalyst. Expect V13 crimping. 12 bolts. *Equipped: Jonathan Siegrist.*

The Discovey Wall (Upper Section)

20. Better Living Through Chemistry** .14c
About 75' to the right of The Catalyst. Enjoy a brief warm up through the first several bolts, then get ready for some thin climbing on bomber stone. It helps to think outside the box on this one. A long draw is helpful at the crux bulge. 8 bolts. *FA: Jonathan Siegrist.*

21. Unnamed open project
Extension off of Better Living to the top. Likely .14d or harder. *Equipped: Jonathan Siegrist.*

22. Turbo 900** .13d
Cryptic movement involving powerful sequences. This route packs a punch. 6 bolts. *FA: Tom Smartt.*

23. Yellow Brick Road*** .13c
Despite several broken holds, this sustained route is one of the most sought after harder routes. Pockets,

side pulls, tricky feet and a little wandering are the name of the game. 5 bolts. *FA: Jonathan Siegrist.*

24. Off To Be The Wizard** .14c
Climbs Yellow Brick Road then keeps going for 5 more bolts. Unique climbing through waves of perfect limestone to the heinous crux – a big move off a left hand pinky mono, followed by more big movement with technical body positioning. 11 bolts. *FA: Jonathan Siegrist.*

25. Skeletor** .12d
Get your crimp game on for this one. 4 bolts. F*A: Peter Heekin.*

26. A Date With She-Ra* .14a
A 3 bolt extension from Skeletor. 8 bolts. *FA: Jonathan Siegrist.*

27. Bushido*** .13a
Classic route. Hard climbing off the ground, 2 distinct cruxes followed by power endurance moves to the anchors. A must do for the 5.13 climber. Shares anchors and last bolt with Mothership. Sport anchors. 10 bolts. *FA: Marc Hanselman.*

Jonathan Siegrist on Better Living Through Chemistry, .14c. Photo by Mike Williams.

143

28. Bare Knuckle Boxer*** .13a/b
5 bolt extension of Bushido that continues past the pod with another crux after the first set of anchors. *Equipped: Marc Hanselman. FA: Jonathan Siegrist.*

29. The Mothership*** .12c
Route angles right then up. Shares anchors and last bolt with Bushido. 8 bolts. *FA: Marc Hanselman.*

30. Mission Control*** .12d/.13a
Climbs Mothership then merges with Boxer. 13 bolts. *Equipped: Marc Hanselman. FA: Jonathan Siegrist.*

31. Hapacholo** .12d
Starts on good holds then veers right through crux followed by fun pocket pulling. Most people clip the chains from the mono. True Hapacholos take the original .13a grade by making the last move to the ledge and then clip the anchors. 5 bolts. *FA: Tom Smartt.*

32. La Cabanita Especial*** .13c
Continue past the anchors on Hapacholo. Head slighty right on decent pockets but poor feet to a ledge. Big moves on pockets lead to a slopey ending. Another one of the area's most sought after harder routes. 11 bolts. *Equipped: Tom Smartt. FA: Jonathan Siegrist.*

33. The Coffee Project Project
Equipped: Tom Smartt.

34. Disco Steppin' Project
Equipped: Tom Smartt.

35. Heads On Sticks** .13b
Located in a wide orange streak. Crimping leads to crux, then big moves on sharp holds to big pod. 4 bolts. *FA: Tom Smartt.*

36. Gulag Dance Party* .12d
Angles slighty left on black streaks through crimps to slopey holds. May require occasional cleaning as the route sees a bit of moisture from runoff. 5 bolts. *FA: Tom Smartt.*

• Project anchors

Yellow Cake Wall

Yellowish colored wall just left of the Discovery Wall. This cuspid shaped wall is the leftmost wall of all the main walls and is the first wall one approaches when hiking from the lower parking area. 25 minute approach from upper parking area or 30 minute approach from lower parking area. Routes are listed from left to right when facing wall.

1. That Fresh Feeling** .11d
Great climbing on edges and occasional pockets. 7 Bolts. *FA: Dave Bingham.*

2. Avatar** .12a
Climbs right leaning seam. 7 bolts. *FA: Dave Bingham.*

3. "51"** .11d
Fun face climbing to pockets and slab. Chain anchors. 5 bolts. *FA: Dave Bingham.*

4. No Country For Old Men*** .13b
Extension to 51. Straight up from anchors on big moves. Main crux is high on the route. 13 bolts. *FA: Ian Cavanaugh.*

5. Yellow Cake** .10d
Starts between two bushes and climbs pockets and edges. Chain anchors. 6 bolts. *FA: Dave Bingham.*

Matt TeNgaio prefers it Shaken Not Stirred, .12a. Photo by Ian Cavanaugh.

144

Yellow Cake Wall

6. Legend Of The Brown Dog***.13d/.14a
Extension off of Yellow Cake. Climb Yellow Cake then fire through gnarly crux after the chains clipping 2 bolts along the way before reaching the crack. From there, start plugging gear. There are 2 more cruxes before the climbing backs off just below the anchors. 9 bolts/gear. *Equipped: Ian Cavanaugh. FA: Jonathan Siegrist.*

7. Separation of Church and Skate*.12a/b
Sharp start leads to better movement up high. Funs moves in the crack. 10 bolts. *FA: Matt TeNgaio.*

8. The Antidote** .13d
5 bolt extension to Separation that climbs to the top of the wall. Great exposure near the end! 16 Bolts. *FA: Jonathan Siegrist.*

9. Techno Pop* .11d
Thin and technical climbing in the upper section. 8 Bolts. *FA: Dave Bingham.*

Burning Spear Area

BURNING SPEAR AREA

Located about .5 mile south of the Discovery and Yellow Cake Walls is an area of seldom-visited slabby/vertical formations.

GETTING THERE: Follow the main Fins driving directions but at about 3.4 miles from the highway (just before the last bend in the road before the lower parking area) park to the left of the road near a power line with a "Danger" sign. Hike diagonally up and left to a shallow dry gully to a cluster of burned pine trees. The routes are on the tall formation directly above the burned trees.

Burning Spear Wall
(Morning sun, afternoon shade)

Climbs are located in a secluded setting. Routes are listed from left to right when facing wall.

1. Burning Spear*   .10a
1st bolt is tan colored. Runout to the anchors. 5 bolts. *FA: Dave Bingham.*

2. Toprope*   .10a
Toprope.

3. Cajun Hot Stick   .10d
Starts just right of water groove/crack. Angles right near the top. Be careful at the top! 7 bolts. *FA: Dave Bingham.*

4. Let it Burn*   .11a
Angles right at mid-way point. 10 bolts. *FA: Dave Bingham.*

5. Matchhead*   .11b
Shorter route just right from Let It Burn. Needs serious scrubbing/cleaning on the upper half. 6 bolts. *FA: Dave Bingham.*

6. X-Crack   .11a/b
Route is located straight up from the parking area past a small sign on the right side of the shallow gully of huge block. 6 bolts. *FA: Chuck Denure.*

Heather Lords on the 2nd pitch of Spirit World, .11a. Photo by Dean Lords.

BOX CANYON

Just north of the small town of Howe lies Saddle Mountain. Its southern slopes are cut by fantastic canyons composed mainly of limestone. A fantastic area to hike and explore, the canyons also offer superb climbing possibilities. Alex McMeekin and friends from the Hailey area developed the sport routes out here in the early-mid '90s. With climbs from 20 feet to 300 feet, Box Canyon has something for everyone.

Box Canyon has great potential for a multitude of more climbing routes. However, being located in a Wilderness Study Area (WSA), future development will have to wait for the WSA status to be changed to one that would allow for new routes. Only time will tell.

GETTING THERE: From Idaho Falls, head north on I-15. Take exit 143 (Rexburg-Terreton), and drive west on State Highway 33. Pass through the towns of Terreton and Mud Lake and continue on until the T-intersection, turn left. Now head south for 4 miles then turn right. Drive west for 9 miles and turn right at the Simplot Farms sign. Head north on a

gravel road for .5 mile, turn left onto 3600 N., head west for another .5 mile and turn right onto 1200 W. Continue north for 4 miles, the road turns into a good jeep track. After about 1 mile on the jeep track, signs about Box Canyon appear and there is a parking area to the right – low-clearance vehicles will want to park here. High-clearance vehicles can continue on – please make sure to stay on the road, there are small parking areas located by each crag – don't create new ones.

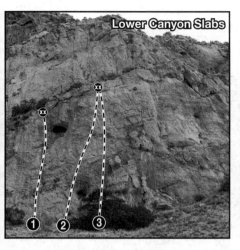

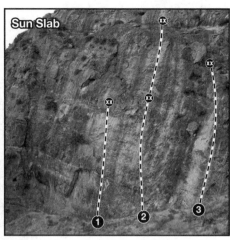

Lower Canyon slabs
(Morning shade, afternoon sun)

Sun Slab
(Morning sun, afternoon shade)

This wall is located at the mouth of the canyon on the east side. Access is gained via a short uphill hike directly to the slabby wall. Routes are listed from left to right when facing wall.

1. Same As It Never Was*   .8
Slab climb to steeper finish at chains. A little runout but easy. Can be set up as a toprope. 4 bolts.

2. Wish List**   .7
Fun slab climb to chains. Can be set up as a toprope. 8 bolts.

3. It Ain't A Perfect World*   .8
Start to the right of a big hole and cruise through fun moves to same anchors as Wish List. 8 bolts.

Sun Slab is an east-facing wall at the mouth of the canyon that is within spitting distance of the road. Routes are listed from left to right when facing wall.

1. Curious George**   .10c
Steep climbing off the deck, route eases up after third bolt. 5 bolts.

2. The Grinch*   .9
Slab climb that eases up at midway anchors then steepens towards the end. 9 Bolts.

3. Ms. Rumphius*   .7
Easy slab climb to chain anchors. 5 bolts.

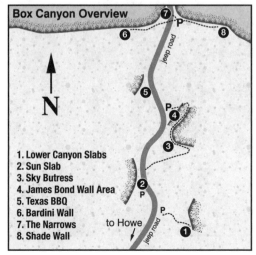

Box Canyon Overview

N

1. Lower Canyon Slabs
2. Sun Slab
3. Sky Butress
4. James Bond Wall Area
5. Texas BBQ
6. Bardini Wall
7. The Narrows
8. Shade Wall

to Howe

Sky Buttress
(Morning shade, afternoon sun)

This wall is located on the east side of the canyon just up the road from the Lower Canyon Slab wall. A steep, but short, uphill hike is used to gain the base of the wall. Routes are listed from left to right when facing wall.

1. Hollowed Ground** .11a
Crux at start on rotten layer, merge with Corpolite at 6th bolt. Rappel anchors. 60m rope recommended. 8 bolts.

2. While You're At It .10d
Toprope.

3. Pocket Full of Corpolite** .8
Climb fun slabby face as it steepens at the top to end at rappel anchors. 60m rope recommended. 8 bolts.

James Bond Wall Area
(All day shade)

This short, steep and aesthetic wall is on the east side of the canyon just around the bend in the road from the Sky Buttress area. Easy 2 minute approach. Home to the canyon's hardest routes. Routes are listed from left to right when facing wall.

1. McMeeken Route* .12d
Tall, thin climb up water streak. Not climbed very often. This route is easier to access from the Sky Buttress area. Bolts.

2. Oddjob*** .10d
Downgraded from original rating of .11c. Follow black bolts to cold shuts. 3 bolts.

3. Dr. No* .12c/d
Hard start, hard finish. 3 bolts.

Tom Smartt on Moonraker, .13d. Photo courtesy Tom Smartt.

4. Thunderball*** .13a
Great stone with fun movement. Some say soft for the grade but some don't...you decide. 3 bolts.

5. Moonraker* .13d
A forgotten and long standing open project sent by Tom Smartt in Feb. 2013. Short, hard and steep. Rap ring anchors. 3 bolts.

6. Barely Legal* .11a
Fun moves with crux by 5th bolt. 5 bolts.

7. High Society .9
Trad climb right leaning crack to the right of Barely Legal. Rarely done. No anchors.

Texas Barbeque
(Morning sun, afternoon shade)

Located on the west side of the canyon. Routes are listed from left to right when facing wall.

1. Texas Barbeque** .12a
Start up face to flake, then negotiate through the sharpest rock known to man. 5 bolts.

2. Weaner Dogs Ripped My Flesh** .10c
Fun route on sharp rock. Shares anchors with Texas. 5 bolts.

3. Acupuncture Slab .9
Toprope face just right of Weaner Dogs. Painfully sharp.

Heather Lords firing it up on Texas Barbeque, .12a. Photo by Dean Lords.

Bardini Wall
(All day sun)

Very tall and impressive wall that starts in The Narrows and continues west for about 500 yards. Routes are listed from left to right when facing wall.

1. Bardini Wall**   .10c/d

Pitch 1: .8 – Starts to the left of big grassy ledge, below a bush. Go up past blocky shelf onto good face climbing and end on anchors at ledge. 90'. **Pitch 2: .10c/d** – Traverse leftward to balanced crux on pockets. Power up face while crimping to belay below horizontal white dike. 90'. **Pitch 3: .10a** – Continue up face on fun moves while taking advantage of good rest holds. Finish on anchors. 120'. Two ropes and about 16 quickdraws are required for this complete route.

2. The Coral Sea***   .10a

Start on grassy ledge, go up slab face, pass to the left of big hole. Cruise through roof section on positive holds and finish on diagonal pockets at chain anchors. An awesome route at 150'; two ropes are needed for rappel. 12 bolts.

Matt TeNgaio on Thunderball, .13a. Photo by Tom Smartt.

The Narrows, left side
(Morning sun, afternoon shade)

Located at the back of canyon where the dirt road passes through a narrow gap in the cliff. Routes are listed from left to right when facing wall.

1. Lemhi Winds***   .10a
Start just left of big flake, breeze through face on fun moves to undercling and finish on positive holds at chains. 7 bolts.

2. The Thread***   .12c
Start just to the right of flake, up to ledge and first crux. Crimp to good holds, clip the threaded sling, then fire second, thin crux to anchors. 60m rope is needed. 10 bolts.

The Narrows, right side
(All day shade)

There used to be 5 high quality routes here. One remains. No topo.

1. Rite of Passage***   .11c
Great climbing that will make you think. Anchors are not visible from last bolt but they are there! Bolts.

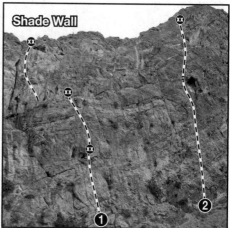

Shade Wall
(All day shade)

Shade Wall is to the right of The Narrows area when heading up the canyon. Routes are listed from left to right when facing wall.

1. Nappy Dread**   .10b
Pitch 1: .7 – Fun pitch that angles slightly right to chain anchors. 80'. **Pitch 2: .9** – From chains veer right then up past horizontal seams to chain anchors below big ledge. 60'. **Pitch 3: .10b** – Traverse left then up face to chain anchors. 75'. 16 quickdraws and two ropes are required.

2. Spirit World***   .11a
Pitch 1: .9 – Climb orange water streak to chain anchors. 195'. **Pitch 2: .11a** – Start off veering slightly left, through thin section, then diagonally right through second crux and finish on chain anchors. 160'. 16 quickdraws and two ropes are necessary.

Gather thee, Virgins of Howe, for the Mothership soon return. Photo by Herschel Smartt.

153

Marc Hanselman on the Main Wall at Cedar Creek.

CEDAR CREEK

The climbing at Cedar Creek offers a pleasant respite from the summer heat of the Lost River Valley. Tucked in amongst tall pines and being a north-facing cliff, Cedar Creek is truly a perfect summer sport climbing area.

Located in the Lost River Range just south of Mt. Borah, the walls are composed of slightly overhung glacially polished limestone. Unlike the pocketed limestone found at The Fins,

Cedar Creek routes tend to have more open hand holds, crimps and sidepulls. The routes on the Main Wall are the tallest at the crag and can leave your forearms with a monster pump well after lowering to the ground.

The routes are closely spaced and well bolted. With the nature of the rock, wearing a helmet while belaying is not a bad idea. A stick clip is useful for a few routes as well.

The authors would like to stress to visiting climbers to help keep Cedar Creek pristine and untrampled. Please tread lightly and remember if you pack it in, pack it out.

GETTING THERE: From Mackay, drive north on Hwy. 93 for about 18 mi. passing the reservoir until you reach the Old Chilly Road sign – turn right and pass through the gate (close it behind you). Follow the rocky two-track dirt road a little over 2 miles to

Parking area for Cedar Creek with Mount Borah on the left skyline.

154

the end of the road, making sure to always stay on the most prominent track.

If you are driving from the north, make your way to the turnoff for Mt. Borah via Hwy. 93 but continue past it for 1 mile – the Old Chilly Road sign is on the left.

If you are driving from Ketchum, take Trail Creek Road almost all the way to Hwy 93, turning left onto Old Chilly Road about a mile before reaching the highway. Follow Old Chilly Road to Hwy. 93, cross the road to reach the Old Chilly Road sign.

The faint trail starts at the end of the road behind a BLM sign and is about 1.5 miles long. Allow 45-60 minutes for the approach. Most of the hiking is rather moderate, however, there is one section that is loose and steep, but thankfully short.

Follow the trail heading east as it climbs and dips it's way between the mahogany, scrub brush and eventually pines and cedars. Keep an

eye open near the start of the trail as it passes right through the fracture line from the 1983 earthquake! Small cairns have been placed to help guide the way but don't rely solely on them to get you there. Keep in mind that the trail stays well away from the creek until the crags are reached.

With the exception of the rightmost routes on the Via Ferrata Wall and the GFC Wall, all routes have all-day shade.

Matt TeNgaio starting up Caught on Tape, .12b. Photo by Marc Hanselman.

Main Wall (Left)

Main Wall

This wall has the highest concentration of Cedar Creek's harder and steeper routes. It is defined by No Hands on the left side and terminates at Ataya, where the mossy area is. A stick clip is useful on a few of the routes as the first bolt is high off the ground.

1. No Hands*   .10c
There are two ways to finish this climb. The left option is easier. 6 bolts. *FA: Marc Hanselman.*

2. Caught on Tape***   .12b
Tough moves down low with a few big moves thrown for good measure. 6 bolts. *FA: Marc Hanselman.*

3. The Jewel Thief***   .12a
Climbs through a bulge halfway up. A must do. 6 bolts. *FA: Marc Hanselman.*

4. The Town Bike**   .12b/c
Climbs over small bulge down low and stays on you until the end. 7 bolts. *FA: Marc Hanselman.*

5. Atreyu*   .11c
Stick clip high first bolt. Powerful moves down low lead to a rightward traverse with a crux move up high. Bolts. *FA: Lucas Hengel.*

6. Song of Nine Winds*.11c
Bolts. *FA: Lucas Hengel.*

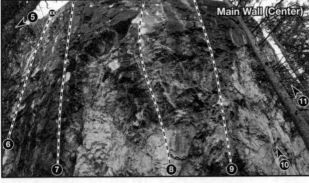

Main Wall (Center)

7. Fingerprints*** .10d
Fun climbing on a variety of holds. Can be a bit cryptic in spots. 8 bolts. *FA: Lucas Hengel.*

8. Drink Up Buttercup** .11b
Starts right of the chossy crack. 9-10 bolts. *FA: Marc Hanselman.*

9. Whisper Pine*** .11c
A Cedar Creek classic that climbs on big holds on a slightly steep angle with a crux up high. 10 bolts. *FA: Lucas Hengel.*

10. 34/24*** .12c/d
Steep jug hauling to continuous crux moves. Another classic. 8 bolts. *FA: Lucas Hengel.*

11. The Nothing** .12c
This is the first route just left of the mossy area. Fun jug climbing to a crux getting to the 5th bolt, then sustained climbing to the anchors. 8 bolts. *FA: Lucas Hengel.*

Approx. 30' right

12. High Water Mark* .10d
Hard start to easier climbing above with a few rests along the way. 10 bolts. *FA: Marc Hanselman.*

13. Vanilla Bean** .11b
Steep start with a crux up high. 8 bolts. *FA: Marc Hanselman.*

14. Ataya*** .11c
Starts just left of the scramble ramp. Fun, powerful moves to a rest then continuous climbing. Be aware of the tree. One of the must-do's. 7 bolts. *FA: Lucas Hengel.*

Scramble

Via Ferrata Wall

The next 7 routes are located up the on the hanging ledge. Access can be gained by scrambling up the low angle slab. Belay from bottom bolts.

15. Thumbs Down** .11b
Fun route that follows endlessly right-leaning holds. 7 bolts. *FA: Ian Jameson.*

16. Ink Well*** .11b
Has a tan belay bolt at the start. Great route that climbs through an obvious 2-finger pocket. 8 bolts. *FA: Marc Hanselman.*

17. Witches Broom** .10c
Shares anchors with Ink Well. 8 bolts. *FA: Marc Hanselman.*

18. Hole Shot** .12a/b
Short route that has a height dependent crux going to the anchors. 4 bolts. *FA: Marc Hanselman.*

19. Dust to Dust** .10a
Crux is getting over the bulge near the top. 5 bolts. *FA: Marc Hanselman.*

20. Dirt Lotus** .11a
Worthwhile route, just avoid the chossy holds to the left. 8 bolts. *FA: Marc Hanselman.*

21. Cold Mountain Poems*** .11a
This is the last route before the fixed line/ via ferrata, just left of the pine tree. Shares anchors with Dirt Lotus. 9 bolts. *FA: Marc Hanselman.*

The next 4 routes are located on the far right side on the hanging ledge. Look for the fixed line after route #21 and to the right of the tree.

22. Ledges and Ladders* .10b
Starts on the first bolt of the fixed line. 8-9 bolts. *FA: Marc Hanselman.*

23. Surya Namaskura*** .10b
Same start as Ledges then heads right. 9 bolts.
FA: Lucas Hengel.

24. Bonsai Tree** .9
Starts on the third bolt of the fixed line. Has a fun traverse section. Bolts. *FA: Marc Hanselman.*

25. Little Dark Cloud*** .9
Starts on the last bolt of the fixed line. Great position overlooking the creek. 9 bolts. *FA: Marc Hanselman.*

These 2 routes are located on small wall before the Main Wall and just below the via ferrata area. They are just to the right where the trail comes close to the creek.

26. Soft Serve** .8
Route climbs leftward and is a bit stout for the grade. The 4th bolt is hidden in the white scoop near the top. No topo. 5 bolts. *FA: Marc Hanselman.*

27. One Rainy Wish** .7
Just around the corner to the right from Soft Serve, behind a tree. Climbs a low angled rounded arete. No topo. 5 bolts. *FA: Marc Hanselman.*

Tom Smartt firing the crux of Caught on Tape.

159

GFC Wall

These 3 routes are encountered just as you enter the rocky part of the trail before it descends slightly, about 200 yards before the Main Wall. This wall could hold a couple more easy routes.

28. Pizza Boys Revenge** .13b
This route is located to the left and around the corner from Crazy Horse. The trail passes directly below it. Stick clip the first high bolt. Very steep start on underclings going to jug at first bolt (crux). Fun 5.11 climbing up the short face to easier ground at the last bolt and anchors. 5 bolts. *FA: Lucas Hengel.*

29. Crazy Horse** .9
Mellow slab climbing to crux getting over the small bulge. Runout from last bolt to the anchors but easy. 6 bolts. *FA: Lucas Hengel.*

30. Pretty on the Outside** .8
Climbs up through horizontal break on good holds. Good for the grade. 6 bolts. *FA: Marc Hanselman.*

This lone route is located about 200' to the right on a very short wall that has a distinct hole on it.

31. Welcome to Cedar Creek** .11d
Easy climbing up to the crux at the third bolt. 4 bolts. *FA: Lucas Hengel.*

Tom Smartt on Los Adalbertos' Especial, .13c/d, Crank Cave. Photo by Ben Spannuth

Ben Rodes going big on Son of Discovery, .13a, The Fins. Photo by Meghan Twohig.

Dean Lords climbing in the Owl Cove at Massacre Rocks with the scenic Snake River in the background. Photo by Nathan Smith.

161

SOUTH FORK AREA

The impressive South Fork of the Snake River flows 65 miles across southeastern Idaho to its confluence with the Henry's Fork near the Menan Buttes. The river supports the largest cottonwood forest in the West.

The area is home to several bird species, including raptors, and various wildlife including moose, deer, elk, mountain lions, mountain goats, black bears, bobcats, coyotes, river otter, beaver, and fox.

The South Fork is best known for it's world class trout fishing, attracting thousands of anglers per year. With several options to enter and exit the river, drift boats are popular during the summer and fall seasons.

Rock climbing has become another popular activity along the majestic South Fork. With five climbing crags established, climbers too can enjoy the beauty of the area while recreating.

The climbing areas are listed in ascending order, following the river upstream. Refer to the maps on the following page to help you locate the climbing areas of interest.

Dean Lords on Occult, .13a, at the Arcane Crag.
Photo by Heather Lords

163

HEISE ROCK

This volcanic plug sits just off the road near the Heise Hot Springs Golf Course. It is also referred to as Elephant Rock.

Spring and fall make for the best climbing at Heise, however, late afternoon summertime sessions are enjoyable as well once the walls receive shade. A 50 meter rope is sufficient for all routes at Heise.

ACCESS: Heise Rock is located on private land and the landowners require climbers to check in at the RV office located across the parking lot from the pizza restaurant. As of press time, there was a daily use fee as well. Please respect their requests when it comes to access of Heise Rock. If the office is closed, you can check in at the restaurant. Be aware that the land that Heise Rock sits on is also a campground and campers have the right of way and a tendency to camp/park right along the northeast side of the crag.

GETTING THERE: From Idaho Falls drive east on Highway 26 for about 16 miles and turn left at the signs for Kelly Canyon Ski Hill and Heise Hot Springs – continue following the signs to the ski hill. At 3 miles, turn right after crossing the Snake River and continue past the hot springs. Just past the golf course, Heise Rock comes into view on the left. There is a small pullout parking area directly in front of it – be careful of oncoming traffic. Routes are listed from left to right when facing the wall.

West Wall
(Afternoon sun)
No topo

Two sets of top rope anchors on this side can be accessed by hiking to the top of the rock around the north side trail. The climbs range from 5.5 to 5.8 depending on the route taken. Bring a few slings and some locking carabiners for the anchors.

South Wall
(Morning shade, afternoon sun)

1. Retro Man** .11a
Face climb to horizontal crack, then over small bulge using pockets to cold shut anchors. Easier if stemmed to the right up to big chockstone. 5 bolts.

2. Pigeon Crack .9
Trad climb big nasty crack. A foul experience.

3. Hanging Humor** .10d
Scramble up slippery ramp, traverse right, work around corner up to undercling. Try to hang on through pockets to cold shuts. First sport route put in at Heise. 6 bolts.

4. Little Ninja .11c/d
Squeezed to the right of Hanging Humor. Bolts.

5. Rock Ninja project
Bolted, unbolted, then bolted again only to be abandoned due to lack of quality.

6. Seeking Sleazy Squeezes***.11d/.12a
Start on jugs, use crack to pull over bulge, face climb to steep pockets then try to hang on through pumpy moves over lip to cold shuts. A classic Heise route despite the guano-filled crack. 7 bolts.

7. Wango Tango*** .12a
Jug start to bouldery section, up to bird crap hold. Continue through somewhat obscure section then left to same finish as Sleazy. A great route that sees little traffic. 6 bolts.

Heise Rock
(South Wall)

Heise Rock (East Wall)

8. Sleazy Tango*** .11d
Climb Sleazy to the 3rd bolt then merge onto Wango. This variation avoids the bat-shit-filled-crack on Sleazy. 7 bolts.

Chelsea Principo on Dark Justice, .12b.
Photo courtesy Chelsea Principo.

East Wall
(Morning sun, afternoon shade)

9. The Devil and Miss Jones* .10b
Diagonally left up ramp, then right over bulge continuing to anchors. 4 bolts.

10. Born to Rock .11c
Wallow through not-so-remarkable moves left of slanted crack to anchors. 6 bolts.

11. Butt Rock .8
Fun, juggy climbing. Shares anchors with BTR. 5 Bolts.

12. Two Minute Crack .7
Trad climb right of leaning crack to chimney, finish on Rock-A-Bye Baby anchors. Can be top-roped.

13. Rock-A-Bye Baby .9+
Possibly the worst bolt line at Heise.

14. Tradmania .10a
Trad climb thin seam, finish on Rock-A-Bye anchors.

15. Todd's Molehill* .10b
Deceptive moves to chain anchors. 2 bolts.

Northeast Wall
(Morning sun, afternoon shade)

16. Clip Me Deadly .11c/d
Short face climb over bulge to anchors. 3 bolts.

17. Buffy Direct* .13a
Single bolt start in thin seam left of Buffy. Used to be .13b until the base of the wall was raised eliminating a few moves. Merges into Buffy at 3rd bolt.

18. Buffy the Tendon Slayer** .13a
A couple of options are available for the crux at the 5th bolt, followed by easier but, sustained finish to cold shut anchors. This route can be plagued by wild rose brushes growing at the base. 6 bolts.

19. Dark Justice*** .12a
Power through first crux to jugs. Work pockets to 2nd crux at 5th bolt. Cruise to cold shuts. A Heise must-do. 7 bolts.

20. Wicked Game** .12d
Start up flake, power through pockets to big move to left-leaning rail, to jugs. Finish on easy terrain at cold shuts. 5 bolts.

21. Traverse From Hell .11d
Start on Dark Justice, through to Wicked Game, to lone gold bolt. Finish on Equilibrium.

22. Equilibrium** .11c
Powerful moves over bulge, traverse right then up flake/seam. Finish on obscure face. 6 bolts.

23. Trad* .12c
Crimpy moves to enormous jugs. Cold shut anchors. 3 bolts.

24. The Good Reverend Christopher Martin* .13a
Stick clip the very high 1st bolt. Powerful crimp moves. 3 bolts.

25. The Bitter End* .11d
Move up to underclings, big moves to slopey ledge. Continue up through steep face and finish with awkward moves to cold shuts. 4 bolts.

Caleb Bohrer climbing Wild Thing, 5.8.

PARAMOUNT

(Morning sun, afternoon shade)

Sitting high above the road, the routes at Para
mount offer great exposure and relief from the
afternoon summer sun. Chuck Oddette, Steve
Reiser and Jed Miller established the routes
from 1989 to 1990. While not the hardest
climbing around, Paramount is home to great
lines in the .9-.10 range – a perfect place for
the budding lead climber. The rock can tend
to be a bit loose in spots, so be mindful while
hanging out at the base of the wall. All routes
except Fly By Night, Positively Negative and
Spraypaint can be done with a 50 meter rope.

GETTING THERE: Use the same directions
for Heise Rock but continue on past Heise
Drive past the first cattle guard and follow the
road as it turns left sharply and begins to climb
– there is a small parking area to the left about
200 yards up the road. Follow the loose trail
up to the base of the climbing area. You can

also park further up the road to the left in the parking area of Little Kelly Canyon just before the second cattle guard. See page ? for access map. Routes are listed from left to right when facing the wall.

1. Aerial Boundaries* .9
Cruise up arete to chain anchors. 5 bolts.

2. Aerial-Fantasy* .9
Start on Aerial Boundaries, at second bolt veer right and clip four more bolts. Shares anchors with Aerial Boundaries.

3. Fantasy** .9
Start on loose rock, up face, sidepull fractured rock to inside corner left of pillar, then sail through fun moves to anchors. There is an alternative finish that climbs on the right side of the bolt line at the last 2 bolts that is about .10b. 7 bolts.

4. Thin Red Line** .10b
First bolt is way up there but easy to get to. Stay right of the bolt line to second bolt then traverse left out onto face and straight up to anchors. 7 bolts.

5. Chuck & Jed's Excellent Adventure .8
Trad climb big inside corner just left of Mr. Rodgers, use last two bolts and chains of Mr. Rodgers. Not shown.

6. Mr. Rodger's Neighborhood* .9
Climb face just right of Chuck & Jed's to chain anchors. 7 bolts.

7. Excitations* .9
Clip two bolts at bottom, then place gear in thin crack to the right of Mr. Rodger's, then clip two bolts at top, finish on chain anchors. Mixed.

8. Wild Thing .8
Scamper up face using cracks just right of Excitations. 3 pitons & 2 bolts.

9. Fly By Night*** .8
Climb face just left of broken arch to chain anchors. Best done with a 60 meter rope. 8 bolts.

10. Take the Heise Plunge .10d
Climb overhung section of broken arch. 4 bolts.

11. Farr Side** .10a
Arete climb on positive holds to small ledge. 6 bolts.

12. Dark Side* .10a
Start on ledge just up and right of Farr Side. Climb face to right leaning crack, then angle left to finish same as Farr Side. 6 bolts.

13. Spraypaint** .10d
Climb slabby fractured face to big roof, angle left and over roof using positive holds. Finish on slabby face. Midway anchors were later added making this route more accessible. Route to midway anchors goes at .10b. If not using a 70 meter rope to the top anchors, 2 rappels will be necessary to lower safely to the ground. 17 bolts.

14. Positively Negative** .11b
First bolt is high off the ground. Climb broken face through small aretes to the double roofs on good holds and sidepulls. Pull over roofs and endure rope drag to chain anchors. Great exposure. 70 meter rope necessary or double 60m rope rappel. 16 bolts.

Victoria Banales Atxirika enjoys a run on Fantasy, 5.9.

169

Heather Lords topping out on The Bicycle Thief, .10a, at the Pointless Crag. Photo by Dean Lords.

POINTLESS CRAG

(Early morning shade, then all day sun)

With a scenic vantage point of the beautiful South Fork of the Snake River that can't be beat, Pointless Crag is somewhat of hotspot for local climbers. Mainly catering to climbers who enjoy the .9 – .10 range, Pointless also is home to a handful of challenging routes in the .11 – .12 range making it an accommodating crag for most local climbers. Take note that the nature of the stone at Pointless is one that should keep all on their toes – do not sit directly below climbers on the wall. A belay helmet is not a bad idea.

GETTING THERE: From Idaho Falls drive east on Highway 26 for about 16 miles and turn left at the signs for Kelly Canyon Ski Hill and Heise Hot Springs – continue following the signs to the ski hill. At 3 miles, turn right after crossing the Snake River and continue past the hot springs and Heise Rock. After passing the big red barn, take the right hand road toward Kelly Island Campground. The road quickly turns to gravel. Follow the gravel road for about 2 miles passing the Stinking Springs trailhead and the Wolf Flats sign along the way and use the big pullout to the right, alongside the river. Locate the climbers trail directly across the parking area. The first route you encounter is Black Betty. Routes are listed left to right when facing the wall.

1. Black Betty***   **.12a**
Steep and powerful climbing up a black bulge with a cool blunt arete finish. This route is about 50 yards to the left of Platypus. 6 bolts.

2. Head on a Silver Platypus*   **.10a**
Overhanging jugs to a fun face above. 6 bolts.

3. Sleepwalker   **.10d**
Get over the bulge at the start and you're home free. 2nd and 3rd bolts have chain draws. 6 bolts.

4. 4 Alarm Fire*   **.10b**
Technical, pumpy and slightly overhanging. Start right and traverse up and left under the small roof to the first bolt. Don't blow the second clip! 4 bolts.

5. Hoppe Hill*   **.10c**
A deceptive and hard to read overhanging pumpy technical experience. 5 bolts.

6. Hustle and Flow**   **.12d**
Steep and Powerful. 6 bolts.

7. Goat Meal***   **.11a**
Climbs on steep jugs to crux at the lip. 6 bolts.

8. Hungry Eyes**   **.9**
Starts on the left side of a roof like arch. A long rambling journey on the tallest part of the cliff. Clipping the anchors might be the crux for shorter people. 8 bolts.

9. Stingray** .10c
Starts on the right side of roof-like arch. Gently overhanging with a crux finish. Tallest route just before turning the corner when following the trail along the base of the wall. 10 bolts.

• *Project*

10. Orbit*** .10d
Difficult third clip. Technical crux to a rest at bolt 5 followed by a pumping juggy finish. A little dirty between the 5th and 6th bolts. 8 bolts.

11. Rock-in My Sports Bra* .9
Angles slightly left then straight up. This route is about 30 yards right of Orbit. 6 bolts.

12. The Disappearing Hat Trick* 9
Cool crack feature mid route. 5 bolts.

13. Crack .8
Clip the first bolt of Black Bear then head left and into a nice inside corner hand crack using trad gear. Mixed.

14. Black Bear** .12c
Arete climb on black bullet stone. Technical and thin crux. 5 bolts to anchors. 5 bolts.

15. What's the Point** .11b
Funky start. Difficult second clip. Tricky overhang. Cool crack finish. 6 bolts.

16. 11 O' Clock* .10a
Straight up fun! Look for the 11 O' Clock pocket if you get stumped! 5 bolts.

17. Team Trailer** .8
Super fun inside corner climb! Dirty start but well worth it once above the second bolt. 5 bolts.

18. The Bicycle Thief** .10a
Be careful between the first and second bolt. Pumpy column finish. 5 bolts.

19. Alien Pod* .8
Cool pod feature. Short and easy. 4 bolts.

Jaren Watson tangles with Black Betty, .12a. Photo by Dean Lords.

171

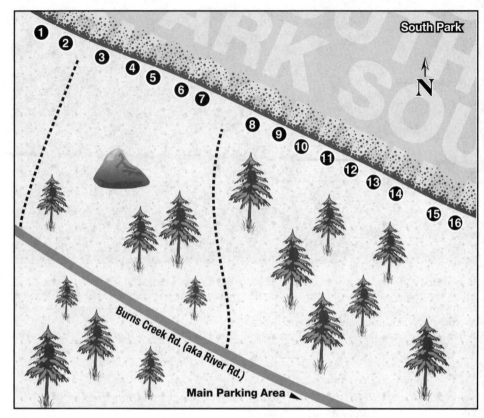

SOUTH PARK

(Early morning shade, then all day sun)

Tucked behind the cottonwoods but clearly visible from the road, the South Park crag has been beckoning climbers for years.

Brian Williams of Rexburg was the first brave soul to bolt a route there in the late 1990's, establishing "Scary Rattlesnake". Years went by before local Dean Lords saw the full potential and figured out what it would take to make the area a legitimate crag. In 2008, he quickly went to work tediously cleaning and bolting, creating what is now known as South Park.

The style of climbing involves a lot of open hand holds, slopers, side pulls, pinches and the use of good footwork.

Be aware that the quality of the stone at South Park is quite chossy. Belay helmets are not a bad idea and if you are not climbing or belaying, do not hang out directly beneath someone on the wall. The routes have been cleaned to their best but choss is choss, so don't rule out an occasional hold breaking.

Also, be aware that the wall scorches in the summer, mainly in the afternoon. Early morning sessions are doable, but be warned that the mosquitoes can be numerous – especially during a hatch. A stick clip is recommended/required for most routes.

GETTING THERE: From Idaho Falls drive east on Highway 26 for about 16 miles and turn left at the signs for Kelly Canyon Ski Hill and Heise Hot Springs – continue following the signs to the ski hill. At 3 miles, turn right after crossing the Snake River and continue past the hot springs and Heise Rock. After passing the big red barn, take the right hand road toward Kelly Island Campground. The road quickly turns to gravel. Follow the gravel road for about 2.7 miles and park in the big pullout area to the left – **DO NOT PARK IN THE ROAD.** Walk back up the road for about 80 yards and locate the short trail to the crag. Routes are listed from left to right when facing the wall.

1. Big Gay Al* .11b
Meander up to big holds to "the schlong" feature, hit crux then keep going. Route has a fixed draw at the 4th bolt. 9 bolts. *FA: Matt TeNgaio.*

2. Who Killed Kenny*** .11a
Fun movement. Crux is at the 4th bolt. Gain a couple of good rests along the way before clipping the anchors. Many use this as a warm up. 9 bolts. *FA: Dean Lords.*

3. Scary Rattlesnake .11b/c
South Park's original route. Not climbed very often. Cold shut anchors. 8 bolts. *FA: Brian Williams.*

4. Smug Alert** .10c/d
Big rest at the chossy ledge at the 3rd bolt. Somewhat devious climbing for the grade. Another route that is used for a warm up. 10 bolts. *FA: Dean Lords.*

5. Cartman** .11b
Fun moves with a sustained crux involving open hand holds and pulling the bulge. 10 bolts. *FA: Dean Lords.*

6. Make Love Not Warcraft*** .12a
The crux on this fun route is encountered well above the ground and has seen many catch air! Have fun. 9 bolts. *FA: Dean Lords.*

7. Hippydigger*** .12b
A tricky start leads to an enormous rest. Try to hang on as you decipher the moves on this pumpy route. 9 bolts. *FA: Dean Lords.*

8. Government Shutdown* .13a
Powerful moves to 4th bolt, techy section, then slopers to the end. 8 bolts. *Equipped: Dean Lords. FA: Sam Perkins.*

9. In Between Days** .12d
Burly moves getting over the bulge. Ring anchors. 7 bolts. *FA: Dean Lords.*

10. Temptation** .12a
Hard start to big holds then an engaging crux. 8 bolts. *FA: Dean Lords.*

11. Drive-By Trucker*** .12c
Fun thuggery from the ground leads to good technical climbing above. 8 bolts. *FA: Dean Lords.*

Stephen Elmer in control of the E.D.S., .12d. Photo by Dean Lords.

12. E.D.S.*** .12d
2nd bolt has a fixed chain draw. Powerful moves to the 3rd bolt, then endurance fest to the end. Don't blow the 2nd clip! E.D.S. is short for "Excited Dog Syndrome". 7 bolts. *FA: Matt TeNgaio.*

13. Ricardo Gets an Anal Probe*** .12b
Great movement from the ground. Many encounter a redpoint crux at the last bolt. 7 bolts. *FA: Matt TeNgaio.*

14. Mr. Hankey*** .12a
Most people start on the 2nd bolt. Move right on underclings to big holds and big moves. Get a good rest at the flake after the crux. Move right then up. A bit chossy in the middle. Sport anchors. 9 bolts. *FA: Matt TeNgaio.*

15. Scuzzlebutt*** .11b
A classic South Park endurance route. A bit cryptic through the lower section. Enjoy the upper half! Ring anchors. 11 bolts. *FA: Dean Lords.*

16. Chef's Meatballs .10d
Somewhat hard to read. Angles right then up. 6 bolts. *FA: Dean Lords.*

ARCANE CRAG

(Morning sun, afternoon shade)

Developed by Dean & Heather Lords with the help of Jaren Watson, the Arcane Crag is the most unique crag in the South Fork Canyon of the Snake River. The volcanic basalt stone has sections of flowstone on its surface; creating a beautiful limestone texture with stripes of black and blue on some of the routes. The climbing is steep, powerful, and difficult to read – making for a great pump!

Chelsea Principo climbs Naiad, .12a. Photo courtesy Chelsea Principo.

GETTING THERE: The shortest way to access the Arcane Crag is by driving past Kelly Canyon Ski Resort and continue 7.6 miles from where the pavement ends at Lift

4. A little over a mile from where the pavement ends is the Y Junction; stay to the right and follow the road down past Table Rock Campground. Just before reaching the river the road turns left and follows the river upstream. From here, continue up river to the Wolverine Creek trailhead and then keep going for another 1.5 miles to reach the Arcane crag.

Another option is to follow the same directions to the Pointless and South Park areas and then keep driving upstream along the river road. The mileage for this option is 10 miles from the right hand turn on to Heise Road/ Burns Creek Road. There is a T-intersection at about 7.5 miles – turn right from here and keep following the river road upstream until the 10 mile point is reached on the odometer.

A small camping/parking area is located between the road and the river on the south side of the road. The Arcane crag is directly across the road and up the hillside to the north. A faint climbers trail can be found on either side of the gully leading up to the cliff.

Deans Lords on Margin Walker, .13a. Photo by Heather Lords.

Lower Ledge	Upper Ledge

1. Proboscis**   .11d

Climb up a wide chimney system for 5 bolts then left through several tiers of an overhang and a powerful crux on crimps. Climb out the big nose and pull onto the "slab" for a rest, then big moves on the final overhang to the anchors. 11 bolts. *FA: Dean Lords.*

2. Naiad***   .12a

Start on Proboscis then veer right after the 5th bolt by climbing a unique ramp/overhang to a good rest. Then pull a horizontal roof and powerful cruxy transition, another small bulge to a big move, and then a rest jug. Continue climbing overhanging terrain with a show stopper crux going to the anchors! Get your burl and pump on! 12 bolts. *FA: Dean Lords.*

3. The Esoteric***   .12d

Perma-draws. The king line of the crag. Steep and WILD! A couple of technical cruxes and massive pump to a big move near the end. An adventure of wander and wonder! Shares anchors with Margin Walker. 13 bolts. *FA: Dean Lords.*

4. Margin Walker***   .13a

Goes through the steepest part of the cave. Merges with the Esoteric after the 7th bolt. Perma-draws. A powerful start right off the deck to reach near horizontal jug hauling for a couple of bolts. Then begins the techy power climbing on smaller, but good holds to reach The Esoteric for the remainder of the route. 10 bolts. *FA: Dean Lords.*

5. Occult**   .13a

Steep, powerful and hard to read. Basically a long boulder problem requiring lots of core strength and good body English. Powerful crux at the lip. Skip the 6th bolt on redpoint attempts. Needs top anchors. Lower from last bolt. 8 bolts. *FA: Dean Lords.*

6. Bitty**   .12a

Hard second clip. Powerful and sequential steep climbing. The 4th bolt is used to assist figuring out the crux but then is usually skipped after learning the sequence and adds a bit of excitement! Make sure your belayer is fully in the game! 5 bolts. *FA: Dean Lords.*

RIRIE RESERVOIR

(Morning shade, afternoon sun)
No topo

The climbing at Ririe Reservoir takes place on a short, basalt cliff overlooking the reservoir. A fun place to hang out in the summer, climbers can cool themselves off with a quick dip in the nearby water. The routes are all top-rope only. Long pieces of webbing are recommended for use as anchors. Use the steel poles cemented into the top of the cliff to set up anchors for routes 4 through 6. A 60 meter rope can be set up on two, side-by-side routes.

NOTE: In recent years, security of the dam at the reservoir has increased. Occasionally, climbers have encountered law enforcement personnel who have threatened climbers with tickets for trespassing. There is no official word yet on whether or not climbing is allowed at Ririe Reservoir. Word is that the campground host at the reservoir won't kick you out but an officer from one of the local Counties may.

GETTING THERE: From Idaho Falls, drive east on U.S. Highway 26 for about 14 miles and turn right at the Ririe Reservoir sign onto Meadow Creek Road. Continue for about 3.2 miles and turn right at the entrance. There is a day use fee of $3 per vehicle on weekdays, $5 per vehicle on weekends. Turn right after the entrance and head north/northeast for about .25 mi. and locate the picnic shelter at the edge of the cliff where there is a parking area. There is a trail to the south of the shelter that descends to the base of the cliff. Routes are listed from left to right when facing the wall.

1. Kings & Queens .8
Face climbing on left side of wall.

2. Ririe Gully .6
Easy climb up gully on the right of Queens.

3. Battle Of The Bulge .8
Small arete climb on the right side of the gully.

4. On The Roof* .10a
Climb through main overhang to shelf above.

5. Aimless Wanderer* .9+
Climb bulges and cracks to the right of the roof.

6. White Dome* .10d
Go up broken face and arete between two roofs using small white dome as a hand hold.

7. Yellow Jacket Crack* .9+
Ascend dihedral and then through the right side of smaller roof. Pull up smearing feet and continue on through the crack to the top.

8. Dean's Torture .10b
Climb arete on the right side of small overhang and smooth face using pocket on the arete.

9. Up Against The Wall .10a
Climb center of face on the left of the small roof then move up sloping face.

10. Down On The Corner .7
Climb open book inside the corner.

11. Howling Coyotes .10b
Arete climb to the right of open book. Cruxes are moving feet up the smooth face below the arete and first move onto the arete with crimpers.

12. Smooth Transitions .10a
Climb face to the right of the arete.

13. Hanging By A Tendon .10a
Short overhanging climb with only three moves on the far right of cliff in the brushy area

176

Heather Lords on Bitchin' Widget. Photo by Dean Lords.

MIDGET WIDGET

(Early morning shade, late morning – afternoon sun)

Another crag developed by Dean and Heather Lords, the Midget Widget Wall sits above scenic Meadow Creek on the east side of Ririe Reservoir. While vertically challenged (30' - 40'), the routes are unique to southeast Idaho – they offer true splitter-crack climbing.

No grades have been given to the routes. Quoting the route developers, "We don't have any suggestions on how difficult the grades are, so just go climbing!"

GETTING THERE: From Idaho Falls, drive east on U.S. Highway 26 for about 14 miles and turn right at the Ririe Reservoir sign onto Meadow Creek Road. Continue past the entrance to the reservoir where the pavement turns to gravel. Follow the gravel road for about 3 miles to a fork in the road where there is a large parking area. Park here. Hike southeast following the rim of the cliff for about 10 minutes. A cairn marks the entry

point to descend to the base of the cliff. Follow the climbers trail as it traverses left and locate the anchors for Get Jiggy Widget. Please use caution out here as some spots of the trail and base of the cliff are loose and anything that is trundled usually ends up on the road below. Needless to say, this area is not very safe for little kids. Also, be very cautious of rattlesnakes.

Routes are listed from left to right when facing the wall.

Bitchin' Widget Section

Bitchin' Widget Section

1. Get Jiggy Widget

The first route you will encounter. Inside corner crack to overhanging hands splitter. Bring small gear (Yellow or Blue TCU) to protect the finger crack getting to the anchors. Gear: Yellow, Orange, Red TCU's – Green, Blue, Purple (Metolius)

2. Bitchin' Widget

Finger crack on nice face to the right and around the corner from Get Jiggy Widget. Ringlocks/fingerstacks, pockets, or lay it back to a boulder crux with no gear. Finish in a good tight hands splitter. Don't reach over the top; clip the anchors from the jam crack. Gear: Blue, Yellow, Orange TCU's – Green (Metolius)

3. Heavy Metal Widget   (project)

About 30 yards to the right of Bitchin' Widget before dropping down and around the corner of the cliff. Mud stone start to a nice inside corner finger crack on bomber stone.

Oz Section

From Bitchin' Widget, walk southeast along the cliff for about 75 yards; dropping down and around a corner. Once around the corner and just uphill is Got Widgets.

4. Got Widgets?

To the right and around the corner from Bitchin' Widget. A single bolt protects the loose mud-stone start. A nice inside corner crack and good pockets to a small roof; then step right and up steep hand crack to a small ledge. Two bolts protect the face moves to the anchors. Gear: Yellow, Red TCU's – Blue (Metolius)

5. Widgets are for Kids

Crack to the right of Got Widgets? A roof crack to wide pod to hand and fist splitter. Shares finish and anchors with Got Widgets. Gear: Black, Green, Blue, Purple (Metolius)

6. Little Widgets

To the right of Widgets are for Kids is a nice face with deep pockets. Protect the climbing with the thin crack on the left side of the face. Gear: Blue, Yellow, Orange TCU's

7. Three Piece Chicken Widget Meal

A short walk from Little Widgets. Likely the easiest route. Climb a slab to a hand size corner crack with a roof. Finish is a wide left leaning splitter. Gear: Green, Blue, Purple (Metolius)

8. Wicked Widget of the West

Just right of Three Piece Chicken Widget Meal. Climbs the inside corner. A fun inside corner. Stem, pull on pockets, layback, and jam up the steep corner. Gear: Blue, Yellow, Orange TCU's – Blue (Metolius)

9. The Widget of Oz

Around the corner to the right of Wicked Widget is an obvious overhanging splitter. The area test piece. A total classic!! Hands to cupping hands splitter. Break left along the rail and into a wide crack. Overhung and powerful the whole way! Gear: Black, Green, Blue (Metolius) #4 Camelot or equivalent size.

10. T- Rad

This route is located to the right of Widget of Oz on the north facing wall and is marked by a single bolt at the start. A nice finger crack through a bulging corner! This one requires a bit of effort.

Crack-a-Lackin' Section

From the Oz Sector, continue southeast along the cliff and around the corner into the next cove. The Crack-a-Lackin Sector is across the cove on the obvious pocketed west facing wall. Or from the upper trail, continue walking easy terrain along the rim of the canyon then descend via a low section of cliff and boulders at the back of the cove.

1. Desert Rats be Damned
A short fun pocketed face protected by a hand-sized crack. Excellent stone!

2. Damn the Man
Some face climbing protected by cracks to reach a thin seam. Protect the upper section well so you don't fall and hit the ledge. Shares anchors with Crack-a-Lackin'.

3. Crack-a-Lackin'
One of the best lines at Midget Widget! A thin inside corner crack leads to an overhanging un-protected face. Pull on some good pockets to regain the crack above.

World Wide Widget Wall
(No topo)

Follow Meadow Creek Road down past the first parking area for about a mile. World Wide Widget will be on your left. Park on the two-track road just past the cliffs and hike up the hill side. Some scrambling required to reach the highest section of cliff where these routes are located. The rock is less quality than that of the main area but still worthy of a visit. No top anchors on these routes (yet) but you can easily walk off the top.

1. Trad Route

2. World Wide Widget
An excellent hands to fist sized crack with a widening finish!

3. Trad Route

Diablo's Tower
(No topo)

To the right of World Wide Widget is another set of cliffs with a tower-like formation. This tower has two columnar-esque trad routes that are worth doing.

Dean Lords on the first ascent of Widget of Oz. Photo by Heather Lords.

Abe Tomco on the decommissioned Pop-a-Bolt. Photo by Nathan Smith.

PALISADES CREEK

Located in the beautiful Swan Valley area, Palisades Creek is home to one the area's best multi-use trail. The non-motorized path gently weaves through the lush canyon bottom mostly hugging the healthy creek as it dodges in and out of the trees. Blanketed by coniferous and deciduous trees, the canyon offers intermittent shade in the heat of the summer and bouts of colorful displays in the fall.

This trail is used to access the 2 lakes that sit up stream from the mouth of the canyon. The Upper and Lower Lakes are big attractions with hikers, trail runners and horse riders. At 7 miles and 4 miles, respectively (one way), the lakes make for a great day hike.

Being one of the tributaries to the South Fork of the Snake River, the creek boasts some great fly fishing too.

NOTE: In a discussion with the Palisades District Ranger, it was agreed upon that with the removal of 2 routes of concern, the rest of the routes at Palisades would be allowed to stay for now. It must be noted that this decision from the ranger was not an official Forest Service announcement. It's more along the lines of a "good faith agreement". As a result, 2 routes to the right of Sasquatch were taken down as they were very close to the trail. There were repeated requests that climbing not be allowed on that small section of rock due to the possibility of rockfall injuring passersby. Please be aware of the sensitivity of the area and be respectful of others.

Also, if you bring dogs of the wandering type, be aware that the trail gets used A LOT by horseback riders so please keep your dogs leashed. Seriously.

GETTING THERE: Make your way to Swan Valley on Hwy. 26 and continue southeast for about 7 miles. Turn left on Palisades Creek Rd. and follow the road to the Palisades Creek trailhead. Parking can be found by taking a left before the campground. There is a pit toilet in the parking area and a foot bridge over the creek.

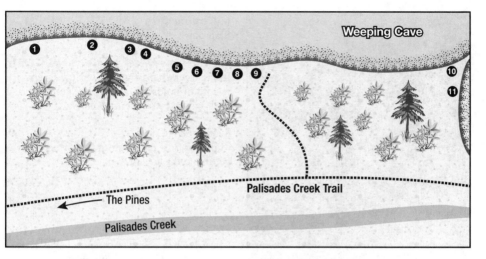

Weeping Cave
(All day sun, late afternoon shade)

Tucked behind the trees and mainly out of view from of the trail, the steep part of Weeping Cave hosts a handful of hard routes. As the wall extends away from the cave, the angle goes to vertical and the routes become easier.

While a couple of the routes in the cave stay shaded all day, the rest of the routes in this sector can be blazing hot when the sun is shining on the wall. The best time to climb here is late in the afternoon when the wall goes into the shade.

There are fixed draws on a few routes that have been donated by various individuals and are meant to be permanent fixtures for all to use. Please be respective of these and leave them in place. Plus, a stick clip for the first bolt on a few of the routes is required/recommended. Routes are listed from left to right when facing the wall.

WEEPING CAVE DIRECTIONS: From the trailhead, the Weeping Cave section is about 2 miles of easy hiking. The halfway point is marked by a bridge crossing. At about 1.7 miles, the trail leaves the trees for a bit and crosses a scree field beneath chossy stone. After the trail re-enters the trees, keep an eye open for an obvious arete that comes somewhat close to the trail. There is a faint trail that leads up to the base of the wall near Kaya.

1. Choss Choking Hoss*   .13a
Links into Hoss at 7th bolt. 7 bolts.

2. Hoss, Moss & Chaos**   .13a/b
Leftward traversing route in the cave. Grade depends on winch start or ground start. A couple of holds near the 1st bolt suffer from seepage in late spring. 8 bolts.

3. Uber Unagi   (open project)
Merges at the 5th bolt of The Basilisk.

4. The Basilisk   (open project)
5.12 climbing that leads to the meat of the route going over the bulge, then easier climbing on the upper headwall to the anchors. 10 bolts.

5. Quart. Of Blood Technique*** .12c
Powerful climbing up awesome limestone. A Classic! The start of the route can be seeping in early summer. 7 bolts.

Dean Lords versus The Basilisk.

181

Matt TeNgaio on Quart of Blood Technique, .12c. Photo by Dean Lords.

6. Chupacabra .12d
Slap-down crux up top. 5 bolts.

7. Nine Cow Wife** .11b
Route veers hard right down low to share a couple of holds with Easy St. before veering back left and straight up. 9 bolts.

8. Easy Street* .9
Mainly 5.7/.8 climbing until the last moves getting to the anchor. 5 bolts.

9. Grovel Road .11a
2 bolt extension to Easy St. The name says it all.

10. Kaya** .10a
Climbs to ledge with crux above ledge. Shares anchors with Grovel Rd. 7 bolts.

The next 2 routes are located to the far right.

11. Backscratcher* .10a
Starts in corner, just left of Sasquatch. 6 bolts.

12. Sasquatch** .10a/b
Right-most route on the wall. 6 bolts.

Heather Lords on the steep start of Ages of You, .13a. Photo by Dean Lords

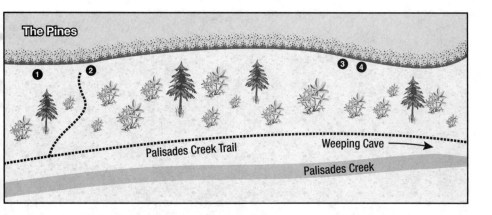

The Pines
(All day sun, late afternoon shade)

The Pines sector hosts a handful of quality routes on steep stone. This cave is also obscured by the trees and makes a nice crag to visit in the summer. Routes are listed from left to right when facing the wall.

THE PINES DIRECTIONS: The Pines section is located about 50 yards before reaching the Weeping Cave and completely hidden from view. Just after the dry creek channel with the rock retaining wall held together with chicken wire, when the trail enters the trees, you can follow a faint path up the hillside to the mouth of The Pines Cave.

1. King of the Road*   **.9**
Starts by the dead tree left of the cave. 4 bolts.

2. Ages of You***   **.13a**
Stick clip the 1st bolt. Fun, powerful crux off the deck to an easier middle section, then another crux on the short headwall. 6 bolts.

3. Toys in the Attic **   **.12c**
A hard start to easier climbing on a leftward traverse, followed by a crux at the bulge. Muy bueno. 7 bolts.

4. Bandwagon   **(project)**
Right-most route.

Riley Rollins climbing Ages of You, .13a
Photo by Dean Lords

Stephen Elmer on Toys in the Attic, .12c.
Photo by Dean Lords

183

TETON CANYON

Located in one of the m ost beautiful settings in the region, Teton Canyon has plenty to offer in the way of rock climbing. Four established walls/areas exist in the canyon. Two of them, Arms Deal Wall and the Grand Wall, are conveniently located side-by-side, with Waterfall Wall being just a short stroll from the Grand Wall. Shady Wall, is located just across the canyon.

GETTING THERE: From Driggs, turn east on Little Avenue/Ski Hill Road and go about 6 miles and turn right onto Teton Canyon Road, which quickly turns to dirt. Drive about 3.5 miles to the end of the road to either the North Fork Trailhead (for Shady Wall) or the South Fork Trailhead (for Arms Deal Wall, Grand Wall and Waterfall Wall).

The road usually opens around Memorial Day and closes about mid-November. This road can have some major potholes in it at times and is heavily used on the weekends. Plus, there can be cattle roaming the meadows and road so be mindful when driving through the canyon.

Arms Deal and Grand Wall access: Take the South Fork trail, which starts just right of the bathrooms, and immediately look for a smaller trail leading left to the big granite formation. The narrow trail eventually forks: Arms Deal Wall is to the left and up while the Grand Wall is to the right.

Waterfall Wall access: Take the South Fork trail for about .4 mi., cross over the footbridge then turn left off the main trail about 20' after crossing the footbridge and follow it to the crag behind the trees to the right of the small waterfall.

Shady Wall access: Park at the trailhead for the North Fork of Teton Canyon (before the end of the road). Walk to the campground and walk south past campsite No. 8 toward the cliffs and cross the creek via two logs that are side-by-side. From there, follow the trail as it crosses the creek about 3 more times via logs. The last creek crossing has 3 logs lashed together. There are a few attractive boulders below the wall.

Arms Deal Wall
(Morning shade, afternoon sun)

Overhung wall located left of the Grand Wall. Some of the steepest and best routes are located on this fine piece of granite. Routes are listed from left to right when facing wall.

Arms Deal Wall

1. G1* .12b**
Sport. Left-most route. Steep start and moves that stay on you until the anchors.

2. G2* .12c**
Sport. Shares the start with G1 then heads right through continually steeper terrain.

3. Unnamed   open project

4. Unnamed   open project
Sport. Except for the start, (which currently remains aid), all the moves have been done on this. So far it's suggested at .13c AO. It's just waiting for the right person to free it completely.

5. Unnamed   open project**
Sport. Starts on Arms Deal then traverses left into G4.

6. Arms Deal* .13b**
Sport. A classic line that cuts straight up through middle of the overhung wall. Get your kneebar game on. Probably THE most sought after hard route in the canyon.

7. Munger Crack* .11c**
Trad. Steep hand crack. A lone bolt is located to the left of the crack for the purpose of stopping the rope from getting stuck in the crack. No anchors. Walk off to the north.

8. Unnamed*   open project**
Sport. About 12' to the right of Munger Crack. Start remains aid. Suggesting grade of .12 AO. Needs to be freed all the way.

9. Jaimé Hole* .12a**
Sport. Steep start on jugs to big pod, then technical face climbing to the anchors.

10. Righteous Spark* .13a
Sport. Starts on underclings through steep section then climbs crack to anchors. There are fixed stoppers in the crack.

11. Bring On The Dopamine* .13a**
Sport. Thin and sustained.

12. Holey Moley .11b**
Sport. Right-most route on upper section. Fun climbing on flakes to anchors.

13. Toprope .7
Anchors.

14. Rat Hole* .12b**
Sport. Fun route on dead vertical face. Single bolt anchor.

15. Springtime* .11c**
Sport. Between Rat and Dr. Hole. Good moves on great stone.

16. Brunhilde .11b**
Trad. Short gear line or highball boulder problem. Small cams or a few crash pads. Shares anchors with Springtime.

17. Dr. Hole .12a**
Sport. Located below Holey Moley. Good technical climbing.

Grand Wall (Z-Crack Area)
(Morning shade, afternoon sun)

Located between Arms Deal Wall and the Grand Wall proper. Identified by prominent "Z" crack feature. There are anchors on routes 1-4 and Wild Kingdom, however, many choose to simply walk off to the climbers left.

1. X Factor* .13 R
Mixed. Starts just left of Z Crack. Climbs up through small roof via a thin crack with the crux just above the roof. Finish on Silver Cougar. Recommended to pre-place gear. 2 rope rappel.

2. Silver Cougar** .11b
Mixed. Climbs the first half of Z-Crack then heads left to gain the short, yet, prominent right-trending crack. Climbs over small roof, then finishes on the steep headwall following left-most black streak. Anchors. 2 rope rappel.

3. Lady Killer* .11b
Mixed. 2 rope rappel. Climbs the first half of Z-Crack then heads straight up following bolts. Shares anchors with Cougar. 2 rope rappel.

4. Z Crack*** .9
Trad. Starts in dihedral to grassy ledge, then follows obvious "Z-Crack" feature. A Teton Canyon classic. Usually done as two pitches. Anchors. 2 rope rappel.

5. Trembleberry* .10b
Mixed. Starts just left of Wild Kingdom on fixed gear, then traverses right and crosses over Wild Kingdom to one more piece of fixed gear in right-facing corner. Dirty finish above the big ledge. Usually done as two pitches. Bring small cams and a set of quickdraws. No anchors. Walk off to the left.

6. Wild Kingdom*** .7
Mixed. 3-pitch route that starts on fixed gear on low angled face. A highly recommended route for the budding lead climber. Bring 1 set of cams and quickdraws. Anchors.

7. Thimbleberry* .5 R
Trad. Route starts about 10' left of Double Cracks. Slabby, unprotectable start. Route just keeps getting better the higher you go. Usually done as two pitches. No anchors. Walk off to the left.

8. Double Cracks* .7
Trad. Starts about 10' left of big tree at the base of the wall. Climb up and slightly right. Usually done as two pitches. No anchors. Walk off to the left.

Grand Wall (Main Area)
(Morning shade, afternoon sun)

Big obvious wall just up the hillside to the left at the start of the Teton Canyon south fork trail. Originally, the Grand Wall area was climbed on traditional gear. With the introduction of sport climbing and well protected routes, the area became the local hotspot for hard climbing in the late 80's and early 90's. Routes are listed from left to right when facing wall.

9. Slope on a Rope*   .11c

Sport. Route angles right and is always pumpy. Anchors.

10. Bambi**   .11b

Sport. Hard start to fun climbing at the top. Anchors.

11. Thumper**   .11c

Sport. Merges with Bambi partway up.

12. Moonlight (Thumper Direct).12c/d**

Sport. Start on Thumper then heads straight up the thin seam. Thin and technical crux. A little runout to the anchors.

A climber on the start of a Teton Canyon classic, Z Crack, 5.9.

the top of the Grand Tower. Three 60m single rope raps to get down or walk off to the left. Anchors.

18. Super Slab .12b
Sport. Single biner marks the end of the route. There is a 5.13 project continuation that merges with Guides Wail.

19. Mayday** .12a
Sport. Long, beautiful line similar to it's neighbor to the right. Two rope rappel. Anchors.

20. High Noon** .12a
Sport. One of the two longest single pitch routes on the wall. A must do. Two rope rappel. Anchors.

21. Afternoon Delight Pitch 1**.9
Trad or Mixed. Original start is in the same corner where High Noon starts, although, more commonly started on Slabadellic, then veer slightly left to crack after second bolt on Slabadellic. Anchors

13. I.Q. Test* .10a
Mixed. Starts on a good ledge and anchors above Bambi and Thumper. Starts on fixed gear then requires trad gear as it traverses the left side of the Grand Tower.

14. Original Route* .9
Trad. Starts on the right side of the ledge for I.Q. Test and climbs to merge with I.Q. Test.

15. S.O.S.** .10c
Sport. Continuous technical liebacking. Anchors.

16. Guides Wail* .13a/b
Sport. Continuation pitch after S.O.S. Route ends at the top of the Grand Tower, where The Prowd starts.

17. The Prowd* .11b
Sport. To access this route climb S.O.S., then if you're feeling spunky climb Guide's Wail or just aid through the 5.13 section to the 5.8 section which signifies the start of The Prowd. Starts at

22. Afternoon Delight Pitch 2*   .12b
Sport. Continuation pitch. Two rope rappel or walk off to the climbers left. Anchors.

23. Slabadellic***   .9
Sport. The name says it all. Shares anchors with Uzi-Waza.

24. Full Sail**   .12d/.13a
Sport. Shares finish and anchors with Slabadellic. Obvious crux at the start pulling over the low roof.

25. Uzi-Waza*   .12a
Sport. Height dependent crux. Anchors.

26. Uzi-Waza Variation**   .10c
Sport. Same start but head right about 8' up to bypass .12a crux, then merge left again.

27. Kinjite*   .11c
Sport. Mellow start to a slap-down crux that can be hard to read. Anchors.

28. Ninjitsu*   .11b
Sport. Easy start to crux steeping out left from notch. Merges with Kinjite.

29. Sepekku**   .11d/.12a
Sport. Same start as Ninjitsu but veers right from notch. Keep your head together at the crux at the last draw. Anchors.

Riley Rollins on the Teton Classic hard route, Arms Deal, .13b. Photo by Dean Lords.

189

Waterfall Wall (Left)

Waterfall Wall
(Partial shade)

This area is located about .4 mi. down the Teton Canyon south fork trail where the short foot-bridge crosses over the runoff from the cascading waterfall to the left. Turn left off the main trail about 20' right after crossing the footbridge and follow it to the crag behind the trees. Easy access to the clifftop can be gained from the left side. Routes are listed from left to right when facing wall.

1. Conifer Crack** .11b/c
Trad. Fixed pin at the start. Steep crack with a few rests along the way. Can be set up as a toprope from pine tree up top. No anchors.

2. Off With His Hands** .13a
Toprope. Starts on Conifer Crack then breaks right at the midway point briefly following the right-trending diagonal break. Main crux is at the ending. Shares anchors with Execution.

3. Public Execution** .13a
Toprope. Starts on Conifer Crack then breaks right at the midway point following the right-trending diagonal break all the way to the rounded arete, then straight up through the crux. Anchors

4. Black Streak* .8
Toprope. Kind of manky and mossy. Can be set up as a toprope from tree up top. No anchors.

5. Trad Line** .11a
Trad. Climbs the clean-looking vertical crack. This is a fun route with good movement. Can be set up as a toprope from tree up top. No anchors.

6. Flare** .10b
Mixed. Climbs the flared crack on the right side of the rounded arete while plugging gear, then clips the 4 draws near the top. Anchors.

7. The Almighty*** .14a/b
Mixed. Climbs the crack on gear then merges with Super G at the last 3 quickdraws. Bring a couple of finger-sized cams and several offset nuts which are difficult to set. This area test-piece was sent by local Ty Mack in 2011 and remains the canyon's hardest route to date.

8. Super G*** .13a
9 draws. A classic hard route on very aesthetic stone. Traverses left after 4th quickdraw. Save some juice for the crux near the top! Anchors.

9. Nordic Man*** .13b
8 draws. Shares first 4 quickdraws with Super G then heads straight up to the business. Another hard classic. Anchors.

10. Free Ride** .12d/.13a
7 draws. Shares first 3 quickdraws with Super G then angles right. Anchors.

11. Super G Variation** .12d
Mixed. Climbs Super G but skips crux by finishing on the draws of Flare. Small gear can be placed to protect link up.

The next 4 routes are located on a small cliff to the right. There are anchors on #13 and #14. Easy access to the top allows for topropes to be set up.

12. 5.9 Crack* .9
Toprope.

13. 5.12 Crack** .12
Toprope. Anchors.

14. The Rightmost Path** .11d
Toprope or trad lead. Anchors.

15. Shortest Crack* .10a
Toprope.

Waterfall Wall (Far right)

191

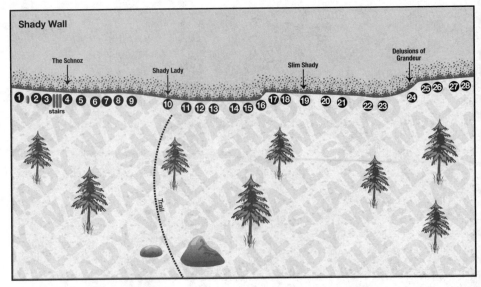

Shady Wall
(All day shade)

Located in a densely forested area Shady Wall is a great crag to escape the hot summer sun. Most of the routes are well protected and thought out. There are a few trad and mixed climbs here, but the majority of the routes are completely equipped. Routes are listed from left to right when facing wall.

1. The Prowler*   .11c/d
Tricky start to tips only crack. Follows thin seam then heads right below the roof. Climbing right of the draw line is easier. Save some juice for the crux below the anchors. 6 draws.

2. Run For Your Money*   .10a
Starts right of the bolt line on chossy section. Rock improves after 3rd draw. Funs jugs through the roof with a crux on the upper face. 5 draws.

3. Unnamed*   .9
Mixed line (2 bolts) up the corner and link into The Schnoz right below the anchors. The direct finish up the dihedral has anchors but is runout. Most people opt to link into The Schnoz at the top.

4. The Schnoz**   .11c/d
Bouldery start leads to an exposed crux with easier climbing above. Route is located at the base of the wooden stairs. 5 draws.

5. Feel the Love***   .10d
Challenging face followed by steep, juggy corner/crack. Finishes with one last steep section. A Shady Wall classic. 9 draws.

6. Made in the Shade**   .12b
Technical face climbing to a hard finger crack crux in the upper half. Sport.

7. Air Johnston*   .12c
A very deceitful crack climb that is hard to protect. Starts the same as Shade but cuts immediately right following the right-trending diagonal seam. It is highly recommended to toprope this route before trying to lead it. Trad.

8. Pumped Up Kicks**   .13b
Starts in corner crack. 9 draws.

9. Big Wray*   .11b R
Steep corner system with a hard to protect crux and a spicy right trending crack finish. Trad.

The next 4 routes are the first routes encountered when approaching the wall.

10. Shady Lady***   .10d
First of the 3 flowstone routes. Edges and pockets give way to an awesome downward-facing flake. A #1 BD cam is optional after the last draw but not necessary. 6 draws.

11. The Ooze*** .11a
2nd flowstone route with left-leaning feature above the flowstone. Hand jams and liebacks gets you to the anchors. 8 draws.

12. Two Faced .12a
Toprope. Climbs the flake feature up to a technical slab finish. Not equipped as of this writing but it has anchors.

13. Flowstoned** .11c
3rd flowstone route with a nice rest before the cryptic crux guarding the anchors. 6 draws.

14. Lovehandles* .11d
Mixed. Starts in bulging hand crack on gear then eases up before the crux from last 2 draws to the anchors. Has a total of 6 draws.

15. Trevor's Crack** .10d
This gear line has 2 starts – either the hand crack on Lovehandles or a finger crack to the right. Both starts lead to the same corner with a tricky bulge in the middle and a hard finish. You can clip the last draw on Bubblebath. Shares anchors with Bubblebath.

16. Bubblebath* .11c
Sport. Start either directly under the first draw or to the left in the finger crack. Route can suffer from dried runoff and be coated with dirt at times.

17. Slaphappy*** .13a
A route featured with hard slopers and 2 cruxes. Shares anchors with Bubblebath. 6 draws.

18. The Great Divide .12a/b
Mixed. Starts on 2 draws then veers right following the arching feature that leads into upper part of Slim Shady that pulls over the small roof.

19. Slim Shady*** .12c
Cool, overhanging start that leads up to the crux at the small roof. Stellar route. 7 draws.

20. The Krakken*** .12a
Aesthetic and tall line that follows the right-leaning diagonal crack, then up the face to one of two small roofs. Lieback to chains. 11 draws.

21. Bad Medicine*** .13a
Sustained hard route with a redpoint crux below the anchors. 9 draws.

22. Slash & Burn*** .12b
Follow diagonally right-leaning crack, then up and left. Exciting mantle move off a pinch awaits near the top. 8 draws.

23. Spider & The Fly*** .12a
Great route with a sustained crux section from the 4th draw to the anchors. 5 draws.

24. Delusions of Grandeur** .12c
Hard start that leads to sustained climbing with a sequential crux just below the anchors. 7 draws.

25. Huec & Bake** .11c/d
Toprope. Climb slab to hueco below the roof, head left using the cracks then up through 2nd roof and up the face to the anchors. The route will likely be equipped in the future.

26. Thug Life project
Toprope. Same start as Huec but instead of going to hueco head right through big roof, then blocky jugs to upper face. Like it's neighbor, this route will probably be equipped in the future.

27. Aggressively Passive** .11d
A short route with a show stopper crux after the last draw. Shares anchors with Black Slabbath. 5 draws.

28. Black Slabbath** .10c
Fun, steep start leads to easier slab moves up higher. 7 draws.

View from the Devil's Staircase in the South Fork of Teton Canyon.

DARBY CANYON

Located on the west side of the Teton range just south of Driggs, Darby Canyon is best known for it's popular hiking trail that leads to the "Wind Tunnel", a cave carved out of the limestone by wind and water. A popular destination for day hikers as well as adventerous cavers. Darby Canyon also hosts some great sport climbing.

Development of the routes began in 2002 by Teton Valley locals. While most of the routes tend to be short and slabby, there are a few that offer steeper angles. The climbs are well protected and the base of the cliff is level, making it an enjoyable crag to visit. Being a southeast-facing cliff, this area makes for a great place to climb on summer afternoons.

GETTING THERE: From Driggs, head south about 3 miles on Hwy. 33 and turn left onto Darby Road, (there is a sign reading "Darby Canyon"). From Victor, head north about 5 miles on Hwy. 33 and turn right onto Darby Road. Follow the pavement as it gives way to a gravel road, take the right fork in the road. At about 1.3 miles up the gravel road, park at the trailhead for the Aspen trail, (signed 034), on the left. Follow the trail past the second switchback then take the climber's trail on the right just before crossing the creek and continue on to the crag. The main trail stays well below the cliffs until routes 2-8 are in sight.

Climbers on Samsonite, 5.9.

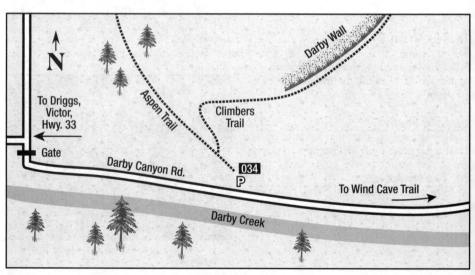

Darby Wall
(Morning sun, late afternoon shade)

Routes are listed from left to right when facing wall.

1. Look Ma, No Hands* .10a
This lone route sits about 100 yards to the left of Samsonite and is best approached by the main trail instead of bushwhacking along the base of the cliff. Angles right and up to big flake by 4th bolt, then finishes on left side of bolt line. 7 bolts.

A climber on Hippies, .11d.

The following routes are located about 80 yards to the right of route 1.

2. Samsonite* .9
Up slabby face to crux at mid-route, then finishes on crimps and good holds. 4 bolts.

3. Stemming For Dollars* .10a
Starts on easy slab, first bolt is way up there. Crimps to small underclings, then finishes on good holds. 5 bolts.

4. Deep Dark Hole** .9
Starts directly below the first bolt, crimp, side pull and pinch your way to the anchors. 6 bolts.

5. Happy, Happy, Happy* .8
Climbs easy, slabby face. Good beginner route. 5 bolts.

6. Sweetish Chest Thrust* .10c
Spicy start to vertical seam, finishes on good holds. 6 bolts.

7. Chubby Rain*** .10a
Crux is low on this route, eases up after 3rd bolt. Chain anchors. 6 bolts.

8. Wango Tango** .11b
Starts directly below first bolt, moves up and over roof to big rest ledge, then up smooth, vertical face. Finishes on good pockets. 7 bolts.

9. Velvet Elvis* .11d**
Powerful, bouldery start to big holds then finishes at roof. A quality route! Rap ring anchors. 6 bolts.

10. Natural Born Drillers .11c
Located near small staircase, behind bush. Sustained route. 6 bolts.

11. Red Headed Step Child* .7
Short, easy route. 3 bolts.

12. Might As Well Jump .10d**
Fun route with crux up high. 6 bolts.

13. Rexquando .11a**
4 bolts.

14. American Idle .10d**
More crimpy, slabby fun. 5 bolts.

15. Stripe* .8
4 bolts.

16. Gizmo .9
Route is equipped with chainlink hangers. 4 bolts.

17. Unnamed .?
Short, slabby-looking route about 15' right of Gizmo. 3 bolts.

18. Hippies .11d**
6 bolts.

19. Duck, Duck, Weird Duck .10c**
Couple of ways to start this one. Main crux higher up. Moving out right at 4th bolt helps. 5 bolts.

20. Unnamed* .12a
Starts below small roof, then angles slightly left over roof. 7 bolts.

Originating near Soda Springs, the 135 mile-long Blackfoot River courses it's way northwest through the Blackfoot Reservoir, then west to join the Snake River southwest of Blackfoot.

Local fisherman and river runners are not the only ones who enjoy the scenic Blackfoot River Canyon. Since the 1980's climbers have been scaling the tall basalt cliffs that frame the river as it snakes its way westward to the Snake River Plain.

Four separate climbing areas are found along the canyon (in ascending order): The Playground, Desperate Wall, Crank Cave, Rapid Wall, and RPM Wall (located in the adjacent Wolverine Canyon).

Heather Lords on a Crank Cave classic, Bride of Crankenstein, .12b. Photo by Nathan Smith.

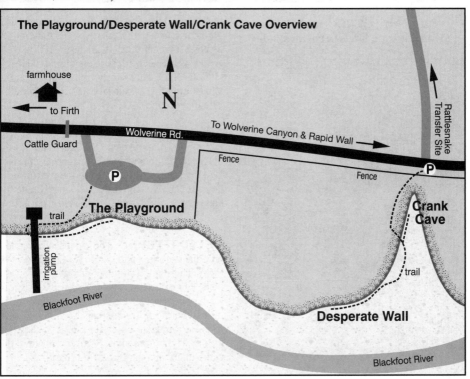

The Playground/Desperate Wall/Crank Cave Overview

farmhouse

to Firth

N

Wolverine Rd.

To Wolverine Canyon & Rapid Wall →

Rattlesnake Transfer Site

Cattle Guard

Fence

Fence

P

P

trail

The Playground

Crank Cave

irrigation pump

trail

Blackfoot River

Desperate Wall

Blackfoot River

197

The Playground
(Morning sun, late afternoon shade)

Heather Lords plugging gear at The Playground.

In the late '80s, local Blackfoot climbers Jim Neilson and Dean Packum were the first to discover and set toprope anchors on this wall. A few years later, Idaho Falls climbers Chuck Oddette and Dean Lords went to work cleaning and bolting this basalt face and aptly named it The Playground.

Topropes can be set before descending or rappelling down to the base. To hike down, follow the steep trail alongside the irrigation pump or take the steep dirt road west of the parking area down to the river and head back upstream to the base of the cliff. Routes are listed from left to right when facing the wall.

GETTING THERE: The easiest driving directions to follow are: Get to the small town of Firth. There are a number of ways to do this. Firth sits directly on U.S. Highway 91. From Firth, take Wolverine Road east for about 9 miles. On the left is a small farm house with mobile homes and a cattle guard in the road – turn right immediately after crossing the cattle guard and park in the dirt parking area.

1. Tied to the Whipping Post*** .11b
Start in columns to shallow open book then through blank section to steep finish at anchors. Best to let your friend climb it first and clean off any dried dirt. Other than that, a Blackfoot River classic. 10 bolts.

2. I'm Too Sexy for My Lycra* .12b
Climb column to smooth open book, over the lip to steep finish at anchors. 8 bolts.

3. Predicaligament* .10a/b
Just right of Lycra, this route climbs it's way up to the wide dihedral with a crack in it all the way to the anchors. 9 bolts. *FA: Erik Jensen, Tom Smartt.*

4. Yo Mama* .8
This used to by a toprope route until bolts were added to it in 2014. Crux start. 9 bolts. *FA: Tom Smartt.*

5. American Gladiator** .10c
Climb columns to small roof, up onto face, shift left to the blunt arete to big rest ledge. Poke the pockets on the way to the chain anchors. 8 bolts.

6. Anchored to the Sky*** .9+
Start in shallow columns to blocky face. Fun moves up fractured plate, then left below roof and finish angling right. 6 bolts.

7. Cure for the Hangover*** .9+
Similar start to Anchored but traverse right at roof on big flake and finish in juggy dihedral at chains. 8 bolts.

8. Tequila Hangover* .12d
Same as Cure but after fourth bolt climb big overhang with glued-on hold, pull the lip and finish on easier moves to anchors. 8 bolts.

9. Tequila Sunrise** .11a
Columns to bulbous section, then up through bulge and finish on hidden jugs. 7 bolts.

10. Toprope Route .7
Climb blocky face to inside corner, fun moves gets you to the top.

11. Toejam* .9
Start up broken face to fun moves in small corner and left to anchors. 5 bolts. *FA: Matt TeNgaio, Mike Benson.*

12. Unnamed .?
Around the corner next to Toejam, this route starts in white column section up to a small ledge and finishes on a short steep white face. 7 bolts.

Located to the left of The Playground and just below the steep dirt road that descends into the canyon are a handful of routes bolted in 2014. This scrappy chunk of gritty Rhyolite has been ignored by route developers in the past due the quality of the stone, or lack thereof. No information was available at press time.

Levi Painter climbing Tied to the Whipping Post, .11b.

199

Heather Lords on Powder Finger, .8. The main cave area is in the background. Photo by Nathan Smith.

Crank Cave
(Routes 1-7 morning sun, routes 8-17 afternoon sun)

Nestled along the basalt cliffs of the Blackfoot River lies Crank Cave. Originally scouted and developed by Chuck Odette and Dean Lords in the early '90s, the cave yielded two routes. It sat dormant for some time afterward until interest in steep cave climbing spurred new development. Beginning in the spring of 2007, Matt TeNgaio and Dean Lords picked up where the previous efforts had left off. Tom Smartt added a handful of hard lines

Crank Cave has a unique style of climbing not normally found in an area that is dominated by face/slab climbing. The routes are very steep, and require powerful sequences using cryptic movements to make it to the anchors.

Routes are listed from left to right when facing the wall.

A stick clip is required/recommended. There is a rotten band of stone at the base of some climbs and the routes were bolted with using a stick clip in mind. Please be courteous about the fixed draws that may seem unattended or left behind – these are permanent fixtures on the routes and open for all to use.

GETTING THERE: Follow the directions to The Playground (Blackfoot River), and continue about .5 mile east. Parking can be found directly across the road from the Rattlesnake Transfer Site entrance. Use the small step ladder over the fence then hike south along the west edge of the cave for about 30-40 yards. Descend via a faint trail through a broken gully, the cave is to the left.

Dean Lords on Riff Raff, .12c/d. Photo by Nathan Smith.

1. Unnamed .7
First route encountered when walking along the base of the cliff. 4 Bolts.

2. Powder Finger*** .8
Climb nice flake to jugs. Finishes on fun pocketed face/open book section. 4 bolts. *FA: Matt TeNgaio, Mike Benson.*

3. Supernaut .10a
Bouldery move onto low ledge, then through fractured rock through open book. Ends under small roof. A non-classic. 4 bolts. *FA: Matt TeNgaio.*

4. Drug Train*** .11a
Either start left of the 1st bolt or winch start to first bolt. Move diagonally right to crux at 4th bolt. Sharp pockets up top. 5 bolts. *FA: Dean Lords.*

5. Bride of Crankenstein*** .12b
Don't let the choss at the start of this superb route detract you from doing this one, it's a classic! Horizontal moves out to the lip of the roof with a demanding powerful crux pulling the lip. 5 bolts. *FA: Dean Lords.*

6. Free Fallin'** .11c
Winch start to first bolt then jug haul through steep section, crux pulling roof. 6 bolts. *FA: Dean Lords.*

Crank Cave
(Powder Finger section)

7. Excretis Maximus .11d
Scramble up chossy mess to gain solid rock. Route veers left then straight up to massive bird shit rest hold. Fire second crux on sharp pockets getting to anchors past the 5th bolt. Another non-classic. 5 bolts. *FA: Matt TeNgaio.*

Crank Cave (left)

Crank Cave (right)

8. El Jefe*** .12a

Same approach as Excretis. Fire crux at the start, then head right on big holds. Powerful moves get you to the top. 6 bolts 6 bolts. *FA: Matt TeNgaio.*

9. Love to Burn*** .12c/d

Start on El Jefe, bust right at 5th bolt and traverse lip of cave for 2 bolts, then finish on Riff Raff. 8 bolts. *FA: Dean Lords.*

10. Riff Raff*** .12c/d

Winch start to starting holds then to steep horizontal hand crack, then powerful moves to pod. Trend right from pod to more powerful moves getting over the lip. 2 bolt hangers mark the anchors. 5 bolts. *FA: Dean Lords.*

11. Wave of Mutilation*** .13c

This route features fun and unique movement. One of the best hard routes in the cave. 7 bolts. *FA: Dean Lords.*

12. Karma Police*** .13c

This route tackles the steepest part of the cave. Big moves on horizontal roof lead to burly crux pulling lip at the cave. One hanger marks the end of the route. Be a man and top out. 5 bolts. *FA: Dean Lords.*

13. Subterrain Homesick Alien** .13b/c

Links into Karma from Karma's third bolt. No fixed draws as of this publication. Just as hard as Karma, but a one move starting crux instead. *FA: Tom Smartt.*

14. Los Aldoberto's Especial** .13c/d

Use the bolt at the very back of the cave to steady the belayer. The climb starts on a corner to the left of the very back bolt. Quite techy and requires some fancy footwork. Links into Karma Police just below the lip of the cave. 6 bolts. *FA: Tom Smartt.*

15. Soul Power*** .12d

Route moves left to crux at 3rd bolt, to pod at 5th, then power endurance moves to the anchors. Ends in open book under roof. Downgraded from original .13a suggestion. 6 bolts. *FA: Matt TeNgaio.*

16. Crank Addiction** .12c

One of the two original routes that opened the cave up in the early '90s. A powerful, technical start leads to jugs. Some don't like that it has a glued on hold, but the movement is well worth it. 6 bolts. *FA: Chuck Odette.*

17. The Hive** .11d

Bouldery start to rest under roof. Use crack above roof and bust through some powerful moves on pockets to anchors. Named after bee hive located to the left of the route in a big hole. 4 bolts. *FA: Matt TeNgaio, Mike Benson.*

Desperate Wall

Desperate Wall
(Morning sun, late afternoon shade)

Another wall developed by Chuck Oddette and Dean Lords back in the early '90s. Despite it's "ghetto" character, (a curse brought on by lazy trash depositing locals), Desperate Wall hosts a handful of fun and worthy long routes. Routes are listed from left to right when facing the wall.

GETTING THERE: Follow the same directions for The Playground but continue past the cattle guard and parking area and drive another .5 mile to the Rattlesnake Transfer site, turn right onto steep dirt road. You can either park here before descending down the steep jeep road or, if you have a high clearance vehicle, continue following the road that skirts the west side of the drainage to the left. Park about 150 yards down the road and look for a gully that cuts down into the drainage. Once in the drainage head toward the river and turn right at the mouth of the drainage. Continue staying by the base of the cliff for about 100 yards until you see the bolts.

1. Cliffhanger*   **.11d**
Toprope. Climb face through to overhang.

2. Desperado***   **.11c**
Column/face climb to overhang then up pocketed face. Chain anchors. 8 bolts.

3. Widow Maker*   **.10c**
Named for loose block on route. Face climb to steep finish at chains. 8 bolts.

4. The Hidden**   **.10a**
Climb face to fun steep pockets to chain anchors. 8 bolts.

WOLVERINE CANYON

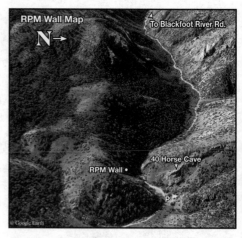

RPM Wall Map

Anyone who has driven through Wolverine Canyon knows that it is filled with limestone – much of it, however, is complete choss and/or vertically challenged. Extensive hiking has yet to produce more abundant quality stone like that found on the RPM Wall.

RPM Wall
(Morning shade, late afternoon sun)

RPM Wall is mainly blue/gray limestone that features slabby-vertical angles that make for thin and technical face climbing. Matt TeNgaio and Mike Benson developed this wall during the '05-'06 seasons.

The crag's east-facing nature coupled with the dense vegetation at the base make it a wonderful place to beat the summertime heat as the wall sees minimal sun. Fall and spring climbing are both excellent as well. Plan on climbing in complete seclusion as the wall sits above the road and is well hidden from motorists.

Routes are listed from **RIGHT TO LEFT** when facing the wall.

GETTING THERE: Follow the directions to get to The Playground and continue heading east. At the fork with the Blackfoot River Road, head left, staying on the paved road. Continue on until the mouth of the canyon is reached and the road turns to gravel.

Follow the dirt road for about 1.5 to 2 miles. until it passes through a narrow section. You'll know you're at the right spot if you can see the big cave, (40 Horse Cave), up to the left of the road just after passing through the narrows. Continue up the canyon and park on the left side at the big pullout just after 40 Horse Cave.

To get to the wall, walk back down the road about 500 feet to the trailhead. Look for the small pile of broken white rock on the south side of the road – the short trail starts just above it and climbs through the trees.

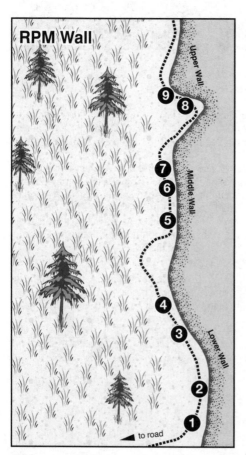

Lower Wall

1. Sweating Bullets***   .11a
Start on jugs then up through crux to big rest ledge. Finish on face with delicate holds. First route encountered when hiking along the base of the wall. 10 bolts. *FA: Mike Benson.*

2. Angel of Death***   .12a
Power through steep start to small rest ledge. Use flaring crack and obscure holds to gain big holds at the anchors. 9 bolts. *FA: Matt TeNgaio.*

The next 2 climbs are located up the hillside from Angel of Death.

3. My Name is Mud   .10d
Hard to read start to slabby crux. Climb right side of the flake to the big ledge at the anchors. Chain anchors with biners. 6 bolts. *FA: Matt TeNgaio, Mike Benson.*

4. Bombs Away*   .10a
First bolt is high. Start in the small crack/flake to the 3rd bolt. Stay left of the bolt line on the slabby face to the big ledge at the anchors. 4 bolts. *FA: Matt TeNgaio, Mike Benson.*

Middle Wall

5. Reach for the Sky**   .11c
Slabby face start to shallow dihedral. Finish on fun face above. 8 bolts. *FA: Matt TeNgaio.*

6. Still Life***   .12b
This routes starts just left of the tree. Ultra thin moves all the way to the 4th bolt. Big jug out right makes a good rest, then fun .10+ moves

Troy Neu keeps his cool on Sweating Bullets, .11a.

all the way to the anchors. 8 bolts. *FA: Mike Benson.*

7. Lateralis*   .11c
Hard to read start to fun middle section on positive holds. Main crux at top getting to anchors. 5 bolts. *FA: Matt TeNgaio.*

Upper Wall

8. Freakie Stylie Direct*   .12d
Stick clip first bolt that is way up there. Burly thin moves to slopey pocket below flake, then straight up on more crimpy moves to anchors. Contrived. 3 bolts. *FA: Tom Smartt.*

9. Freakie Stylie***   .12b
Use seam and traverse right to gain flake at 3rd bolt, then merge with Freakie Stylie Direct. A short but fun route. 4 bolts. *FA: Tom Smartt, Matt TeNgaio.*

Mike Benson on the thin crux of Still Life, .12b.

Rapid Wall
(Morning shade, afternoon sun)

This oft-forgotten, seldom visited, short and obscure basalt wall sits high above the scenic Blackfoot River and was named after the rapids in the river below. The scenery may be better than the actual climbing experience at Rapid Wall but don't let that discourage you. Routes are listed from left to right when facing the wall.

GETTING THERE: Follow directions to The Playground and continue driving east. At the intersection of Wolverine Road and Blackfoot River Road, turn right onto the gravel road and set your odometer to zero. Follow the road as it climbs the foothills and heads upstream. At about 6.6 miles park alongside the road and hike out toward the edge of the cliffs. At the top of the cliffs, anchors will be found and one can either rappel from the right-most anchors or brave the steep descent down the gully just downstream from the climbs. This same gully is used to hike out.

This crag is not the best place to bring your dog or little ones because of the nature of the descent/ascent out of the canyon. Beware of rattlesnakes.

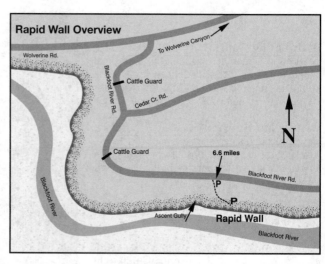

Rapid Wall Overview

1. First Chalk**   .10a
Start on broken face to ledge, lieback flake to steep face to chain anchors. 6 bolts. *FA: Matt TeNgaio, Mike Benson.*

2. Ginsu***   .10d
Up choss, negotiate big flake to face climb to chains at ledge. 5 bolts. *FA: Matt TeNgaio, Mike Benson.*

3. Lichensmear**   .8
Climb inside corner of lichen covered arete to chains at big ledge. 5 Bolts. *FA: Matt TeNgaio, Mike Benson.*

4. Around the Bend**   .10c/d
Climb blocky section to ledge, use flake to get to pockets and face to big jug and crux; end on jugs. 5 bolts. *FA: Matt TeNgaio, Mike Benson.*

5. Who Let the Bugs Out*   .11d
Negotiate way to ledge, straight up fin to big rest, fire through crux and finish on .10b section to chains. 6 bolts. *FA: Matt TeNgaio, Mike Benson.*

6. Under the Hood**.10d
Start up face on positive holds, work through crux in right-facing corner, finish on good holds below roof. 5 Bolts. *FA: Matt TeNgaio, Mike Benson.*

Open Climb at Ross Park's Sunny Side wall.

ROSS PARK

Conveniently located in the town of Pocatello, Ross Park is home to more than 140 climbs.

Located on the northeast side of the park, the Shady Side offers toprope climbs ranging from 5.7 to 5.12c – plus many fun boulder problems.

On the southwest side of the park, the Sunny Side offers great toprope, lead climbs and a few boulder problems as well.

The routes were put in by the Idaho State University Outdoor Club and the area is maintained by the Pocatello Parks and Recreation.

Routes can be easily identified by their numbers painted at the base of the cliffs and/or stamped plates at the anchors on top. There are also a few stamped plates attached to rocks along the base of the cliffs. Once a week during the summer, the outdoor club sets up top ropes for climbers to use in the evenings (usually on Thursdays). Find the ISU Outdoor Club on the Internet for precise schedules of climbing nights and which side of the park will be set up. Most routes are short enough that one rope will service two routes.

GETTING THERE: Take I-15 to Pocatello and take the 5th Street exit. Drive west for about 1 mile and the Shady Side cliffs will come into view on the left. There is limited parking along 4th Street. Extra parking is available in Upper Ross Park by the covered shelter. For the Sunny Side, follow the signs along 5th Street to Ross Park, drive through the park, passing the big swimming pool (on your right) and just after exiting on the south side, there is a big parking area on the left.

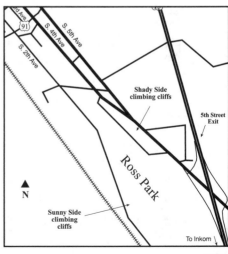

Climbers enjoying a morning session at Ross Park's Shady Side.

Shady Side
(Morning sun, afternoon shade)
Routes are listed from <u>right to left</u> when facing the wall.

1. (.11c/d)	21. (.11b)	41. (.10c)
2. (.7)	22. (.10b) J Crack	42. (.10c)
3. (.9)	23. (.8)	43. (.9)
4. (.8)	24. (.10b)	44. (.9)
5. (.8)	25. (.10c)	45. (.11b)
6. (.9)	26. (.8)	46. (.9)
7. (.12b)	27. (.9)	47. (.9)
8. (.10b)	28. (.8)	48. (.9)
9. (.9)	29. (.10b)	49. (.10a) Z Crack
10. (.9)	30. (.7)	50. (.9)
11. (.10c)	31. (.7)	51. (.10a)
12. (.7)	32. (.7)	52. (.10a)
13. (.8)	33. (.9)	53. (.11a)
14. (.10c)	34. (.10b)	54. (.9)
15. (.10b) Big Cut	35. (.11a)	55. (.10c)
16. (.12b) Degal's Nose	36. (.11a)	56. (.10c)
17. (.9)	37. (.11b)	57. (.8)
18. (.8)	38. (.10a)	58. (.8)
19. (.12c) Star Search	39. (.9)	59. (.10a)
20. (.10a)	40. (.10b)	60. (.9)

Sunny Side
(Morning shade, afternoon sun)
Routes are listed from left to right when facing the wall.
(routes 1 to 8 are on private land)

Main Wall

9. Not So Bad (.10d)	21. (.10d) 3 bolts	34. (.10b)
10. Bad (.11b) 3 bolts	22. (.8)	35. (.9+) 4 bolts
11. Badder (.12a) 4 bolts	23. (.9) 5 bolts	36. (.10a)
11A. (.12b) 3 bolts	24. (.7)	37. Rubber Arete
12. Baddest (.11b) 2 bolts	24A. (.11b) 3 bolts	(.11c) 3 bolts
12A. (5.?)	25. (.7)	38. (.9)
13. (.10d) 3 bolts	26. (.8)	39. (.9)
13A. (.12c) 4 bolts	27. (.9-) 5 bolts	40. (.8) 4 bolts
14. (.10c)	28. (.8) 5 bolts	41. (.8)
15. (.8)	28A. (.7)	42. (.9) 3 bolts
16. (.11a) 4 bolts	29. Silver Bolt (.11a) 3 bolts	43. (.10c) 3 bolts
17. (.9+)	29A. Ruthlessly Wired (.12a) 4 bolts	44. (.12a) 3 bolts
17A. (.10b) 4 bolts	30. (.10a)	45. (.10c)
18. (.7) 5 bolts	31. (.9-)	46. (.9)
19. (.9+)	32. (.10a) 4 bolts	46A. (.10d)
20. (.10a) 3 bolts	33. Two Fingers (.10b) 4 bolts	

Middle Wall

46B. (.9)	52. (.10b) 5 bolts	58. (.11) 3 bolts
47. (.7) 5 bolts	53. Monkey Arete (.11c) 5 bolts	58A. (.12b)
48. (.8)	54. (.10a)	59. (.10a) 4 bolts
48A. (.10a) 4 bolts	54A. (.12a/b) 5 bolts	60. (.10)
48B. (.10a) 6 bolts	55. (.11a) 5 bolts	61. (.10a) 4 bolts
49. (.9)	55A. (.12b) 4 bolts	62. (.?)
50. (.11?)	56. (.9+)	
51. (.10c) 5 bolts	57. (.11a)	

Ivy League Wall

62A. Multi Face (.10) 5 bolts	67. (.10a) 4 bolts	72. (.9+) 3 bolts
63. (.6)	68. (.8) 5 bolts	73. (.11c) 2 bolts
64. (.10c) 4 bolts	68A. (.8) 4 bolts	74. (.10b/c) 3 bolts
65. (.10a/b) 2 bolts	69. (.9+) 3 bolts	75. (.12a) 3 bolts
65A. Lep of Faith (.12a) 4 bolts	70. (.9+) shares 69's bolts	
66. Route 66 (.10a)	71. White Line (.10d) 3 bolts	

Nick Vitale on Toxic Socks Syndrome, .10d. Photo by Mike Engle.

Massacre Rocks

Located in the heart of southeastern Idaho, Massacre Rocks is home to 760+ routes. Heralded by some as "one of the best sport climbing areas" in the West, Massacre Rocks has something for everyone. While it hosts grades from 5.8 to 5.13, a majority of Massacre's fame comes from it's nickname "five-eleven-heaven".

One of the aspects that makes Massacre so attractive is the convenience of being able to climb at the same wall all day. Areas like Wild Onion Wall, Red Light District and the popular All American Area all host routes from 5.9 – 5.12+, with a majority of those being 5.10-5.11. It truly is a fantastic place for the those seeking quality routes in those parameters.

Like most areas in southeastern Idaho, the main climbing seasons at Massacre are spring and fall. However, afternoon shade can be found at some walls in the summer making it tolerable during the scorching months. Climbing on sunny windless days in winter is usually tolerable as well.

MASSACRE ROCKS AREA HISTORY: Massacre Rocks was a landmark along the Oregon and California Trails during the mid-19th century. Immigrants alternatively used the names

Massacre Rocks, Gate of Death, or Devil's Gate to the trail's narrow passage through the rocks from the fear of a possible attack by Indians. While there was an ambush that resulted in 10 immigrants perishing, the actual attack was located east of the State Park. Nonetheless, the name Massacre Rocks stuck.

GEOLOGY: The park and it's surrounding canyons were created during the repeated volcanic activity on the Snake River Plain. The big boulders near the interstate were deposited in their present location about 14,500 years ago, during the massive flood known as the Lake Bonneville Flood.

When ancient Lake Bonneville breached it's northern shoreline near Red Rock Pass, ID, the estimated discharge of the water was 15 million cubic feet per second, with an average speed of 16 mph. The peak flow only lasted about 3 days, while the lake continued to drain for up to a year. The Portneuf Narrows near Inkom, ID was completely flooded with the waters reaching a soaring height of up to 400'. The water followed the Snake River all the way to it's confluence with the Columbia River as it scoured and exposed previously buried canyons in the basalt along the way.

Troy Neu doing his best impersonation of the All American Man, .12b, All American Wall.

Terran Engle on the start of I-Chi-Hua-Hua, .12b, South of the Border Wall. Photo by Mike Engle.

Climbers enjoying a fine late winter day at the Rural Wall, All American Area.

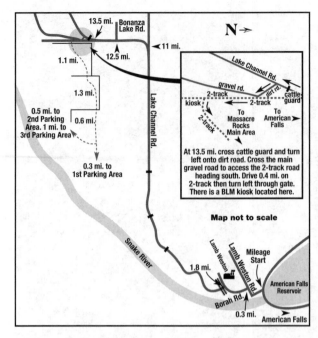

Map content:
- 13.5 mi.
- Bonanza Lake Rd.
- N→
- 11 mi.
- 1.1 mi.
- 12.5 mi.
- Lake Channel Rd.
- 1.3 mi.
- gravel rd.
- 2-track
- kiosk
- 2-track
- dirt rd.
- cattle guard
- Lake Channel Rd.
- 0.5 mi. to 2nd Parking Area. 1 mi. to 3rd Parking Area
- 0.6 mi.
- 2-track
- To Massacre Rocks Main Area
- To American Falls
- 0.3 mi. to 1st Parking Area
- At 13.5 mi. cross cattle guard and turn left onto dirt road. Cross the main gravel road to access the 2-track road heading south. Drive 0.4 mi. on 2-track then turn left through gate. There is a BLM kiosk located here.
- Map not to scale
- Snake River
- Lamb Weston Rd.
- Mileage Start
- 1.8 mi.
- American Falls Reservoir
- Borah Rd.
- 0.3 mi.
- American Falls

There should be a water trough just on the other side of the gate.
• The road turns sharply left (north) then east again and continues for 1.3 miles. Here you pass through another fence/gate.
• Drive for another 0.6 mi. and:
• **1st Parking Area** - Take the left fork in the road heading east for about another .3 mi. until a 90 degree left turn in the road. Located at the sharp turn is an area to park before walking through the opening in the fence. This is the parking area for the Main Wall, The Outback, Down Under and Windmill Wall. Pass through the fence and hike the old road, now closed to motorized traffic.
• **2nd & 3rd Parking Areas** - Take the right fork in the road heading south. Drive for another .5 mi. to the 2nd parking area. To get to the 3rd parking area continue another .5 mi. past the 2nd parking area until the two-track ends. Park here and hop the wire fence.

Please note that 4WD is not necessary to access the parking areas, however, a high clearance vehicle is recommended. That being said, it's not unusual to see an occasional sedan at the parking areas.

River Access: The quickest and easiest way to reach the Main Wall and Owl Cove, if you have access to a boat, is to cross the Snake River at Massacre State Park. Drive about 11.5 miles west of American Falls on I-86. Take the Massacre Rocks exit #28. Park where the road T's and pack your boat about 200 yards to the river, or drive to the boat ramp and boat 1/4 mile back upriver. Camping and showers are available at the State Park for a fee.

FINDING YOUR WAY AROUND: As with many of Massacre's walls, there are faster approaches if one knows the area well. For the sake of simplicity, however, access directions to individual walls are described from starting at the 3 main parking areas.

Routes are listed from left to right when facing the wall.

RATTLESNAKES: Be aware that the area is home to rattlesnakes and sightings are quite common. Keep an eye on your dogs and kids.

GETTING THERE
Driving Access: From the town of American Falls, take State Highway 39 across the American Falls Reservoir dam. Take the first left, Lamb-Weston Road. Listed mileage starts here:
• 0.3 miles: Turn left onto Borah Road
• 1.8 miles: Turn left onto Lake Channel Road, cross the railroad tracks heading south. The road has 3 sharp corners on it before angling southwest, then straight west.
• 13.5 miles: Look for a cattle guard where Lake Channel Road starts to gently angle right. Once across the cattle guard you will see a dirt road on the left, turn onto this road. The road will then merge onto the gravel road. Cross the gravel road and pull onto the 2 track dirt road that parallels the main gravel road and head south. See map above.
• After 0.4 miles on the 2 track dirt road you should see a place in the fence on the left that you can pass through. Put the fence/gate back up after passing through. There is a small outcropping of stones to the right of the gate. There is a BLM kiosk located here.
• Heading east/northeast, drive on a dirt road for 1.1 miles and pass through another fence/gate.

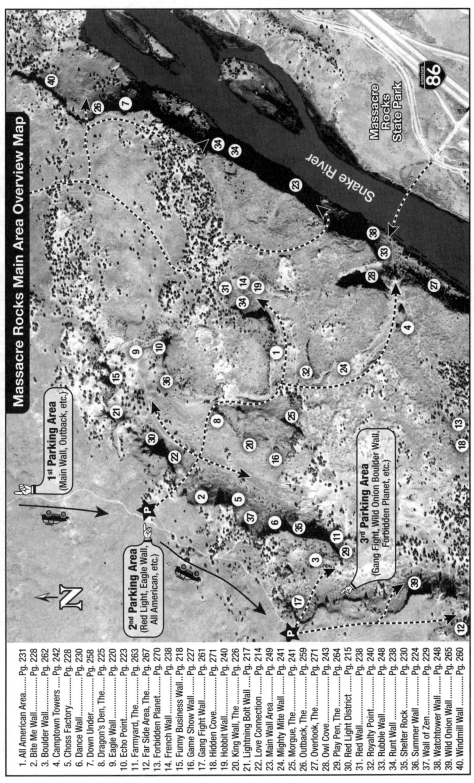

Massacre Rocks Main Area Overview Map

1st Parking Area
(Main Wall, Outback, etc.)

2nd Parking Area
(Red Light, Eagle Wall, All American, etc.)

3rd Parking Area
(Gang Fight, Wild Onion Boulder Wall, Forbidden Planet, etc.)

Snake River

Massacre Rocks State Park

INTERSTATE 86

Love Connection
(Early morning shade, all day sun)

Short, steep wall, south facing wall located to the left of Red Light District.

APPROACH: Park at the 2nd parking area and locate the trail heading southeast to the canyon's rim. Pass through a gap in the fence and keep descending for about 300' – Love Connection wall is on the left.

1. French Connection*   **.11c/d**
Steep jug hauling. Good Stuff. 4 bolts.

2. La Femme Nikita**   **.12a**
Pumpy pocket pulling. 4 bolts.

• 2 bolt ending variation for La Femme Nikita?

3. Aphrodisiac**   **.13a**
Fun start then the slap-down begins. Hard footwork. 5 bolts.

4. Aphrodite*   **.13a/b**
Link-up, starts on French Connection, then Aphrodisiac finish.

5. Love Connection***   **.12a**
The wall's namesake and a very worthy route. 4 bolts.

6. Love On The Rocks**   **.12b**
More short and powerful cranking. 4 bolts.

7. Kama-Sutra*   **.13b**
7 bolt traverse from French Connection to L.O.T.R.

8. One Night Fling*   **.12c**
Clip the first bolt of L.O.T.R., then right & up for three bolts. 4 bolts.

9. Nothing But A 2-Bit Whore   **.12c**
18'. This would be a boulder problem were it not for the small jutting rock at the base. 2 bolts.

Red Light District (left)

Red Light District
(Morning sun, late afternoon shade)

East-to-Southeast facing wall, right of Love Connection Wall.

APPROACH: Park at the 2nd parking area, locate the trail heading southeast to the canyon's rim. The trail drops and passes through a gap in the fence and keeps descending, heading southeast past Love Connection Wall. At this point there are 2 trails. For easier access to Red Light District, hike to the base of Love Connection Wall then follow the trail east as it contours the cliff. The center area of Red Light District is about 250' from Love Connection Wall.

Routes 1-5 are located down and left of Love Canal, about 100' right of Love Connection Wall.

1. Trundler   .8
Long route broken up by a few ledges. 12 bolts.

2. Felix*   .8
Similar to Trundler. 12 bolts.

3. Twisted*   .10c
Alpine-style climbing to fun upper dihedral. 12 bolts.

4. The Matinee*   .10a
Starts at the left corner of the east facing wall. 6 bolts.

5. Adults Only**   .12b
Climb Matinee and keep going past 3 more bolts. 10 bolts.

Routes 6-8 are accessed via rappeling from the clifftop to the hanging ledge.

6. Paw Prints   10a
Crux down low to easier climbing above. Bolts.

7. Bow Wow*   .8
Sustained climbing for the grade. 3 bolts.

8. Dawg Daze   .10b
Tough start then mellow climbing near the anchors. 3 bolts.

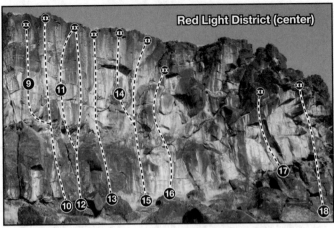

Red Light District (center)

17. Sweaty Betty**.12c/d
Starts on "coral lava" ledge, up overhanging white dihedral. Steep and powerful. 4 bolts.

18. Tension Forever** .11a
Starts on chossy-looking section to white, blocky upper section. Has a tag on first bolt. 5 bolts.

Short broken section of wall

Routes 9-17 are located around the bend and uphill from The Matinee. Approach from beneath Boy Toy and head west along the base of the cliff.

9. Love Canal* .11d/.12a
Start on first 2 ring bolts of Kinky, then cut hard left across loose ledge, then straight up on clean stone. Hard crux! 6 bolts.

10. Kinky* .11b/c
Shares start with Canal. 6 bolts.

11. Love Slave** .10c
Climbs to ledge, then up dihedral to face finish. 6 bolts.

12. Barbara Dare*** .11a/b
Shares start and anchors with Slave. 6 bolts.

13. Girly Mon*** .10d
Up to ledge, then up right-leaning dihedral. 6 bolts.

14. Immaculate Deception** .11b/c
Thin dihedral start, finishes over left side of obvious roof. 6 bolts.

15. Jail Bait** .11c
Same first 3 bolts as Immaculate, then right, up prow. 6 bolts.

16. Boy Toy* .10d/.11a
Climb to ledge then up right-leaning column. 5 bolts.

19. Hollow Weenie*** .12a/b
Down and 20 yards right of Sweaty. White face, thin moves. 5 bolts.

20. Lip Service* .11c
Hard 2nd clip. 3 bolts.

21. Private Dancer* .12c/d
Climbs blunt prow. Short and hard. 3 bolts.

22. The Tease* .10d
4 bolts.

23. Slam, Bam, Thank You Ma'am!** .10c
Blunt arete start. 5 bolts.

24. Scared Stiff*** .11a
Up brown "hourglass" face on small holds, then same finish as Slam. 5 bolts.

25. Every Crimp Needs A Good Ho* .10c
Climb the face just left of the ledge of #22 and finish going over the bulge at the top. Has a tag on it. 4 bolts.

26. WTF* .8
4 bolts.

27. Woody in the Woods** .9
Climb crack to chain anchors. 5 bolts.

28. Marathon Man** .10b
Slab bulging to vertical at top. Shares anchors with No Hips. 5 bolts.

Sue Parsons is not a Girly Mon, .10d.

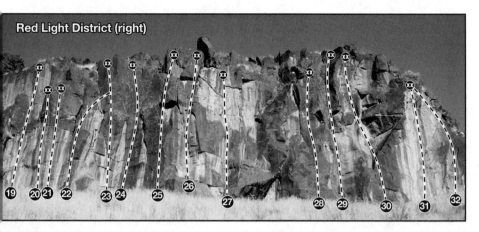

Red Light District (right)

29. No Hips, Hands or Butts** .9
Fun dihedral to hook anchors. 4 bolts.

30. Lay Back and Enjoy* .10b
Bulge to sport anchors. 4 bolts.

31. Tricks Ain't for Kids** .12a/b
Thin, technical white face, hard from the
ground up. 4 bolts.

32. What A Climb, Max!** .12a
Tricky moves, same anchors as Tricks. 4 bolts.

Lightning Bolt Wall
(Morning sun, late afternoon shade)

South-facing wall about 100 yards west of Funny Business Wall.

APPROACH: Follow the approach for Funny Business Wall. Lightning Bolt Wall sits up the
hillside to the left of Legends of the Fall and Samurai Warrior.

1. Lights Out* .9
Begins to the right of white streak. 4 bolts.

2. Lighten Up* .9
5 bolts.

3. All 'Lit Up* .9
4 bolts.

4. Lightning** .10a
Climbs to the left of roof.
4 bolts.

5. Thunder** .11b
Veers right and goes over
small roof. 4 bolts.

**6. Tripping the Light
Fantastic** .10a
4 bolts.

7. I Saw the Light .10a
4 bolts.

8. Light My Fire .10a
4 bolts.

9. Light in the Loafers** .10a
3 bolts.

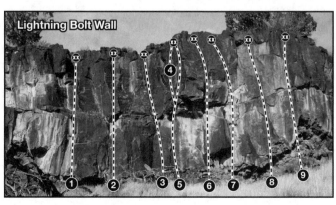

Lightning Bolt Wall

Funny Business (left)

100' to the left

Funny Business Wall
(Morning sun, late afternoon shade)

South-facing wall about 100 yards northwest of Eagle Wall.

APPROACH: Follow the approach for Eagle Wall. Funny Business Wall is located just before reaching Eagle Wall and is up the hill to the left.

1. Legends of the Fall*   .11d
Left side of short, very steep wall. 4 bolts.

2. Samurai Warrior*   .12c
Same anchors as Legends. 4 bolts.

About 100' right

3. Daffy*   .10a
Climbs to a ledge followed by funky movement. 7 bolts.

4. Mickey*   .10c
Up left side of big block, then angle right. Has a name tag on the first bolt. 6 bolts.

5. Minnie*   .10a/b
Right side of block, up blunt arete. Has a name tag on the first bolt. 5 bolts.

6. Goofy*   .12a
Up layback/flare, short and mean! Has a name tag on the first bolt. 4 bolts.

Short broken section of wall

7. What A Crackup*   .10a
Slab to crack to face. Has a name tag on the first bolt. 4 bolts.

8. Die Laughing*   .10b
Slab to dihedral. Has a name tag on the first bolt. 4 bolts.

9. Kamikaze   .13a/b
Drilled mono-digit pockets. 3 bolts.

10. Sick Humor*   .11b
2 cruxes. 7 bolts.

**11. Joke 'Em if They Can't
Take A Fuck*   .11c**
Slab crux. 7 bolts.

12. Vegematic*   .10b
Has a name tag on it. 6 bolts.

13. Slap Stick*   .10d
Arete behind big juniper tree. Has a name tag on first bolt. 5 bolts.

14. No Laughing Matter   .9**
Starts beneath a low roof, climb slab then corner crack. 8 bolts.

15. Jokes On You   .10b**
Climbs the corner. 9 bolts.

Funny Business (right)

16. The Improv* .11b
Climbs funky, blocky arete. 7 bolts.

17. Kermit the Frog** .10c
Good flared dihedral, look for "frog-head" profile at base. 7 bolts.

18. Good for a Laugh or Two* .11c
Bulge start, short dihedral up right side of block, steep face finish. 7 bolts.

19. Funny Business** .10c
Climbs dihedral then shares 2 bolts with Good For A Laugh..., then veers left to a ledge. Lay-back the crack from the ledge then cruise to the anchors. 8 bolts.

20. Yuk It Up* .12b/c
Up to blunt arete, hard moves over bulge, easier but sustained to the anchors. 8 bolts.

21. Giggles*** .11a
Clip the first 3 bolts on Yuk, then 4 more bolts to anchors. 7 bolts.

22. The Punchline* .10c
Up the middle of the face. 7 bolts.

23. Stand Up Comedy* .11c/d
Up prow/slab, several technical, thin cruxes! Clip the first bolt of Laughs. 7 bolts.

24. Just for Laughs** .10b
Starts in short dihedral. 7 bolts.

25. Hee-Haw* .10c
Right-most bolt line. Clip the first 2 bolts of Laughs. 6 bolts.

#26 is located to the right about 20 yards on a short and steep section of a chossy-looking cliff.

26. Pathological Technology** .13a
Short, steep and hard. 3 bolts.

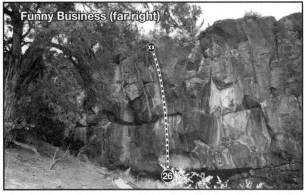

Funny Business (far right)

Eagle Wall (left)

Eagle Wall
(Morning shade, afternoon sun)

West-facing wall at the head of the main canyon. Eagle Wall is home to some of Massacre's longer routes.

APPROACH: Park at the 2nd parking area, locate the trail heading southeast to the canyon's rim. The trail drops and passes through a gap in the fence and keeps descending, heading southeast past Love Connection Wall. At the bottom of the canyon, hike east following the wide sandy trail straight to the head of the canyon. Eagle Wall is the tall, wide formation at the back of the canyon. Average hiking time is around 15 minutes.

1. Stumped** .12a
Left-most bolt line. Short, tricky. 4 bolts.

2. Free as a Bird* .10d
Corner to wide crack to face. 100'. 12 bolts.

3. Rap-Tour* .10a/b
Finishes on left side of pretty brown face. 10 bolts.

4. Eagle Feather* .11c
Variation finish between Rap-Tour and Ruffled Feathers.

5. Ruffled Feathers** .10c/d
Somewhat funky start leads to good climbing up right side of brown face. 10 bolts.

6. Bearly There* .11b
Climbs flare to dihedral. 9 bolts.

7. D.O.A. (a.k.a. Dan's Out of Action)** .12b
Hard flare start, steep, pumpy middle, wild finish, named in honor of "busted finger" first ascent. 9 bolts.

8. Air of the Dog** .11c
Climbs past huge flake, quite sustained and good. 10 bolts.

9. The Eagle Has Landed** .11b/c
Classic stemming. 5 bolts.

10. She's A Screamer** .11d/.12a
Starts left of "cave", over roof, then left to great arete climbing. 11 bolts.

11. My Main Squeeze* .11c/d
Up and right into dihedral. Shares 1st bolt of Screamer. There is a lone red bolt above the 1st bolt of Helter Skelter that appears one could start on Helter then link into either Screamer or Squeeze. 12 bolts.

12. Helter Skelter* .12a
Climbs out of cave, then up and right to halfway anchors. 7 bolts.

13. The Perch*   .11c
Funky start leads to fun moves around left side and up onto jutting horizontal flake, then laybacks up shallow dihedral. 10 bolts.

14. The Diving Board*   .11d
Shares start and finish with The Perch; goes straight up right side of jutting flake. 9 bolts.

15. Bullets and Butterfly Wings***.13a
Finger crack through roof, steep slabs above. Chain anchors. 9 bolts.

16. Big Balls in Cow Town**   .12b
Up left-trending dihedral. 9 bolts.

17. Cowtown Stud**   .12a
Variation start of One Bad Stud. Clip the first 5 bolts of Big Balls, then right and merge with Bad Stud. 9 bolts.

18. One Bad Stud*   .12a
Same start as She Ain't Pretty, then diagonal left and up steep face; sustained and excellent. Shares anchors with She Ain't Pretty. 8 bolts.

19. She Ain't Pretty, She Just Looks That Way**   .11b
Climbs shallow, sustained corner. 8 bolts.

20. Layla*   .11c
Just left of small arete. 9 bolts.

21. Big Hair*   .11d
Up face, over crux roofs at top. 10 bolts.

22. Free Bird*   .11b
Up to tricky right traverse, good steep finish. 1st bolt is on bottom of arete. 9 bolts.

23. Smooth Talker*   .11b/c
Move right up slab start, into slot, steep face finish. 10 bolts.

24. Wildfire**   .12a
Up face/arete/face. 9 bolts.

25. Fire Away**   .12a/b
Shares the first 4 bolts and anchors of Tour, then up the blunt arete/face. 8 bolts.

26. Tour de Pump**   .11b
Up left-leaning, steep ramp, then traverse right across face to slot. 8 bolts.

27. Flies on a Hotdog**   .10a
Starts in big dihedral. 8 bolts.

28. Scary Little Crack   .11a
Mixed. Clip the first 3 bolts of Birdcage then plug gear to the anchors for Birdcage.

Eagle Wall (right)

29. Birdcage .11a
Up left crack for 3 bolts, then traverse right and up right dihedral. 8 bolts.

30. Sideswiped .11c
2 bolt variation of Sidewinder. 8 bolts.

31. Sidewinder** .11d
Traverse right into flare, up face/arete. 8 bolts.

32. Easy Does It* .9
12 bolts.

33. Cornholio .10d
Up corners to steep slabs. 8 bolts.

34. Sudden Down Syndrome* .13a
Climbs blank-looking overhanging corner. Just plain hard! 5 bolts.

35. Barney Rubble* .11b
Climbs up through flare to wide slot to face. 8 bolts.

36. Zippity-Do-Da* .12b
Climbs thin crack/seam crux. 100'. 13 bolts.

37. Prairie Dog .11c
Funky moves up bulge, then up big dihedral with a big, loose-looking block. 11 bolts.

38. Bird of Prey* .12a
Clip the first 6 bolts of Prairie, then right to nice sustained arete/face. 11 bolts.

39. Daydream Believer** .12b
Up hard layback, up flare, then good climbing up face, same finish as Bird of Prey. 11 bolts.

40. The Disease .11d
Tall route with a blocky finish. 12 bolts.

41. Happy-Happy-Joy-Joy** .10d
Up discontinuous dihedrals, 100'. 13 bolts.

42. Good and Plenty* .10d
Clip the first 7 bolts of Happy, then move right into fun dihedral for 5 more bolts, 95'. 12 bolts.

43. Overseer* .12b
Tricky bulge to crux liebacking through roof. 10 bolts.

44. Bladerunner** .11d
Up huge flake, wild!! 7 bolts.

45. Blood, Sweat and Beers** .12c
Wild .12a roof leads to hard crux moves at last 2 bolts. 7 bolts.

46. Father Time* .10a
Right-most line on the wall. Climbs blocky features. 7 bolts.

Echo Point
(Early morning sun, then all day shade)

North-facing wall across the gully, just to the right of Eagle Wall.

APPROACH: Follow the approach for Eagle Wall, then ascend the steep sandy trail to the right. Break off of the trail and climb up the grassy hillside to the base of Echo Point.

1. Echo Phobia   .12a
Climbs prow then 3 bolt face finish. 7 bolts.

2. Out of the Flying Pan*   .11d
Hard start on gray face, step left to pillar, then same finish as Echo Phobia. 7 bolts.

3. Flambé***   .12d
Funky start then up center of overhanging face. One of Massacre's best hard .12's. 9 bolts.

4. Flame On**   .12a
5 bolts up crack/corner then finish on last 3 bolts of Flambé. 8 bolts.

5. Yo-Yo-Ma-Ma*   .11a
Climbs up face/slot/prow. 8 bolts

6. King Kong**   .12b/c
A worthy climb that goes up a hard face and corners. 7 bolts.

Troy Neu feeling the heat on the crux of Flambé, .12d.

223

Summer Wall
(All day shade)

North-facing, red and white streaked wall located directly across the canyon from Funny Business Wall.

APPROACH: Follow the approach for Eagle Wall, however, once at the bottom of the canyon and right after passing Red Light District, look to the right (west) and locate a small alcove: Summer Wall is just left of the alcove. Easy cross country travel will get you to the base of the wall.

1. Summer Hummer**   **.11b**
Left-most route on grayish rock. Fun and sustained climbing. 9 bolts.

2. The Weenie Roast**   **.12a**
Goes up the left side of the dihedral with a crux up high. 7 bolts.

3. The Picnic*   **.10a**
Climbs the right dihedral using the crack and face holds and ends just beneath the big block. Solid for the grade. 6 bolts.

4. Shady Lady**   **.11d/.12a**
Climbs the reddish-brown face. Like other routes on this wall, the crux is low but the climbing is sustained above. 7 bolts.

5. The Air Show*   **.11d**
Climbs the thin crack then up to slabby section. 7 bolts.

6. Summertime Blues**   **.11b**
Engaging and sustained movement throughout. 8 bolts.

7. School's Out*   **.11b/c**
Kind of dirty at the start. Crux down low then good sustained climbing to anchors. 9 bolts.

8. Dog Daze**   **.12a/b**
Right-most route. Starts in the crack then climbs face. 8 bolts.

The Dragon's Den
(Morning shade, afternoon shade)

North facing wall, about 1/4 mile west of Summer Wall.

1. Draggin' Lady**   **.11c**
Boulder up blocky ledge to first bolt, then thin crack to crux face above. 6 bolts.

2. A Fright In Tiny Armor**   **.11d**
Climbs hand crack to thin, bulging face, to dihedral finish. 6 bolts.

3. What The Heck Do I Do Now?*   **.10c**
Climbs right up the snout and the middle of the dragon's forehead. 7 bolts.

Dean Lords on Special Olympics 5.11b, Owl Cove.

225

The King Wall (left)

The King Wall
(Morning shade, afternoon sun)

West facing wall across the canyon from Dance Wall.

Jerry Painter raises the roof at The Party, .10b, King Wall.

1. Here Comes The Sun** .11a
4 bolts.

2. I Am The Walrus** .11c
Shares anchors with Here Comes. 4 bolts.

3. Bad Dog* .11d
Technical jamming above low roof. 3 bolts.

4. Hard Day's Night** .12b
Climbs up hard flare. 3 bolts.

5. Come Together** .10d
5 bolts.

6. King Of Swing* .12b/c
Up brown bulge. 3 bolts.

7. Black Velvet Elvis** .10c
5 bolts.

8. Burning Love** .11c/d
Shares the first 2 bolts with The King. Steep laybacks, same anchors as Black Velvet. 6 bolts.

9. The King** .11a
Climbs through good dihedral. 5 bolts.

10. Don't Be Cruel* .11b/c
More dihedral climbing, shares anchors with The King. 4 bolts.

11. Now Or Never** .12a
Climbs prow. 4 bolts.

12. The Hound Dog* .11a
Thin dihedral. 5 bolts.

13. Jailhouse Rock* .11a
Climbs dihedral, shares 1st bolt and anchors with Hound. 5 bolts.

14. Graceland** .10c
Dihedral to left side of roof. 4 bolts.

15. Got My Mojo Working** .12b
Up blunt arete. 5 bolts.

16. Love Me Tender** .11d
White bulge to roof/layback crack. 4 bolts.

17. The Party* .10b
Shares anchors with Love Me. 4 bolts.

Game Show Wall
(Morning shade, afternoon sun)

West facing wall about 100 yards south of The King Wall.

1. What's My Line?* .10d
Scramble up ledge to first bolt. 5 bolts.

2. T.S. Productions* .10d
Blocky start, through slot, stem the roof, finishes on the face. 6 bolts.

3. Password* .11b
Tough slot start, funky stand-up, face finish. 6 bolts.

4. The Gong Show** .12b/c
Stemming crux low leads to harder, sustained face climbing above. 8 bolts.

5. What's Behind Door #3?** .11c
Stemming start to pumpy block/crack above. 5 bolts.

6. The Price Is Right* .9
Angles right, up corner. 4 bolts.

Bite Me Wall
(Morning sun, afternoon shade)

Located to the right of Choss Factory.

APPROACH: Park at the 2nd parking area, locate the trail heading southeast to the canyon's rim. The trail drops and passes through a gap in the fence. From here turn right and bushwhack southwest for about 150 yards staying near the top of the steep hillside. Bite Me Wall is the first small cliff band encountered.

1. Slap The Bitch* .10b
Left-most route. 5 bolts.

2. Bite Me* .9
Climbs up through orange lichen then left side of prow. 5 bolts.

3. Lichen It* .8
Passes the prow on the right before the anchors. 4 bolts.

4. Whip Me With Barbed Wire** .10d
Follows the fun crack in the middle of the wall. 4 bolts.

5. Eat Me* .9
Angles left then straight up following seam. 4 bolts.

6. Lick Me* .8
Starts in short white dihedral then angles slightly left. 4 bolts.

Choss Factory
(All day sun)

South facing just left of Bite Me Wall.

1. The Chossimator* .10c
Climb up for two bolts and then move left. 5 bolts.

2. Choss Production** .10b
Shares first two bolts with Chossimator then moves left, cool fin holds. 5 bolts.

3. Chossimatic 2000** .11a
Climb up right side of bulbous/chossy roof, use long draw on first bolt then move left. Technical moves to ledge then moderate upper headwall. Shares first bolt with Haulic and anchors with Production. 5 bolts.

4. Choss-A-Haulic** .10a
Shares anchor with Production and 2000, shares first bolt of 2000, fun moves. 5 bolts.

Wall of Zen
(Morning Sun, afternoon shade)

Short, east facing wall about 100 yards right of Dance Wall. These short routes pack a punch.

1. Funky Buddha .9
Deceptive climbing for the grade. 3 bolts.

2. Confusionism** .12a
Tough moves using the seam/crack. 3 bolts.

3. Yen*** .12c
Powerful moves all the way to the anchors. 3 bolts.

4. Yang*** .12b
Shares the first bolt of Yen, then angles right for three more bolts finishing on the obvious sidepull near the anchors. 4 bolts.

5. Zen*** .12d
Hard climbing right off the ground that doesn't let up until the anchors. 3 bolts.

Troy Neu seeks Zen, .12d.

Dance Wall
(Morning Sun, afternoon shade)

East facing, about 150 yards right of The Play Pen.

APPROACH: Park at the 3rd Parking Area. Hop the fence and follow the trail southeast for about 60'. From there the trail drops down into the large alcove that houses the obvious Gang Fight Wall. From Gang Fight, hike cross country due east directly to the visible cliff band, Boulder Wall. From Boulder Wall, stay along the base of the wall passing The Farmyard, The Play Pen and the small Shelter Rock. Dance Wall is about 50 yards right of Shelter Rock.

1. The Side Step**   .11a
Climbs the white face with the crux getting to the first bolt. 4 bolts.

2. The Twist*   .11b
10 yards right of Side Step. 6 bolts.

3. The Fast Waltz*   .11d
Dihedral to blunt arete. 6 bolts.

4. Can-Can*   .10a
Stem the big inside corner about 30 yards right of Waltz. 4 bolts.

5. All Tangoed Up*   .11b
Tricky climbing down low to crack then technical face moves on pockets and edges. 5 bolts.

6. Burley Ballet**   .11a
Big move to hueco at the start then crux in the upper arete. 5 bolts.

Shelter Rock
(Morning Sun, afternoon shade)

About 50 yards left of The Dance Wall. This short, slightly steep wall is usually dry on a rainy day. Use Dance Wall approach.

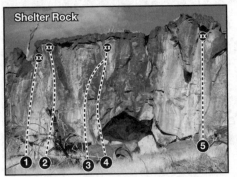

1. The Brat*   .11b
Technical climbing. 4 bolts.

2. Weatherbeater**   .12a
Short but sustained. 4 bolts.

3. Total Denial**   .13b
Bouldery start out of little roof. Shares anchor with Jewel. 4 bolts.

4. Jewel of Denial**   .13a
Climbs out from left side of roof. Powerful! 4 bolts.

5. Shakin' at the Shelter*   .11b
Climb up light tan prow on thin edges to crack finish. 3 bolts.

All American Wall

All American Area

This wall faces south and is broken up into 4 different sections. It is one of the more popular walls at Massacre due to the variety of grades. It is a great area to climb on cooler days.

APPROACH: Park at the 2nd parking area, descend into the canyon heading southeast past Love Connection Wall. At the bottom of the canyon, hike towards the wide gap via a singletrack that heads uphill towards the Dragon's Den but passes it on it's left. Follow the wide sandy trail through the gap heading due south then contour left into the All American Wall area. Average hiking time is around 15 minutes.

All of the walls in this area receive all day sun.

All American Wall
The left-most wall at the All American Area.

1. If I Had An English Accent .9
Blocky climbing. 8 bolts.

2. Little Big Man* .10b
More blocky climbing. 6 bolts.

3. A Sticky Situation** .11d
Fun moves from the ground, up through crack. Keep it together for the crux at the end. 6 bolts.

4. Banana Splits** .11b
Traverse in from the right up into fun dihedral. There is a direct start variation with 2 bolts that looks like holds broke on it that supposedly goes at .12a/b. 6 bolts.

5. Fried Chicken* .11c/d
Dihedral right of Splits. 6 bolts.

6. Wall Street* .10b/c
7 bolts.

7. Main Street* .9
Shares last bolt and anchors with Wall Street. 7 bolts.

8. Kitty Hawk* .10b/c
The bolt count includes the fixed pin for the 2nd clip. 8 bolts.

9. Rockabilly* .11a
Thin slab to bulge, shares 1st bolt, pin and anchors with Kitty Hawk. 8 bolts.

10. Lock And Load Variation* .8
Single bolt easier start to Gear Jammer. 7 bolts.

11. Lock And Load* .11b
Bulging crack at the start that used to be a gear route and named Gear Jammer. 8 bolts.

12. Ugly Old Man* .10b
Shares first 3 bolts of Pretty Woman then cuts left and up into dihedral. 9 bolts.

Rural Wall (left)

13. Pretty Woman*** .11a/b
Starts just right of brown bulge. Hands down one of Massacre's best 5.11's. Sustained! 10 bolts.

14. All American Man*** .12b
Nice face climb to thin crux at mid-route. Great climbing on stellar stone. 10 bolts.

15. Fireworks on the Fourth*** .11a/b
Great face climbing to vertical seam. Sustained. 9 bolts.

16. Miss American Pie** .12a
Climb Fireworks to top of white face then traverses right at 5th bolt and up bulge. Anchors could use relocating. 8 bolts.

17. Snickers* .10c
About 15 yards right of Fireworks. Scramble up past one bolt to big platform to belay. 4 bolts.

18. Peanut Gallery* .10d
Shares start with Snickers. 4 bolts.

Rural Wall
30 yards to the right of All American Wall.

1. Sunny Side Up** .8
Scramble up and belay on ledge. 5 bolts.

2. Burnt Toast** .12b
Up blunt prow, thin!! Belay on ledge. 4 bolts.

3. Biscuits & Gravy** .10a
Climb crack/inside corner. 4 bolts.

4. Butt Cleavage*** .10d
Face just left of arete, hollow flakes. 6 bolts.

5. Totally Agricultural** .10d
Blunt arete, shares anchors with Cleavage. 6 bolts.

6. Prize Fight*** .10c
Fun steep headwall finish. 6 bolts.

7. Wide Load* .7
Top rope up wide slot to Rodeo anchors.

8. Rodeo Queen** .10a
5 bolts.

9. Migrant Labor** .10d
Same finish as Rodeo. 5 bolts.

10. Coyote Bait** .11b
6 bolts.

11. Rawhide*** .9
Starts in corner/slot, up through fun face moves. 6 bolts.

12. Whining Babies** .8
Brown slab start. 7 bolts.

13. Lolita** .10b
Same finish as Whining. 6 bolts.

14. G.I. Joe*** .10c
Fun bulge at top. 5 bolts.

15. Barbie* .10b
Same finish as G.I. Joe. 5 bolts.

16. Fire Inside** .11c
Left-leaning arete. Much better if you climb the direct line on the arete. 6 bolts.

17. Fire Flies .10a/b
Trad climb with fixed pin at top. No anchors.

18. Rosie the Riveter** .11a
Up bulge/face. 6 bolts.

19. Working Man** .10a
Up box dihedral. 6 bolts.

20. Tick Fever** .11c
Fun pockets up top. 7 bolts.

21. Famous Potatoes** .11c
Ends on arete. 6 bolts.

22. Cracker Jacker** .9
Climb the shallow left corner. 7 bolts.

23. Sunshine* .10b
6 bolts.

24. Moonbeam* .10b
5 bolts.

Mike Engle punches the clock on Working Man, .10a.

233

Thelma & Louise Wall

Thelma & Louise Wall

To the right of Rural Wall.

1. Loco-Motive**　　　　　.11a
Fun climbing on nice face. 5 bolts.

2. Derailed*　　　　　　　　.11d
Face to arete. Crack to the left makes it much easier. 4 bolts.

3. Caboose**　　　　　　　.10a
Stem up left side of big block, crux finish. 5 bolts.

4. Kitty's Corner*　　　　　　.9
Climbs dihedral. 5 bolts.

5. Women on the Loose**　　.10c
Block start, bolts up face/shallow arete. 4 bolts.

6. Thelma***　　　　　　.10b
Fun moves up the left side of arete. 6 bolts.

7. And*　　　　　　　　　　.11d
3 bolt start to Thelma-Louise. Tough moves.

8. Louise**　　　　　　　.11a
Up the right side of prow, same finish as Thelma. 6 bolts.

9. The Terminator**　　　　.12b
Climbs the white face to roof. Crux pulling roof. 5 bolts.

10. Border Town*　　　　　.11b
6 bolts.

11. Dream On**　　　　　.12b/c
Starts on ledge behind juniper tree. Easy climbing to crux at bulge. 5 bolts.

South of the Border Wall

To the right of Thelma & Louise Wall.

1. Pasta La Poopa**　　　　.10a
4 bolts.

2. Jalapeño　　　　　　　　　.9
Finishes up wide crack. 3 bolts.

3. Fiesta*　　　　　　　　　.8
Climb up corner. 5 bolts.

4. Cartoon Violence**　.11d/.12a
Tackles the blunt arete at the start to a no-hands rest followed by fun steep headwall finish. 6 bolts.

5. Roadrunner Roof***　　.11d
Starts in white dihedral, exits out left side of big roof, shares anchors with Cartoon. 7 bolts.

6. The Tick**   .13a
Climbs the white face, then directly over roof (crux) to jugs. 6 bolts.

7. Run for the Border***   .11b
Good face/dihedral, just right of the roof. 7 bolts.

8. El Grande Corvette**   .11a
Climbs shallow dihedral. 5 bolts.

9. I-Chi-Hua-Hua***   .12b
Starts out left side of low roof, then up shallow dihedral. 6 bolts.

10. Cinco De Mayo**   .10b
Climbs aesthetic white streaked face to slabby ending. 5 bolts.

11. Stella*   .9
Starts on broken plates then angles left up to fun face. 8 bolts.

12. Zorro**   .10a
Fun and long climb. Angles left near the last 2 bolts. 8 bolts.

13. Speedy Gonzales**   .9
Starts on boulder/ledge. 7 bolts.

14. Dos Equis*   .10a
Starts on big block, just right of Speedy. 7 bolts.

Brandon Barlow on Hasta La Poopa, .11c

Terran Engle mid-crux on I-Chi-Hua-Hua, .12b. Photo by Mike Engle.

15. Low Rider*   .10a
4 bolts.

16. Hasta La Hoopla*   .11c
First bolt has a tag on it. 6 bolts.

17. The Breeze***   .9
Climbs wide corner. 6 bolts.

18. Jose Can You See***   .10c
Up steep face. 6 bolts.

19. Star Spangled Banger***   .10a
Climbs blunt arete. 6 bolts.

20. Easier Said Than Done**   .10d
Climbs dihedral, shares anchors with Star Spangled. 6 bolts.

21. Mexican Standoff*   .10c
Climbs fun face to left side of the arete. Chain link hangers. 7 bolts.

Routes 20-22 are located up and to the right in a small alcove.

22. Acapulco Cliff Diving**   .11b
Climbs right side of arete. 5 bolts.

Lisa Safford starting up Speedy Gonzales, .9.

23. Little Miss Muffet*   **.9**
Starts on ramp about 20 feet right of Acapulco.
5 bolts.

24. The Hobo**   **.11a**
Fun steep face. 4 bolts.

Routes 23-25 are located down and to the right.

25. Tres Hombres**   **.11d**
Short, fun climb up brown prow. 3 bolts.

26. Caca-Mongo**   **.11b**
Steep face. 7 bolts.

27. Tequila Sunrise**   **.13c**
Overhanging white face, around the corner from Caca. 5 bolts.

Le Petite Covette

Southwest-facing cirque about 1/8 mile east of All American Area. The Covette area includes Runt Wall, Red Wall, French Wall and Hobbit Wall. The individuals walls are listed clockwise, starting with Runt Wall.

APPROACH: Follow the directions to All American Area and keep hiking past the South of the Border area toward the back of the canyon. Average hiking time is around 20 minutes.

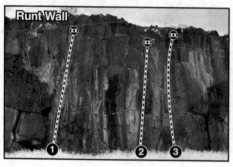

Runt Wall
(All day sun)

Red Wall
(Early morning shade, then all day sun)

APPROACH: Follow the directions to All American Area and keep hiking past the South of the Border area toward the back of the canyon. This small wall is located directly across the canyon from Hobbit Wall and left of the Red Wall.

These 3 routes on the short south-facing wall to the left of French Wall on the left side of the big sand hill.

1. El Rojo* .10b
Starts in white streaked corner then up steep section and left to anchors. 5 bolts.

1. Half Pint* .10a
3 bolts.

2. Crimson Ghost** .10a
Starts in white dihedral. 4 bolts.

2. PeeWee* .10a
3 bolts.

3. Bloodshot Thighs*** .8
Starts just right of white dihedral. Shares anchors with Crimson. 4 bolts.

3. Small Fry .10a
3 bolts.

French Wall
(Morning shade, afternoon sun)

Located in the back of the canyon on the right. French Wall is home to a handful of Massacre's best routes.

1. Unknown* .11c
Left-most route behind tree. Has 2nd set of anchors higher up. 4 bolts.

4. Solitaire* .11c/d
Just left of manky/wide crack. 5 bolts.

5. Whee-Whee** .11c
Hard start out of small roof, hard finish if you go up from 4th bolt; off-route finish if you hand traverse right after 3rd bolt. 4 bolts.

2. French Kissing** .9
Used to be a trad route. 5 bolts.

3. Mon Amie* .11d
Climbs arete/face. 6 bolts.

6. Truffles** .11a
Fun start to steep finish on typical Massacre micro pockets. 8 bolts.

7. Totally French*** .12b
Steep face left of big roof. A route with a bit of everything. One of Massacre's best .12's. 8 bolts.

8. All Naturale** .10c
Climbs the left side of the roof via crack. Used to be trad. 8 bolts.

9. Pepe La'Peau** .10d
Just right of roofs. 7 bolts.

10. This Smoo is for You** .10c
Fun route. If you're old enough, you may recognize the SMOO feature at the start of the route. 7 bolts.

11. Mr. McGoo** .10b
Dihedral just right of SMOO. 6 bolts.

12. Honor Amongst Friends** .11d
10 yards right of SMOO, starts just right of little roof, then up sustained face, good! 8 bolts.

13. The Guillotine* .10d
Stemming start, over small roofs, to crux bulge. 8 bolts.

14. French Toast* .10a
Same start as Guillotine, then right and up slot. 7 bolts.

15. Water Lilly** .10b
Better than it looks. 5 bolts.

16. Water Louie* .12b/c
Hard laybacks! 5 bolts.

Matt Reymann near the top of Water Lilly, .10b.

239

6. What's It's Gots In It's Pockets*** .11b/c
Great finger pockets, thin moves, steep face. Classic. 8 bolts.

7. Hobbit Forming* .10a
Trad/Mixed. Crack just right of #6. Finishes on last 2 bolts of #6.

8. Menage-a-Trois** .12b/c
Crux start, sustained middle, juggy finish. 3 bolts.

• 2 projects

Royalty Point
(All day shade)

This north-facing wall is south of All American Wall across the canyon.

1. In Search Of The Holy Flail** .11d
Climbs up long face that goes over small roof half-way up. 7 bolts.

2. Sir Laughs-Alot** .10d
Another fun line just right of In Search Of. 8 bolts.

3. King Sighs* .11b
Finger crack start. 7 bolts.

4. Queen Sighs* .11b/c
Technical stemming. 6 bolts.

Hobbit Wall
(Morning shade, afternoon sun)

To the right of French Wall, faces northwest.

1. Magic Rings** .11b
Funky 2-bolt start to big ledge, then 6 bolts of fun climbing up crack/face. 8 bolts.

2. Gandalf Takes A Wiz* .12a
Start on Magic Rings, then straight up from big ledge to crux arete moves, then sustained climbing finishing near big nest. A bit dirty up top. 7 bolts.

3. Hobbit Heaven*** .10c/d
Great face climb. Clip 1st bolt then scramble up to big ledge and head left. 7 bolts.

4. Gollum*** .11c/d
Sustained climbing on steep arete. Another classic Massacre 5.11. 10 bolts.

5. Bilbo On A Bungee*** .11a
5 bolt start variation to What's It's Gots. Merges at the 6th bolt.

Royalty Point

Mighty-Mite Wall
(Morning shade, afternoon sun)

This wall is about 150 yards south of Royalty Point. Mighty-Mite is short and west facing.

1. Fearless Fly*   .10c
4 bolts.

2. Atom Ant*   .9
3 bolts.

3. Under Dog**   .11b
Good route with an exciting finish. 3 bolts.

4. Mighty Mouse**   .12a
Fun but contrived for the grade. 4 bolts.

The Morgue
(Morning sun, afternoon shade)

Short, steep, southeast facing wall about 100 yards southwest of All American Wall.

1. Near Death Experience*   .12b/c
Long first move, height dependent. 4 bolts.

2. Rigormortis**   .13a
Stick clip first bolt, shares last two bolts and anchor with Near Death. 4 bolts.

3. Sex After Death*   .12d
Short and hard. 3 bolts.

4. R.I.P.**   .10b
Bulge start to fun crack. 3 bolts.

5. Final Wresting Place***   .12a
Starts in crack then angles left below the anchors on fun moves. 4 bolts.

6. Movin' On Up*   .10a
Stemming corner. 3 bolts.

7. Pine Box Derby**   .11d
Crux finish. 4 bolts.

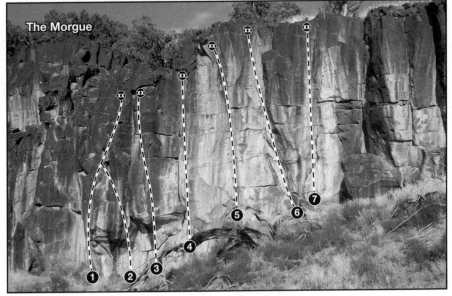

Camptown Towers

About 100 yards west of the southwest corner of the Owl Cove are short towers, named for the nearby remains of an old camp stove.

East Tower
(All day shade)

Four short routes on the overhanging north side.

1. Musket Balls*   .11c
Left route, kind of gritty. 3 bolts.

2. Beaver Trap*   .12a/b
Take a poke in the hole, then get a good pump gettin' over the hump! 3 bolts.

3. Mountain' Men**   .11d
A rough and rowdy ride! 4 bolts.

4. Buffaloed Gals*   .10d
Tricky moves at both ends. 3 bolts.

West Tower
(Morning shade, afternoon sun)

Three short routes on the west side.

1. Poker Face**   .12a
You'll crack a smile getting up the slab/arete! 4 bolts.

2. Buckshot Dan*   .11d
Burly bulge! 4 bolts.

3. Full Quiver**   .11c
Shoot up the bulge, then aim for the right-side arete. 4 bolts.

242

Owl Cove

U-shaped cove about 1/4 mile west, down river, of the Main Wall.

APPROACH: Access is gained from parking at the 2 parking area, hiking southeast toward the All American Area, then south to Mighty Mite Wall followed by the Camptown Towers. From there the mouth of the cove is obvious as the wide trail veers northeast into Owl Cove. Average hiking time is around 25 minutes.

Climbs are listed clockwise, starting at the mouth of the cove on the west wall.

Cling/Clang Wall
(Morning sun, afternoon shade)

East facing wall on the west side at the mouth of Owl Cove. The left half of the wall features shorter, steeper routes on white, blocky featured basalt.

1. Dry Hump*   .11a
Crux getting over roof. 4 bolts.

2. Pink Slip*   .8
Somewhat inconspicuous climbing until 3rd bolt. 3 bolts.

3. Bolter's Ed**   .9
Fun climbing up big holds to right leaning flake/crack. 4 bolts.

4. Cling**   .11a/b
Steep start to easier climbing above. 5 bolts.

5. Clang**   .11c
Climbs directly above 2nd bolt (crux) then merges with Cling. 4 bolts.

6. Spring Spawner**   .11c/d
Goes straight up and over bulge at 3rd bolt. 5 bolts.

7. Jabberwocky*   .10c
Tricky climbing at 4th bolt to anchors. 4 bolts.

8. Wild Thang**   .12a/b
Funky climbing for first 2 bolts then powerful crux at 5th bolt using undercling. 6 bolts.

9. The Wild Side**   .11a/b
Starts in corner. Move left onto arete/face, then climb right-leaning slab to bottom of headwall. Fun headwall finish. 9 bolts.

10. The Vile Side*   .11d/.12a
4 bolt variation to the start of Wild Side.

11. The Mild Side*   .10d/.11a
Short-but-fun face. Anchors? 3 bolts.

Owl Wall

Owl Wall
(Morning sun, afternoon shade)

East-facing wall on west side of Owl Cove. About 30 yards right of Cling/Clang Wall.

1. Bitch Slap*　　　　　　　.10a
Ends on top of big block. 5 bolts.

2. 5.8'sh*　　　　　　　　　.8
Climbs fun blocky section. 6 bolts.

3. Bad Date*　　　　　　　　.8
Climbs crack and blocky section. Trad.

4. Get Laid**　　　　　　　.10d
Tricky layback crux. 10 bolts.

5. Heavy Petting**　　　　.9/.10a
Starts beneath small roof. Shares anchors with Get Laid. 6 bolts.

6. First Date**　　　　　　　.9
Climbs the corner and crack through small roof. Trad.

7. DV8**　　　　　　　　　.11b
Blunt corner to face, thin crux! 9 bolts.

8. Space Violator***　　　　.11a
Climbs the center of the face. Pumpy top section. 8 bolts.

9. Black Mamba**　　　　　.11b
Same start as Space Violator, then right and up, tricky laybacks. 6 bolts.

10. Project?　　　　　　　　.?
2 bolts at start of crack. Shares anchors with Face Shot?

11. Face Shot*　　　　　　　.10c
7 bolts.

12. Space Shot*　　　　　　.10b
Tricky blunt arete/face. Runout between 4th & 5th bolt. 6 bolts.

13. Jeff-Boy-R.D.　　　　　　.10b
Climbs left-facing corner to blocky face. Left side of slab. 6 bolts.

14. Holey Trojans**　　　　.12a
Middle of steep slab, thin moves! 4 bolts.

15. Hot Date**　　　　　　.11a
Right side of slab, shares anchors with Holey Trojans. 4 bolts.

16. Date Bait*　　　　　　.9/10a
Climbs the corner. 3 bolts.

17. Wet Dreams**　　　　　.10b
Up blunt prow. No anchors. Must belay from Date Bait anchors. 4 bolts.

18. Tow Job　　　　　　　　.12d
Climbs the steep slab on micro thin crimps. 3 bolts.

19. The Slob*　　　　　　.11b/c
Funky moves. 3 bolts.

• *project to the far right of #19*

Asylum Wall Upper Ledge (left)

Asylum Wall
(Morning shade, afternoon sun)

West-facing wall on east side of Owl Cove. The wall is broken up into 2 sections: The Ledge section and the Lower Section.

The Ledge Section

1. ADHD** .10a
Starts on the 1st bolt of Sociopath then veers left and up. 8 bolts.

2. Sociopath** .10b/c
The slash grade depends on which side of the bolt line you climb. Left side is easier. 8 bolts.

3. Psychopath** .10c
Has a tag on 1st bolt. 9 bolts.

4. Coma Toes** .10d
Short arete route. 5 bolts.

5. Waiter, There's A Fly In My Supe*.10a
7 bolts.

6. Welcome to the Funny Farm** .11d
Good face moves. 8 bolts.

7. Chalk Therapy** .10b/c
7 bolts.

8. Straight Jacket** .12a
Climbs the black bulge to face. Funky moves. 6 bolts.

9. Committed* .13b/c
Direct start to Straight Jacket. Joins at 3rd bolt. 6 bolts.

10. Brain Dead But Good in Bed* .10c
Up overhanging flare, weird moves! 9-10 bolts.

11. Acrophobia* .11b
Starts on crack/slot. 6 bolts.

12. Psycho Billy* .11c/d
Up left side of huge block. 6 bolts.

13. Sweethearts of the Rodeo* .11a/b
Up right side of block. Shares last bolt and anchors with Psycho Billy.

14. Perverts Pleasure** .12a
Sustained, up two parallel seams to dihedral finish. Easier if you use the block out to the left. 6 bolts.

15. Cat-a-tonic** .12a
Thin face climb. 6 bolts.

16. Pavlov's Dogs** .12b
White face just left of obvious roof, great!! 8 bolts.

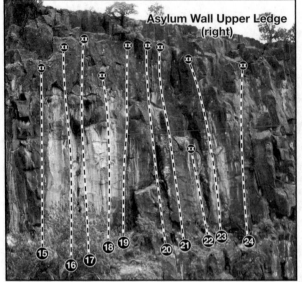

Asylum Wall Upper Ledge (right)

17. Oedipus Complex* .11b
Climbs through big roof. 6-7 bolts.

18. Maniac** .12d
Climbs white face, one of Massacre's best hard routes. 6 bolts.

19. Amnesia** .11c
Climbs up through crux flare. 7 bolts.

20. It's Time for Your Medication .11c
Kind of contrived. 10 bolts.

21. Pathological Flyer* .11c/d
Excellent and varied moves. 10 bolts.

22. Zigman Void** .11d/.12a
Z-seam face. 4 bolts.

23. Freudian Slip** .11a
Great concave crack/face. 8 bolts.

24. Off Your Rocker* .10d
Sustained. Last route on the right side of the ledge. 9 bolts.

The Lower Section

25. Still Crazy After All These Years* .11d
Blunt arete, sharp crimps. Located directly below #24. 4 bolts.

26. Demonic Possession .11c/d
Second crack right of Still Crazy, behind big juniper. Trad.

27. Delirious* .11a/b
Next crack to the right. Trad.

28. Seizure* .12c
Climbs arete. Easier (.11c) if you use the crack to the right. 4 bolts.

29. Nut Case* .10a
Tall route. Used to be trad and named Slippin' Post. Has a rusted tag on first bolt. 14 Bolts.

30. Serial Driller**.11d/.12a
Long with several cruxes. 15 bolts.

31. Crack Baby** .10b
Tall route that used to be trad and named Rattled-er. 14 bolts.

32. Nurse Ratchet* .10a
Climbs funky shaped plates. Gritty in spots. 4 bolts.

33. Dr. Feelgood* .11c/d
11 bolt extension of Nurse Ratchet.

34. Ted's & Marty's Wonderful Adventure* .10d
Long pro crack, left of obvious large face. Trad.

Asylum Wall Lower Section (left)

35. Sketch-O-Frantic .11c
Up right side of face, kind of loose rock at start, gets better, funky moves, steep finish. 14 bolts.

36. Daddy Needs His Medicine* .10c
Nice tall route that used to be trad. 16 bolts.

37. Yo Riley Crack* .11a
Starts on left side of short pillar. 12-13 bolts.

38. No Mo Natural Pro* .11d
Starts on short pillar, then right, stemming start to crack, crux face finish. 11-12 bolts.

39. Split Personality** .12b
Starts in corner left of the arete, to ledge, then wild finish. 8 bolts.

40. Airhead** .11c
Up hand-jam crack to great, steep finish. 11 bolts.

41. Pain Thriller** .11c/d
Starts in thin, tough finger crack, then up and left for steep face finish. 8 bolts.

42. Loco* .10d
6 bolts.

43. Unnamed* .10b
Climbs the corner crack to the left of Everybody…and shares anchors. Either trad or toprope.

44. Everybody and Their Dog** .11a
Climb wild, detached pillar. 5 bolts.

45. Lunatic* .10c/d
Starts on first 2 bolts of Delirium, then left for 4 bolts, finishes on same anchors with Delirium. One of Massacre's best stemming climbs. 6 bolts.

46. Delirium Tremens* .11a
Face right of pillar. 5 bolts.

47. Wild Virus** .10d
Fun route. 6 bolts.

48. Special Olympics** .11b
Climb crack to blunt, brown arete, crux is thin finish. 7 bolts.

49. Dead Man Walking* .10c
This route can be used an alternative approach route to access the routes on the Jail House Wall routes on the upper ledge. However, Red Shank on Rubble Wall is more commonly used. Has a tag on first bolt. 7 bolts.

Rubble Wall

Watchtower Wall

Jail House Wall
(Morning sun, afternoon shade)

These next 3 routes are perched high above the ground on a big hanging ledge that runs from Asylum Wall to Rubble Wall. Access is gained by climbing either Dead Man Walking, Red Shank (Rubble Wall), or rapping in from above. See Asylum Wall Lower Section (right) topo.

1. Jail Break**   **.10c**
Left-most route. 6 Bolts.

2. Back On The Chain Gang***   **.10c**
6 Bolts.

3. Chain Breaker***   **.11a**
Climbs nice-looking brown stone. 6 Bolts.

Rubble Wall
(Morning sun, afternoon shade)

Located on the right, outside point of Owl Cove.

1. Barn Stormer*   **.9**
Climbs a corner to a ledge, then up dihedral to a face. Finishes on stemming moves in wide corner. Has a tag on first bolt. 7 bolts.

2. Lone Ranger**   **.10a**
Climbs to the left of the bush following a pillar-like formation then through dihedral. 12 bolts.

3. Red Shank**   **.9**
Climbs to the right of the bush. This is the usual approach pitch to access the Jail Break Wall. Has a tag on first bolt. 7 bolts.

4. Puppy Chow*   **.10a**
Climbs past a chain link bolt to ledge, then to a series of corners, then finishes at anchors in large roof. 7 bolts.

5. Double-Dog-Dare**   **.11c/d**
Climbs the first 3 bolts of Puppy Chow, then moves right and up over the hard bulge past 5 more bolts. 8 bolts.

Watchtower Wall
(Morning sun, afternoon shade)

Broken looking area between Rubble Wall and the Main Wall. Best approached by traversing from Owl Cove.

1. Watchtower*   **.10b**
Starts on gritty section to broken face, and finishes on prow. 12 bolts.

2. Cryday the 13th*   **.11a**
The rock quality and movement gets much better after the first few bolts. There is a belay anchor on the ledge about 16' off the ground. 8 bolts.

3. The Whinery**   **.11c/d**
Starts on Cryday, then veers right after 3rd bolt up hard finger crack and over bulges. Finishes on nice, steep reddish face. 9 bolts.

The 1/4 mile long, 200' tall Main Wall as seen from the Snake River. Photo by Mike Engle.

Main Wall Area

(Morning sun, afternoon shade)

This long wall faces southeast, just above the river and is broken up into 8 different sections. However, with the first 6 sections there really is no defining differential separating them.

Some of the routes have tags on the 1st bolt to help climbers get their bearings.

NOTE: Some of the routes require a 2-rope rappel to lower safely to the ground. Make sure to have an extra rope on hand and place a knot in the end of the lead rope. Also, some of the bolt counts on these routes are a visual estimate from the ground – make sure to pack a few extra draws.

APPROACH: The most direct way to access the Main Wall area is to canoe from the State Park directly across the river. However, most climbers choose to drive in from the north (the "back-side") using the main driving approach for all of the other areas and parking at the 1st Parking Area. From there pass through fence and hike along the main 2 track road for about .4 mi. as it heads south toward the river. Make sure to adhere to the main road and do not take any of the intersecting ATV paths. At about .4 mi. there is a faint 2-track that veers

left marked by a cairn – that is the route to Windmill Wall, The Outback and Down Under Wall. Keep on the main dirt road as it cuts right and heads southwest for about .3 mi. before veering south again making sure to stick to the main road. At this point there should be a shallow depression that flows toward the river. Bushwack toward the edge of the cliff and locate the break in the cliffs to scramble down to the base of the walls. Left-Wing Wall is immediately to the left.

Alternatively, one can hike to the mouth of Owl Cove and head upstream along the river to the beginning of Left-Wing Wall.

Left-Wing Wall
Left-most climbs on the Main Wall.

1. Arch Enemy* .10b
Starts above the small natural stone arch. Formerly called GRIM R.P.er rated 5.9+ with a fixed pin, it is now fully bolted. 8 bolts.

2. Sundance** .10b
Climbs arete. 11 bolts.

3. Moonstruck** .11a
Angles left at the start and climbs over funky, blocky roof. Has a fun upper face. 11 bolts.

4. Ice Breaker .8
Top-rope face/crack.

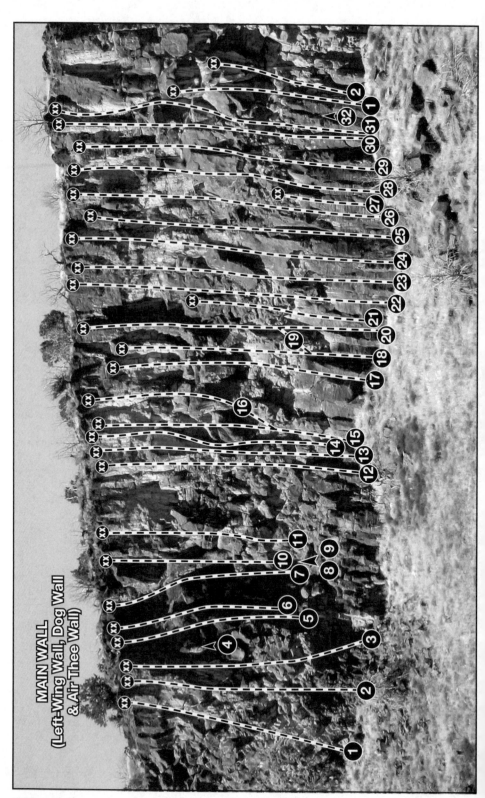

MAIN WALL
(Left-Wing Wall, Dog Wall
& Air Thee Wall)

5. Three Dogs For A Dollar* .11a
Bolted slab/face, starts on upper ledge. 9 bolts.

6. Hole-In-The-Wall .7
Chimney in deep corner, upper ledge start. Trad.

Dog Wall

7. Outlaw Trail .8
Large crack, right side. Trad?

8. Deputy Dog .10c(R)
Climbs the crack on trad gear. Located ? Trad.

9. Chili Dogs .10b/c
Crack system. Located ? ? bolts.

10. Lethal Rejection* .11c/d
Bulge to steep headwall, upper ledge start. 9 bolts.

11. Dog Fight* .11c
Starts on upper ledge. Trad.

12. Obedience School* .11a
Climbs crack. 10 bolts.

13. The Dog Pound* .11a/b
Climbs through prow/arete. 11 bolts.

14. The Mad Dog .11a/b
Wild crack climb. Trad.

15. The Mongrel* .11b
Several cruxes. Bolts.

16. Birddog** .11c/d
Starts on first three bolts of The Mongrel, then straight up, over funky bulge to steep, fun face. 12 bolts.

17. The Dog Catcher** .11d
Starts in wide crack, up bulge, steep upper face/corner. Bolts.

18. Dog At Large* .11b
Fun route. Bolts.

19. Dog Slide** .10c
Link-up. Start on Dog At Large, finish on Slip Slide'n Away.

Air Thee Wall

20. Slip Slide'n Away* .11a
Climbs steep slab (crux), then fun, but somewhat run-out climbing up arete, left of large, right-facing corner system, 90'. 11 bolts.

21. Grease Monkey* .11b/c
Slab climb, 60'. 9 bolts.

22. Air Thee Well** .11b/c
Crack to slab, to overhanging headwall, classic. Trad.

23. Be Scared And Hold On Tight* .11b
Wild slab, through roof, to overhanging crack. 100'.11 bolts.

24. Off-Ramp** .12a
Start on short block, up slabby column to wild whitesh scoop. Finish on steep arete. 11 bolts.

25. Overpass* .10c
Good moderate line that climbs up through open book/crack then through the roof (crux). Used to be trad. 14 bolts.

26. Country Rhoads .10a/b
Crack through bulge. Direct finish would be good, harder but would need bolts. Trad.

27. Cruise'n The Strip* .11a/b
5 bolts.

28. Freeway* .10a
1 bolt start. Wanders, finish in steep open book. 120'. Mixed.

29. Streets Of Fire* .11a
Finishes on arete. 14 bolts.

30. Sherlock Moans* .10c
100'. First half rather loose and blocky, excellent arete finish. 15 bolts.

31. Ted's Date Route* .9
Gear line through bulge, up nice slot/book. Trad.

32. All Riled Up .10c
Top-rope.

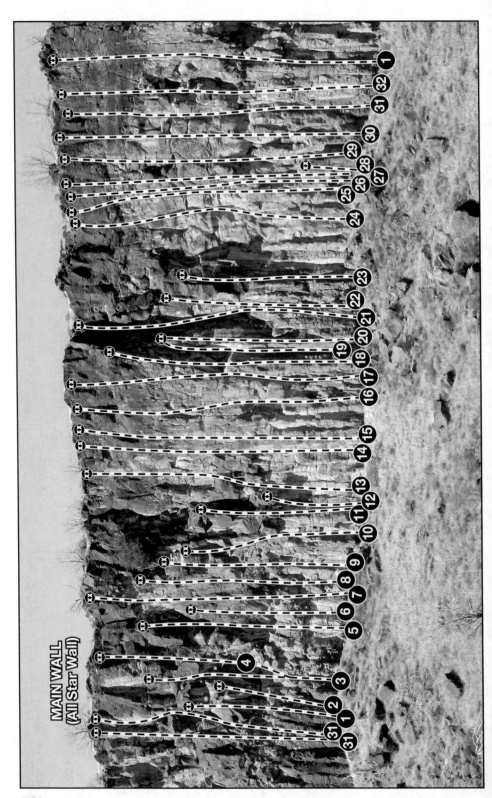

MAIN WALL
(All Star Wall)

All Star Wall

1. Get Primate Or Fly Mate*   **.12a/b**
Climbs thin, flared crack, then face finish, 70'. 8 bolts.

2. Voodoo Child*   **.12a**
Short, steep and fun! 7 bolts.

3. Castles Made Of Sand*   **.10b**
Climb first 3 bolts of Dirty Dancing then veer left for 6 more bolts up right facing corner. Steep with big holds, a good warm-up. 9 bolts.

4. Dirty Dancing*   **.10d**
Up and a bit right through overhanging plates and cracks, 90'. 11 bolts.

5. Wingin' In The Rain*   **.12a**
Crack through roof, face finish, steep and hard. 10 bolts.

6. Debra Winger*   **.11c/d**
Classic face and laybacks, 75'. 6 bolts.

7. Lock-Up*   **.11b**
Long with lots of climbing, wild finish, 110'. 11 bolts.

8. Jack The Whipper*   **.11d/.12a**
Classic overhanging face to finger crack, 85'. 10 bolts.

9. Disturbing The Peace*   **.11d**
Continuously steep. 12 bolts.

10. Gravitron   **.11a**
Kind of dirty, starts in dihedral. 75'. 10 bolts.

11. Get A Grip*   **.11c**
Continuously cruxy, 75'. 8 bolts.

12. White Trash*   **.12a**
Short and hard. Crux from 4th to 5th bolt. 5 bolts.

13. Mommy's Little Monster*   **11b/c**
Rap-chain halfway, upper part is easier and real fun, 110'. 13 bolts.

14. Nasty Dread Locks*   **.12a**
Long and hard, with several variations; right finish is the best & hardest. 15 bolts.

15. Missing Link*   **.11c**
This was the first bolted route at Massacre and one of it's best. 115'. 15 bolts.

16. Honey Come Down*   **.11c**
Climbs through roof/bulge, up headwall, continuously cruxy, 115'. 12 bolts.

17. Meltdown*   **.11b**
Pro crack to headwall, then left and up on 3 bolts, and finish on trad. 120'. Mixed.

18. The Bully At Muscle Beach*   **.12b/c**
Starts just right of arete. First crux (Muscle Beach) is .12a; overhanging headwall finish (The Bully) has crux at the top, 120'. 13 bolts.

19. Totally Tubular*   **.11b**
Finish on bolted headwall(?) or finish on Good Flyday. Pro crack.

20. Good Flyday*   **.12b**
Overhanging face, several cruxes, good for a pump! 80'. 11 bolts.

21. The Mummy   **.10c**
Pro crack through roof. Trad.

22. Ho! Yo-Yo-Yo!*   **.11c**
Starts on poor rock, finishing moves are worth the climb, 60'. 8 bolts.

23. Time Keeps On Slip'n, Slip'n, Slip'n*.12a
Crux at upper arching finger crack, sustained, 60'. Trad.

24. Crank Calls*   **.11c**
Climbs through funky slots, then left to steep headwall, 120'. 14 bolts.

25. Joy Ride.**   **11c**
Shares several moves with Crank Calls, then goes right, up through wide slot, 120'. 13 bolts.

26. Snow Job*   **.11c**
Climbs face and flared crack, shares a move or two with Toxic Socks. Pumpy, steep crack/face finish, 125'. 13 bolts.

27. Toxic Socks Syndrome*   **.10d**
Starts just left of short free-standing pillar, pumpy. 125'. 14 bolts.

28. Waylaid Pillar   **.11d**
Hard clips. 2 bolts.

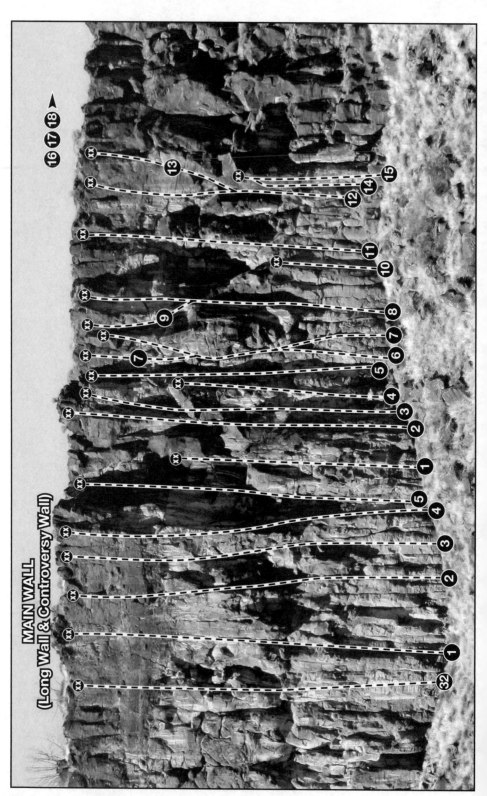

29. Waylaid* .11b
Starts on the right side of the pillar, through crux at flare/roof, 120'. 15 bolts.

30. Career Of The 90's*** .11c/d
Great moves, 120'. 12 bolts.

31. Mass-A-Crack* .11b
Great gear route in crack through flared roof, to bolts on overhanging headwall. Trad.

32. Yolanda** .11d
Hard face at bottom, wild bulge, good steep headwall finish, 125'. 15 bolts.

Long Wall Area

1. Firefall* .12a
Climbs through bulge/roof, sustained, continuously technical, good in spite of some flaky rock, 130'. 14 bolts.

2. Dale's Roof
Top-rope project up corner to roof/headwall.

3. Black Tide* .11d
Long & steep. 16 bolts.

4. Danger Zone** .12a
One of the best long routes at Massacre; good for a monster forearm pump! Original line goes straight up to a rest ledge, then a wild traverse left, (.11d). Best variation diagonals left, avoiding the rest ledge. Take your pick. 18 bolts.

5. All Jammed Up .11c
First part is somewhat dirty, past pin, to right-facing corner; upper face is fantastic, pumpy climbing, 130'+. Trad.

Controversy Wall Area

1. The Stranger* .11c/d
Funky moves, step left at crux, then up and right. 12 bolts.

2. Ambushed* .11c
Crux at bush, lots of good climbing. NOTE: climbs over a Canadian goose nest. Don't climb this route in the spring if geese are around. 16 bolts.

3. Deluxe Aggravation .10d/11a
Starts in corner, through roofs and bulges, past fixed pin, finish on steep headwall, 130'. Trad.

4. A Surprise For Mom** .12a
Climbs steep face/arete. Great power moves off small holds, 60'. A Mother's Day gift! 9 bolts.

5. Public Enema #1** .11a/b
Crux is from second-to-third bolt, steep, pumpy finish. 14 bolts.

6. Cooked Goose* .11c
Face to overhanging crack to arete finish; plenty of great, hard climbing, 125'. 14 bolts.

7. Chasing Wild Geese* .11a
Pro crack, shares overhanging crack with Cooked Goose, then left up crack system. Trad.

8. The Slot Machine** .11d/.12a
Hard and sustained from the start, the crux is above the mid-way anchors, arete finish, 125'. 16 bolts.

9. The Slots* .11c
Natural cracks above the mid-way anchors on The Slot Machine, straight up or left into corner. Mixed.

10. Robbin' The Cradle* .11c
Thin crack, short but fun, 35'. 4 bolts.

11. In Your Face* .12a/b
Dirty start, good crux moves over bulge, good 5.11 climbing above. 11 bolts.

12. Swing Dancing* .11a
Start in corner/wide crack with sharp chockstone, up chimney, then go left to face with thin crack,120'. Trad.

13. Chorus Line* .8
Same start as Swing Dancing, but go right after chimney, good natural pro, varied, 120'. Trad.

14. The Pillar** .11c
Natural crack line, using only the top bolt for finish face moves, 40'. Mixed.

15. The Weenie* .11a/b
Controversial bolt addition to The Pillar. Stemming left and clipping bolts makes it easier and wimpy. 5 bolts.

16. Airwaves* .10c
About 30 yards right of The Weenie, beyond the old fence, 50'. Not pictured. 8 bolts.

17. Stand By For Technical Difficulties* .11b
Not pictured. 9 bolts.

18. AM/FM* .11c
50'. Not pictured. 8 bolts.

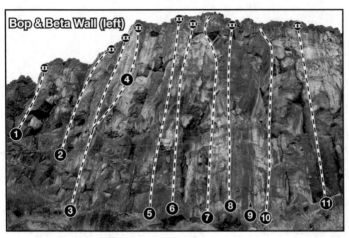

Bop & Beta Wall (left)

7. The Austin Shuffle* .11b
Natural crack/corner system through left corner/roofs, 125'. Trad.

8. Ah Vue Reggae* .11a
Climbs face, through roof/bulge, onto slab face, 125'. Has a tag on the first bolt. 10 bolts.

9. Marty's Wild Idea
Project on right side of slab.

Bop and Beta Wall

APPROACH: Follow the directions to The Outback but do not descend. Stay on top of the cliff following the trail as it parallels the rim heading southwest for about 1/4 mi. looking for a somewhat obvious shallow drainage that leads to a wide break in the cliff. There is a trail on the left that allows access to the base of the cliff. The Wild Life Preserve is just to the right. Bop and Beta Wall is about 100' downstream.

1. If You Ain't Crankin' It You Must Be Spankin' It** .11d
Starts on upper ledge, 60'. 6 bolts.

2. A Face In The Crowd** .10b
Fun face climb, starts on right edge of upper ledge, 75'. 8 bolts.

3. The Beta Garden** .10c
Starts on first two bolts of Dorque Convertor, then up and left, finishes on great arete, 95'. 9 bolts.

4. Dorque Converter** .12a/b
Shares start with Beta Garden, then right and up overhanging headwall. Technical and pumpy! 110'. 12 bolts.

5. Bop'Til You Drop* .11d
Climbs through bulges, wild layback crux, hard clip!, 125'. 12 bolts.

6. Life Of Riley* .11c
Starts off boulder, crux is bulge half-way up. 13 bolts.

10. If You're Not Pro'n It, You're Blowin' It* .9
Natural crack line/corner system inside right facing corner, through roof, 100'. Trad.

11. Critical Mass** .11d
Crux is above ledge, then sustained face; technical and pumpy, 90'. 13 bolts.

20 yard break in routes

12. Vanna White .11b/c
Top rope project on ledge above broken rock.

13. Dancing With Myself** .10c
Roof start to slab/face to steep finish. 12 bolts.

Bop & Beta Wall (Salty Boogers section)

Wild Life Preserve

14. Salty Boogers*   .11c/d
Several cruxes. Has a tag on the first bolt. 9 bolts.

15. Calling Elvis**   .11c/d
Short, blunt arete. 4 bolts.

16. Twist & Shout*   .10c
Pro-crack to anchors. Trad.

17. Recreational Vehicles***   .10b
About 25 yards right of Salty Boogers. Gritty start leads to great face climbing. 9 bolts.

18. Born To Be Wild*   .11c
Climbs white face and arete. 20' to the right of Recreational. 8 bolts.

The Wildlife Preserve
APPROACH: See Bop and Beta Wall.

1. Something Wild**   .11a/b
Climbs slab/face on colored hangers. 9 bolts.

2. Wily E. Coyote**   .10c
Natural crack line, right facing corner/crack, past huge, loose-looking block. Trad.

3. Doggy Style Arete***   .12a
Wild arete, pumpy headwall, 75'. 7 bolts.

4. Wild At Heart***   .11b/c
Climbs bulge to arete to headwall, great pumpy top section, 75'. Has a tag on the first bolt. 9 bolts.

5. Above The Law**   .11c
Roof/slot crux start to fun upper climbing. 9 bolts.

6. Hosstyle*   .11d
Climbs left-facing corner. Has a tag on the first bolt. 6 bolts.

Down Under
(Morning sun, afternoon shade)

The Down Under wall is 80' to the left of The Outback.

1. Crocodile*   .10b
Big ledge between 4th & 5th bolts. 6 bolts.

2. Aborigine*   .9
Starts on orange lichen-covered slab to ledge at 5th bolt. 6 bolts.

3. Wake & Bake*   .10a
5 bolts.

4. Cultural Revenge*   .8
Climbs dihedral. 5 bolts.

5. BLM*   .9
6 bolts.

6. Men At Work*   .11d
Climbs steep dihedral. Bolts.

7. 5.10, Eh?**   .10c
Has a tag on 1st bolt. 6 bolts.

8. Duckbill Platypus**   .8
Start at base of Juniper tree. 4 bolts.

9. Never Trust A Waleroo**   .8
Starts in short left-facing corner. 5 bolts.

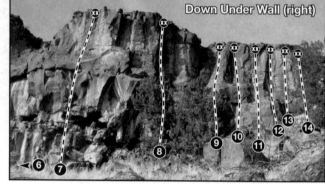

10. The Wanker*   .8
Slabby start to short dihedral. 3 bolts.

11. The Dingos Ate My Baby*   .8
High 1st bolt. 3 bolts.

12. Boomerang*   .9
Climbs blunt arete to ledge, then slabby dihedral. 4 bolts.

13. Worthog*   .9
Starts on pointed flake then up short face. 3 bolts.

14. Wombat*   .7
Climbs cracks and pockets. 3 bolts.

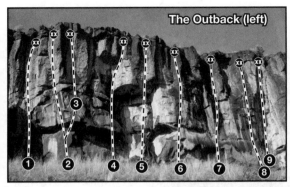

6. Dingo** .12b
Steep start, thin moves up the steep slab. 4 bolts.

7. The Walkabout** .11c
Hard start. Angles right then up on easier terrain. 4 bolts.

8. Waltzing Matilda** .11b
Great moves. 5 bolts.

9. The Diggery-Doo* .10c
Climbs dihedral. 4 bolts.

The Outback
(Morning sun, afternoon shade)

The Outback is an east facing wall, upriver from the Wildlife Preserve and about 80' right of the Down Under wall.

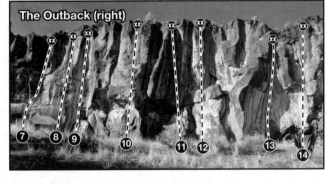

APPROACH: Park at the 1st Parking Area. From there pass through fence and hike along the main 2 track road for about .4 mi. as it heads south toward the river. Make sure to adhere to the main road and do not take any of the intersecting ATV paths. At about .4 mi. there is a faint 2-track that veers left marked by a cairn. Tun left here and follow the 2 track for about 400' toward the edge of the cliff, then turn right and locate the faint trail that descends through the broken area in the cliff. The Outback Wall is about 100' to the right.

1. Wallaby Wannabee* .10a
Climbs crack/stem. 4 bolts.

2. Great Barrier Reef** .11b
Left side of roof. 4 bolts.

3. The Land Down Under** .11a
Same start as Barrier, then move right, over the roof. 5 bolts.

4. Wooly* .10c
Up face/corner to left side of roof. 4 bolts.

5. G'Dday Mate** .10d
Fun moves over right side of roof. 4 bolts.

10. Another Shrimp On The Barbie .11c
Starts on prow, right of roof. 5 bolts.

11. Hop Like A 'Roo** .11b
Starts in dihedral, then move left up pocketed face. 4 bolts.

12. Bloody Yanks* .11a
Climbs to ledge, then up crux arete/face. 5 bolts.

13. Sticky Wicket** .11a
Climbs right-leaning dihedral. 4 bolts.

14. Attack Of The Killer Koala* .11b
Starts just left of rubble pile. 4 bolts.

Clayton Collins visits The Land Down Under., .11a.

Windmill Wall
(Morning sun, afternoon shade)

This wall is about 250' to the right of The Outback.

1. Unknown   .?
20' route that starts on gritty, sculpted pockets to short dihedral finish. 3 bolts.

2. Kill A What**   .10a
Starts on black, gritty rock to small ledge, then follows crack to anchors. 5 bolts.

3. Tilting At Windmills*   .10c
Begins on white corner to dihedral. 5 bolts.

4. Idaho Power***   .11a
Hard start to crack then arete. 6 bolts.

5. OMG, It's A Dragon**   .11a
Thin lower section to slabby face with curving crack. 6 bolts.

6. Snake Bones   (project)

short broken section of cliff.

7. Locomotive Breath**   .10a
Dihedral to crack. 6 bolts.

8. Rockhead*   .9
Decent warm up. 5 bolts.

Heather Lords on Nurse Ratchet, .10a, Owl Cove. Photo by Nathan Smith.

Gang Fight Wall
(All day sun)

South facing wall that is usually sheltered from the wind and a great place to climb on colder, sunny days.

APPROACH: Park at the 3rd Parking Area. Hop the fence and follow the trail southeast for about 60'. From there the trail drops down into the large alcove that houses the obvious Gang Fight Wall.

1. West Side Story*   .11b
3 bolts.

2. Cement Shoes*   .12a/b
4 bolts.

3. Hit Man*   .11c
Crux near 3rd bolt. Shares last bolt and anchors with Cement. 4 bolts.

4. The Rumble**   .13a
Finger pockets up bulge, fun and athletic moves. 5 bolts.

5. Zip Gun**   .11c
3 bolts.

6. Mean Streak**   .12d
Climbs black water streak. Easy moves give way to hard climbing at the midway point. 4 bolts.

7. Gang Fight**   .11c
4 bolts.

8. Graffiti***   .11a
Classic route with crux near the 4th bolt. 5 bolts.

9. Caught In The Line Of Fire   .10b/c
Groove to the right of Graffiti, shares anchors with Graffiti. 4 bolts.

10. Do the Right Thing*   .11a
4 bolts.

11. The Switchblade***   .12b/c
Another classic Massacre route. 5 bolts.

12. Drooling   (open project)
4 bolts.

13. The Knife Fight**   .11b/c
Several struggles. 5 bolts.

14. Gang Bang**   .10b
A 4th bolt was added to this years after the F.A. making it much more safe and appealing. 4 bolts.

15. Twin Peaks   (project)

16. Drive-By*   .12a
Fun moves off the ground. Crux is moving through the crack. 4 bolts.

17. Trigger Happy**   .10b
4 bolts.

18. The Chump*   .9
Around corner by pile of rocks. Has a name tag on first bolt. 5 bolts.

150 yards to the right on a small southwest-facing cliff.

19. Cocky Young Men**   .13a/b
Hard moves over bulge. 4 bolts.

20. Grumpy Old Men**   .12b/c
Great route with the crux at mid-height. 4 bolts.

261

Boulder Wall
(Morning shade, afternoon sun)

West facing wall that offers great morning shade.

APPROACH: Park at the 3rd Parking Area. Hop the fence and follow the trail southeast for about 60'. From there the trail drops down into the large alcove that houses the obvious Gang Fight Wall. From Gang Fight, hike cross country due east directly to the visible cliff band.

1. Doggie Doo*** .11c
Diagonals right on good holds to thinner crux finish. Surprisingly pumpy for the length. 4 bolts.

2. The Horror .11c
Climbs corner, hard third clip. Could use another bolt. 3 bolts.

3. Happiness is a Warm Gun** .12a
Powerful start to long reaches and sustained. 4 bolts.

4. Hands Up* .10b/c
Right leaning crack to top anchors. Trad.

5. Dukes of Hazard* .11a
Thin pro crack, same anchors as Hands Up. Trad.

6. Your Hine Ass** .11b/c
Low crux, good thin face. 4 bolts.

7. Little Miss Can't Be Wrong* .10a/b
4 bolts.

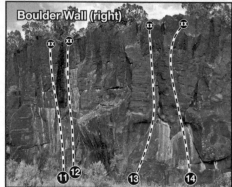

8. Resistance Is Futile .11c/d
Natural pro, 1 pin and 1 bolt. Out right side of low roof. Shares anchors and last bolt of Path-Illogical. Mixed.

9. Path-Illogical* .12a
Climbs arete right of Resistance. 4 bolts.

10. Cat On A Leash** .10d
Climbs crack, arete finish. 5 bolts.

11. Lonesome Dove* .11b
Climbs prow. 4 bolts.

12. Comeback Kid* .10a
Crack to box corner. 4 bolts.

13. Anchors Away* .10c
Check out the original anchors in the big block at the base! 4 bolts.

14. Termite Velocity** .10b
4 bolts.

The Farmyard
(All day sun)

South facing wall just around the corner and to the right of Boulder Wall and to the left of The Play Pen.

1. The Old Grey Mars (she's still what she used to be!)*　　　　.11b/c
Climbs white dihedral. 3 bolts.

2. Rooster in the Hen House　　.10b/c
4 bolts.

3. Runt of the Litter　　　　　.9
3 bolts.

4. The Nag*　　　　　　　.10c
Crux start, then fun crack moves. 6 bolts.

5. Pot-Belly Pig**　　　　　.12b
Use the flat-topped flake to clip the third bolt, then move right on thin face holds. 6 bolts.

6. Holy Cow*　　　　　　.11a
4 bolts.

7. Chicken Little*　　　　.11a/b
3 bolts.

Sue Parsons deals with the Rooster In The Hen House, .10b/c.

The Play Pen
(Morning Sun, late afternoon shade)

South-Southeast facing, short, white wall with shallow dihedrals. Right of The Farmyard.

1. Maiden Voyage*   .11a
Climb corner system, traverse right after last bolt to Youthanasia anchor. 6 bolts.

2. Youthanasia**   .11d/.12a
Just right of the corner where the east facing wall turns to southeast facing, starts off big boulder. 4 bolts.

Chelsea Principio powers through The Pacifier, .11d.

3. Death by Chocolate   .10a
Starts behind the big boulder, up big brown corner, big flake to second bolt. 5 bolts.

4. Mary Had A Little Jam*   .10a
Chimney/stem start to sharp crack. 3 bolts.

5. Rock'n the Cradle*   .10b
Crack/dihedral. 3 bolts.

6. The Pacifier***   .11d
Bulge to very thin finishing moves. 4 bolts.

7. Kid Stuff**   .10a
Shares anchors with Pacifier. 3 bolts.

8. Patty Cake*   .9
Climbs face/corner. 3 bolts.

9. Baby Face**   .10c
Surprisingly sustained climbing for the grade. 4 bolts.

10. The Bull Pen*   .10b
4 red bolts

11. Humpty-Dumpty**   .10b
Climbs dihedral. 3 bolts.

12. Teeter-Totter*   .10b
Another dihedral climb. 3 bolts.

13. Merry-Go-Round**   .10a
Brown arete/face. 3 bolts.

• 3 sets of top anchors/projects

Wild Onion (center)

Wild Onion (left)

Wild Onion Wall
(Morning sun, afternoon shade)

East to north facing wall, about 1/4 mile south of Gang Fight Wall. Wild Onion Wall is a great area to climb on hotter days as the cliff is completely shaded by early afternoon.

APPROACH: Park at the 3rd Parking Area. Hop the fence and locate the trail that stays on top of the cliff heading south. About a 1/4 mile from the car, locate a faint trail that gradually descends to the right side (north-east facing) of Wild Onion Wall.

1. Drill 'Em And Fill 'Em*   .9
Starts on orange lichen covered corner. 4 bolts.

2. Hüsker Dü*   .10a
4 bolts.

3. Massacre Master Beta   .10b
Starts on slabby section. 4 bolts.

4. Pussy Riot   .10c
4 bolts.

5. Blockbuster   .10c
Starts in a dihedral. 4 bolts.

30 yard break in the cliff

6. Magic Mushroom**   .9
Fun arete climb. 4 bolts.

7. Black Widow Crack   .7
Pro crack. Trad.

8. Early Bird**   .10a
Climbs face. 3 bolts.

9. Red Skies in the Morning**.   11b/c
Climbs reddish face/finger crack. 5 bolts.

10. Let It Shine**   .11b
Share first bolt and anchors on Rise & Whine. 6 bolts.

11. Rise & Whine*   .12a
Climbs slab/prow. 5 bolts.

12. Something Special***   .10c
Corner to steep face with great pockets. 5 bolts.

13. Wild Onion Crack*   .9
East facing pro crack to anchors. Trad.

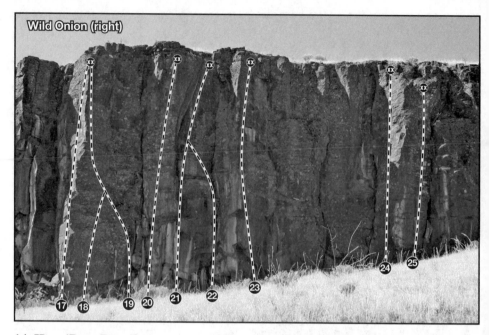

Wild Onion (right)

14. How 'Bout Dem Onions** .10b
Face/arete just right of the crack, shares anchors with the crack climb. 5 bolts.

15. Three Bucks A Clip* .11d
Climb great arete, then finish on prow to the left. 6 bolts.

16. Buttercup* .10c
Seamed off dihedral start to crack/face. 5 bolts.

17. Looking Through A Glass Onion*** .11b
Nice northeast facing arete with a low crux. 5 bolts.

18. Mark's Flying Time** .12a
1 bolt variation, stick clip a bolt to the left of Crying Time and to the right of the arete. Cool throw and climb into Crying Time.

19. Crying Time* .11c
Left-most climb on north face, same anchors as Looking Through. 5 bolts.

20. Yellow Bells** .10d
Undercling small roof, then climb up prow. 5 bolts.

21. Show Me the Way** .10d
Climb face to crack then up arcing dihedral. 6 bolts.

22. Onion Rings* .10b
3 bolts up right crack, then same 3 bolt finish as Show Me. 6 bolts.

23. Dog Gone* .11b/c
Crux moves off the ground to face right of arete. 5 bolts.

24. Wall Flower* .12a
Bouldery start. 5 bolts.

25. Go Johnny Go** .10a
Good warm up climb. 3 bolts.

Chris Tennant floats the thin crux of Rise And Whine, .12a.

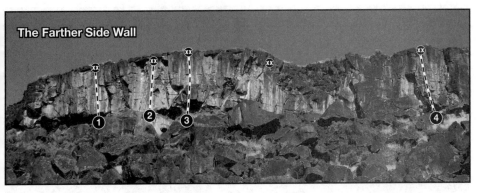

The Farther Side Wall

The Far Side Area

(Morning sun, afternoon shade)

East-facing crag, about 1/4 mile south of Onion Wall.

APPROACH: Park at the 3rd Parking Area. Hop the fence and locate the trail that stays on top of the cliff heading south. About a 1/4 mile from the car, pass the access point for Wild Onion Wall and keep hiking south for about 500'. When you come to a big side gully, descend and go south along the base of the cliff for about 200'. Routes are listed left-to-right.

The Farther Side Wall

These routes are located to the left of The Far Side Wall. Access is gained by traversing the boulder field to the left of Blizzard.

1. Barracuda**   .10b
Watch for the barracuda with a mouthful of teeth. 4 bolts.

2. The Third Platform**   .10c
Clip the anchors from the diving board for added pleasure. 3 bolts.

3. Atlas***   .11d
You may find the world resting upon your shoulders. 4 bolts.

• project anchors

4. Three on the Tree**   .9
Start at the steering wheel, shift gears and enjoy the ride. 3 bolts.

The Far Side Wall

(Morning sun, late afternoon shade)

1. Blizzard*   .11d
Steep white rock. 5 bolts.

2. Typhoon*   .11c
Same start as Blizzard. 5 bolts.

3. Twist & Pout*   .11c
Thin diagonal crack start. 5 bolts.

30 yard break in the cliff

Far Side
(Blizzard Section)

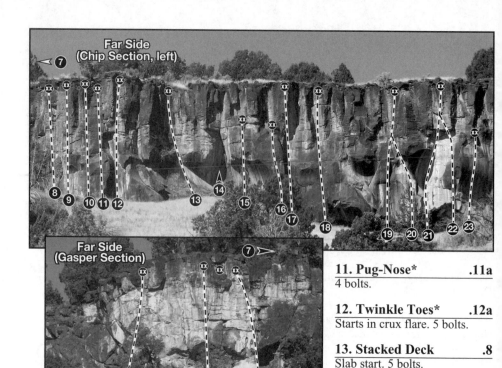

Far Side
(Chip Section, left)

Far Side
(Gasper Section)

11. Pug-Nose* .11a
4 bolts.

12. Twinkle Toes* .12a
Starts in crux flare. 5 bolts.

13. Stacked Deck .8
Slab start. 5 bolts.

14. Honey Vee (project)
Climb slot left of Chip. No hardware.

4. Ghouly-Mon* .11d
Climbs white face to short steep crack finish. About 30 yards right of Twist. 5 bolts.

15. Chip Off The Old Block*** .12a
Starts up huge, free standing flake. A must do. 4 bolts.

5. Gasper The Friendly Toast** .12b
Scramble up 15 feet to first bolt on flakey rock. Great pockets. 4 bolts.

16. Killer Wail* .12a
Hop up on the slab, then try getting on the face to the right. 3 bolts.

6. Bouldergiest* .11a
Goes up through crux slot. 5 bolts.

100 yard break in the cliff

17. Humpback* .10d
Same start as Killer, then up corner to arete above. 6 bolts.

7. Holey Moley** .11a
100 yards right of Bouldergiest. Climbs overhung prow on fun holds. A bit gritty. 4 bolts.

18. Slight Of Hand* .10a
Hand traverse start. 6 bolts.

50 yard break in routes

19. Seal Clubber* .11d
Starts out of low cave, 2 bolts up prow, then angle right and up for 4 more bolts. 6 bolts.

8. Good To The Last Drop .10c
50 yards right of Holey. 4 bolts.

20. Save The Wails* .11b
Cave start, up and left to same finish as Seal Clubber. 6 bolts.

9. No-Doze* .11b
5 bolts.

21. Attitude Adjustment* .11c
Low cave start, then up right-leaning dihedral. May want to place pro (#0.5 Camalot) between bolts four and five. 6 bolts.

10. Bull-Doze* .11b
Several cruxes. 4 bolts.

Far Side
(Chip Section, right)

22. Thanks For The Ankors** .12b/c
Starts on flat boulder at edge of low cave, hard moves through the first three bolts, then worthy finish. Shares last bolt and anchors with Attitude. 6 bolts.

23. Bad Style (project)
An improbable, yet attractive, piece of stone that was "chipped" by one person and then "filled in" by another, rendering it useless and unattractive. 5 bolts.

24. Around The World In 80 Ways*.11d
High first bolt, undercling right around flake, then angle left to steep headwall finish. 6 bolts.

25. U-Turn* .10d
Same start as Around, then right and up hand crack. 6 bolts.

26. Funnel Vision* .11b
Scramble up ramp to high first bolt, struggle up the body-snacher slot until you can escape right to the face. 4 bolts.

27. Hilti Goes To Heaven* .11b
Right-leaning corner. 5 bolts.

28. Crunch Time** .12a
Steep prow, same finish as Hilti. 5 bolts.

29. The Oasis .11a
Up inside corner, about 30 yards right of Crunch. 4 bolts.

30. Lost In The Desert .12a
4 bolts.

31. The Mirage** .11d
Aesthetic, steep face. 4 bolts.

32. Woof Direct* .11b
About 30 yards right of The Mirage. 2 bolt direct start, bypasses roof on the left side. 4 bolts.

33. Big Woof*** .12a
Horizontal climbing at Massacre! A unique route for the area. 6 bolts.

34. Momma, Don't Let Your Babies Grow Up To Be Climbers!** .10a
Starts just right of Big Woof. 4 bolts.

35. Yapper* .11b
Climbs up corner. 4 bolts.

36. Top Dog* .11c
Funky bulge start. 4 bolts.

37. Pooch* .11c
Brown bulge start, then angle right up steep face/arete. 4 bolts.

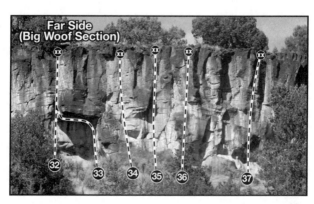

Far Side
(Big Woof Section)

Forbidden Planet
(All day shade)

Forbidden Planet is a north facing wall about 1/2 mile west and a bit south of Camptown Towers. The easiest way to access this wall is from the 3rd Parking Area. USE WILD ONION DIRECTIONS. Then head south toward the obvious wide, shaded wall. The main area is accessed via the right side of the wall. Routes 1 and 2 are best accessed from straight below the lone section where they reside, as traversing from the main area is somewhat of a struggle.

1. The Crow** .10b
Climbs just to the right of the crack. 5 bolts.

2. Rave-on** .10d
5 bolts.

75 yard broken section

3. Man In The Moon** .10b
4 bolts.

4. The Thing* .11b
Up wide crack to prow. 6 bolts.

5. The Predator** .11d
Flared crack start. 6 bolts.

6. The Alien* .11a
Jump-start off pointed boulder. 6 bolts.

7. Forbidden Planet* .11a/b
Starts in lichen-filled chimney, then left to fun arete. 5 bolts.

8. Forbidden Fruit .9
Toprope. Shares start with Forbidden Planet, then right, up face.

9. Earth Girls Are Easy .9
Starts right of big chimney. 5 bolts.

10. Men Are From Mars** .10b
Same anchors as Earth Girls. 5 bolts.

11. Rocket Man** .11a
Climbs dihedral. 4 bolts.

12. Flash Gordon* .10a
Up arete, same anchors as Rocket Man. 4 bolts.

13. The Force (May It Be With You!)* .11b
A bit gritty at the bottom but worth it. 6 bolts.

The Overlook
(no topo)
(Morning sun, afternoon shade)

This crag faces the Snake River and is about 1/4 mile down-river from the Owl Cove. Approach by switch-backing up from the river, or contouring in from the Camptown Tower area. Some say the routes here are not worth the effort. You decide. There are 2 separate toprope anchors left of Fancy Feet.

14. G-Force**   .12a
Overhanging face between two cracks. 4 bolts.

15. Life Force**   .11c
Climbs pretty, steep face. Anchors could use relocating making for a better clipping stance. 4 bolts.

16. Final Frontier*   .11b
4 bolts.

17. UFO   .10b
Same anchors as Final Frontier. Cool features on gritty basalt. 3 bolts.

Hidden Cove
(Morning shade, afternoon sun)

Southwest-facing cove that is accessed by hiking right from UFO and up through the small boulders.

1. You Break It, You Buy It**   .11a
Steep start that angles left on cool, but fragile flake-features. Finishes on fun pockets. 4 bolts.

2. Everything Will Be O.K.**   .11c
Climbs to right of the ledge at the 2nd bolt. Follows crack to slabby dihedral. 4 bolts.

3. This Is A Relaxing Climb**   .12a
Starts on white streaks, angles slightly left. 5 bolts.

4. He Died Instantly**   .12a
Steep steep start to big sidepull below 4th bolt. 5 bolts.

1. Fancy Feet*   .11b
Slab start. 7 bolts.

2. Out In Left Field*   .11d
Belay on ledge/ramp. Moves left after 3rd bolt to face/blunt arete. 7 bolts.

3. Right On**   .12b
Shares first 3 bolts with Out In Left Field, then up for 4 more bolts on fun movement. 7 bolts.

4. Mag-Neat-O!*   .10b
Climbs red/brown face. 6 bolts.

Clayton Collins on Forbidden Planet, .11a/b.

Westworld Area

The Westworld Area was one of the last sections to be explored and developed at Massacre Rocks. While not frequented as much as other areas at Massacre, the routes are well worth the drive.

Erin's Wall and Berlin Wall are included in this section as they roughly share the same driving directions as the Westworld Area. The Gunfighter Wall is included in this section as well as it is most easily approached on foot via the Westworld Wall area.

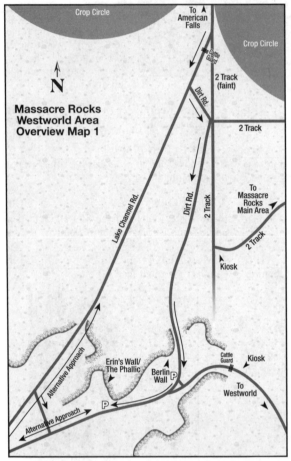

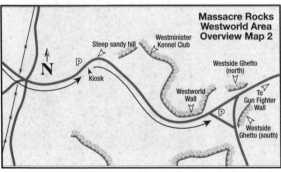

GETTING THERE
Driving Access: From the town of American Falls, take State Highway 39 across the American Falls Reservoir dam. Take the first left, Lamb-Weston Road. Listed mileage starts here.
• 0.3 miles: Turn left onto Borah Road
• 1.8 miles: Turn left onto Lake Channel Road, cross the railroad tracks heading south. The road has 3 sharp corners on it before angling southwest.
• 12.8 miles: Once across the cattle guard you will see a dirt road on the left, turn onto this short road then turn right onto the main gravel road and head south. You will encounter a gate right before the dirt road turns to back to pavement. Make sure to close the gate behind you.
• 13.7 miles: Turn left off the pavement onto a two-track dirt road.

Zero out odometer. 4WD or AWD is required beyond this point.

• .02 miles: Ascend a short sandy hill and cross over a cattle guard. There is a kiosk to the left. Follow the main track.
• 1.5 miles: Pass through the gate and go straight, heading east.
• 1.6 miles: A 2nd kiosk is to the right. Parking can be had here if one chooses not to descend the sandy hill.
• 1.9 miles: After passing the main Westworld Wall, parking can be found at the intersection of the 2 dirt roads. However, there is one more steep sandy hill to negotiate if one chooses to park here.

Westminister Kennel Club
(Morning shade, afternoon sun)

1. Bark**   .12c
Fun powerful start moves. 3 bolts.

2. Bite*   .12a
Head up huecoed crack then veer left. Shares last bolt and anchor with Bark. 3 bolts.

25 yards right to next route

3. Dogged Determination*   .12a/b
Climbs technical, fingery arete. Look for hidden holds. 3 bolts.

30 yards right to next routes on a south facing section of the wall

4. Dog Nelson*   .12a/b
Climbs up streaked face. Bouldery move off ground. Left crack is off. 2 bolts.

5. Wag The Dog**   .12b
Steep crack with a bulge start. Leave the crack at the third bolt and hang on to the top. 4 bolts.

Westworld Wall

(Sun/Shade varies on sections of wall)

1. Refer (.12b)** – 3 bolts. Cool face climbing with neat lift "The Refrigerator Move." This route is on a west facing corner with a tan crack to the right of it.

70 yards right to next route

2. Low Rider*   .11c/d
Face with crack to the left, funky moves. Route is about 15' left of a big nest. 4 bolts.

10 yards to next route

3. Lotta Mo!**   .12a
Stick clip 1st bolt. A bit runout to the 2nd. Great arete climbing. 4 bolts.

4. The Streak**   .11b
Great, steep jug-haul to fun headwall finish. 4 bolts.

5. TNT   .11b
Climbs face. 4 bolts.

20 foot broken section

6. The Chimp***   .12a
Fun bulge start to thin moves. 5 bolts.

7. Come As You Are*   .11c
Wide crack start, same anchors as The Chimp. 4 bolts.

40 foot broken section

8. Iron Man**   .11c/d
Climbs wide corner. 4 bolts.

70 foot broken section

9. Downward Spiral*   .10b
Climbs steep chimney. 3 bolts.

10. Jug-Aholic**   .9
Fun, steep jug haul. 4 bolts.

11. Dazed And Confused*   .10c
Step right after first bolt. 3 bolts.

12. Sports Action**   .13a
Gently overhanging route with smooth face on bottom to a more featured headwall, long powerful moves, right behind free standing pillar. 5 bolts.

13. The Real Thing**   .11a/b
Left dihedral, just right of free-standing pillar. Shares anchors with Sports Action. 5 bolts.

14. Power-Age*   .11c
If your legs are long enough you can stem the upper half – it not, then get ready for a struggle. 5 bolts.

Westworld Wall (right)

15. Dudes On Ludes*** .11d
Great moves. One of the best routes at the Westworld area. 4 bolts.

16. Dudes On Butt** .12a
The bastard child of Dudes On Ludes and Putty Butt. Climb and clip first 2 bolts of Putty Butt then head left climbing steep pocketed arete. Clip two more bolts and continue left to the anchors of Dudes On Ludes. 4 bolts total.

17. Putty Butt* .10c
Climbs wide crack, 3rd bolt could be lowered a bit. 3 bolts.

18. Cara's Toy* .10a
Funky featured basalt at the start. 3 bolts.

19. Livin' High On The Heel** .11b/c
4 bolts.

20. One Bad Bunny* .12d
Climb and clip first 3 bolts of Thumper then head left around arete clipping 1 link-up bolt using a long draw and then clip last bolt and anchors of Livin' High. 5 bolts total.

21. Thumper*** .11d/.12a
5 bolts.

22. Chunky Shuffle** .10d
Crux start using crack then climbs dihedral. 4 bolts.

23. Sin City* .10a
Thuggish start leads to delicate climbing near the anchors. 4 bolts.

Matt TeNgaio on Lotta Mo!, .12a. Photo by Leigh Collins.

275

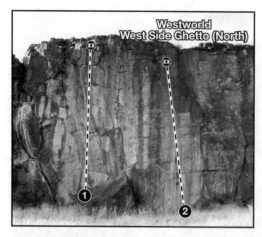

West Side Ghetto (north wall)
(All day sun)

This wall is about 110 yards east of the furthest right route on the West World Wall. This wall is about 30 feet tall, tan and south facing.

1. Shots Fired**   **.12c**
Climbs up left side of overhanging prow. Crack 6 feet left of bolts is off route. 3 bolts.

2. Pimping Is Easy*   **.12a/b**
Up cool vertical face with thin left arcing seam up it. 3 bolts.

West Side Ghetto (south wall)
(Morning/mid-afternoon shade, late afternoon sun)

90 yards to the south across the road from PIMPING IS EASY is a steep north facing wall.

1. Homie Don't Play That***   **.12b**
Angles left up steep huecoed face. Cool finishing moves. 4 bolts.

2. Skeezer**   **.12a**
Steep face, angles left with crux at last bolt. 4 bolts.

3. Ghetto Superstar**   **.12c/d**
Hard bulge start, L crack is off. Stick clip first bolt. 3 bolts.

4. Deal Gone Bad*   **.12b/c**
Starts off block right of first bolt. Sustained climbing arcing up and left. Note the two bullet holes 2 feet left of third bolt. 5 bolts.

Gunfighter Wall
(Morning shade, afternoon sun)

The easiest approach to this wall is from the parking area for Westworld. Hike east between the West Side Ghetto walls passing around the barrier across the sandy road. Follow this road due east for about .3 mi. Gunfighter Wall is the short, southwest facing wall. Easy 10 minute approach.

1. Doc Holliday**   **.12b/c**
Climbs brown arete. 4 bolts.

2. Aces and 8's*   **.8**
About 70' right of Doc. Jug haul. Starts left of tree stump. Reputed to being THE best 5.8 at Massacre. 3 bolts.

3. The Shootist**   **.13b**
Overhanging white/black streaked face with micro thin holds and pumpy finish. 4 bolts.

4. Jesse James**   **.12b**
Fun route on overhanging wall. 4 bolts.

**5. William Bonney
(aka Billy The Kid)****   **.12a**
Merges with Jesse after 3rd bolt. 4 bolts.

Troy Neu busts a move on Homie Don't play That, .12b.

277

BERLIN WALL AREA

The following 2 areas are located near the turnoff to the Westworld Area. They both sit on private property. Please be respectful.

GETTING THERE
Driving Access: Use the same directions for Westworld but at the turnoff from the pave-

Matt TeNgaio is a Chip Off The Old Block, .12a, Far Side Wall. Photo by Bruce Black.

ment, park on the right in the small pullout. Berlin Wall is the obvious cliff behind the pullout.

To access Erin's Wall/The Phallic, continue past the pullout for Berlin Wall for about .01 mi. and find a place off the dirt road on the right to park. Erin's Wall is directly to the right (north) of the road.

Berlin Wall
(All day sun, late afternoon shade)

1. Ouch-Wich** .11b/c
A bit dirty and chossy between 3rd & 4th bolt. 7 bolts.

2. West Berlin** .11c
Fun face climb. 4 bolts.

3. East Berlin** .11b
Slab start to good face climbing Same anchors as West Berlin. 5 bolts.

4. Fire In The Hole* .10a
4 bolts.

5. Look Out Below!** /9
4 bolts.

Erin's Wall/The Phallic
(Morning shade, afternoon sun)

1. Erin's Cool Route** .11b
Starts in large broken dihedral heading left into large hueco, pull steep bulge then finish on slab. 4 bolts.

2. Pharm D Candidate** .11d/.12a
Climbs up steep crack to a hard lock off move to easier finish. 5 bolts.

3. Drug Pusher** .12b/c
Clip two bolts and then finish on the last 2 bolts of Pharm D. Steep bulge hard crank at lip to easier finish. 4 bolts.

Next 3 routes are on the free standing pillar out in front of Erin's Wall.

4. On The Verge Of Orgasm** .11d/.12a
Devious, technical climbing up north face of pillar. Starts on slab 15 feet up. 3 bolts.

5. Richard Head's Route*** .12b
Climbs up west side of pillar. Steep overhanging face up positive crimps. 5 bolts.

6. Viagra Popin'** .10b/c
South facing route up shallow dihedral. 4 bolts.

Nick Vitale handles The Brat, .11b, Shelter Rock. Photo by Mike Engle.

Useful Addresses and Phone numbers

Caribou-Targhee National Forest
- Ashton Ranger District, Box 228, 30 South Yellowstone Highway, Ashton, ID 83420, (208) 652-7442
- Dubois Ranger District, P.O. Box 46, Dubois, ID 83423 (208) 374-5422
- Island Park Ranger District, P.O. Box 220, Island Park, ID 83429, (208) 558-7301
- Palisades Ranger District, 3659 East Ririe Highway, Idaho Falls, ID 83401 (208) 523-1412
- Teton Basin Ranger District, P.O. Box 777, Driggs, ID 83422, (208) 354-2312
- Malad Ranger District, 75 South 140 East, P.O. Box 142, Malad, ID 83262 (208) 766-4743
- Montpelier Ranger District, 431 Clay, Montpelier, ID 83254, (208) 847-0375.
- Pocatello Ranger District, Federal Building, Suite 187, 250 South 4th Avenue, Pocatello, ID 83201, (208) 236-7500
- Soda Springs Ranger District, 421 West 2nd South, Soda Springs, ID 83276, (208) 547-4356

State Parks
- Harriman State Park, HC-66 Box 500, Island Park, ID 83429, (208) 558-7368
- Massacre Rocks State Park, 3592 N. Park Lane, American Falls, ID 83211, (208) 548-2672

Bureau of Land Management
- Idaho Falls office, 1405 Hollipark Drive, Idaho Falls, ID 83401, (208) 524-7500

Other agencies
- Department of Recreation, City of Pocatello, P.O. Box 4169, Pocatello, ID 83205-4169, (208) 234-6232

Idaho Falls Ski Club
- Web site: www.ifskiclub.com/

Idaho Alpine Club
- Web site: www.idahoalpineclub.org

Idaho State University Outdoor Program
- Web site: www.isu.edu/outdoor

Southeast Idaho Climbers Coalition
- Web site: www.seiclimbing.com

ABOUT THE AUTHORS

Matt TeNgaio has called Idaho Falls home for 30 years. Since relocating from Hawaii as a teenager, Matt fell in love with the region and it's outdoor recreational opportunities. While he enjoys several outdoor pursuits, his main passion for the past 17 years has been rock climbing. He is married and has 2 kids. He can be reached at mtengaio@postregister.com.

Jerry Painter has lived in Idaho Falls since 1988 with his wife. He is an outdoor columnist for the Post Register newspaper. He enjoys being scared to death on top of the region's highest peaks and keeping up with his children on their latest 5.11 projects. His other books include "Great Trails for Family Hiking: The Tetons" (out of print), "10 Peaks in 10 Weeks" and "Trails of Eastern Idaho" with Margaret Fuller. He can be contacted at jpainter@postregister.com.

Jerry Painter and Matt TeNgaio on the summit of Mt. Borah via the North Face route.

280